D0953567

KILLING A KING

KILLING A KING

The Assassination of
Yitzhak Rabin
and the Remaking of Israel

Dan Ephron

W. W. NORTON & COMPANY
Independent Publishers Since 1923
NEW YORK • LONDON

For information about permission to reproduce selections from this book,
write to Permissions, W. W. Norton & Company, Inc., 500 Fifth Avenue,
New York, NY 10110

For information about special discounts for bulk purchases, please contact
W. W. Norton Special Sales at specialsales@wwnorton.com or 800-233-4830

Manufacturing by RR Donnelley Westford
Book design by Brooke Koven
Production manager: Anna Oler

Library of Congress Cataloging-in-Publication Data
Ephron, Dan, author.
Killing a king : the assassination of Yitzhak Rabin and the
remaking of Israel / Dan Ephron.—First edition.
pages cm
Includes bibliographical references and index.
ISBN 978-0-393-24209-6 (hardcover)
1. Rabin, Yitzhak, 1922-1995—Assassination.
2. Israel—Politics and government—1993– I. Title.
DS126.6.R32E54 2015
95694.05'4—dc23
2015025695

W. W. Norton & Company, Inc.
500 Fifth Avenue, New York, N.Y. 10110
www.wwnorton.com

W. W. Norton & Company Ltd.
Castle House. 75/76 Wells Street, London W1T 3QT

1 2 3 4 5 6 7 8 9 0

For my daughter and son,
Who make every moment better and more interesting
And for Nancy—
My partner in this and all things

According to Judaism, killing a king is profoundly significant. It affects the entire nation and alters its destiny.

—HAGAI AMIR,
in a letter from prison, days after
his brother assassinated Yitzhak Rabin

Contents

Introduction

In early 2012, during one of those YouTube click binges that can eat up an afternoon, I came across an old video showing Israeli investigators interrogating Yigal Amir, the young man who had assassinated Prime Minister Yitzhak Rabin. I was serving as the Israel bureau chief for *Newsweek* magazine and looking for subjects to write about—new ways to understand a country I had covered intermittently over two decades. The excerpt, from the night of the shooting in 1995, drew me in. Though the murder had been one of the most dramatic events in Israel's history, Amir had largely faded from view in the years following his trial. Prison officials had barred journalists from interviewing him. The short clip, which had surfaced in the Israeli media on one of the anniversaries of the murder, seemed to have come from a mounted surveillance camera. It occurred to me that more existed—that somewhere in the country, there must be hours of interrogation tapes.

Eventually, I tracked down those tapes and, in several sittings, watched the long sessions that investigators conducted with Amir. Even by the standards of murder cases, of political murders, they seemed extraordinary. Yigal Amir shot Rabin in a Tel Aviv parking lot on the evening of November 4, 1995, plunging the country into a state of shock and grief. That a Jew had assassinated the leader of the Jewish state made it especially dreadful to Israelis. But at police headquarters in Tel Aviv that night and in the weeks that followed, Amir seemed impervious to the turmoil around him—to the trauma he had caused. He leaned back much of the time, cocked his head, and recounted how he had stalked Rabin over two years, luxuriating in the details. He explained the religious doctrines that motivated him, the zealotry that could not abide Rabin's peacemaking with the Palestinians. At one point he asked for a drink so that he could toast the prime minister's death.

The murder came at a critical juncture for Israel. Rabin's diplomacy had already produced two accords with the Palestinians and a momentum that made a final peace agreement feel almost inevitable, however difficult and complicated. It had also triggered a violent backlash by both Palestinians and Israelis opposed to the conciliation process. For reporters based in Israel at the time, it wasn't unusual to cover a peace ceremony one week and a shooting or bombing attack the next. The assassination itself exemplified the bewildering zigzag: Amir had shot Rabin at the end of a huge peace rally, one of the largest Israeli gatherings on record. I attended that rally and later covered the murder trial. Though it wasn't clear at the time, Amir had set off a chain reaction that would shift the power in Israel from the pragmatists to the ideologues. Two decades later, the coveted peace remains elusive.

Killing a King is a detailed account of the murder and the two years leading up to it—a narrative about a twentysomething law student, smart and exceedingly radical, who set out to alter the slope of history and succeeded. In a broader sense it is about Israel at a unique point in its existence, a moment when the isolation and hostility that had defined its position in the region for decades seemed to finally lift—but only temporarily. Through the lens of the murder, much can be gleaned about Israel today.

In my reporting for the book, a counterfactual history question came up again and again: would Rabin have succeeded? There's no doubt that he faced huge obstacles: not just the obstructionists on both sides but a problematic partner in Yasser Arafat, a waning popularity at home, and his own misgivings about the concessions that peace required of Israel. Yet all those factors must be weighed against the circumstances that favored peacemaking in 1995. The opponents of compromise in both camps had nowhere near the power and influence they hold now. The process itself had yet to be contaminated by sustained waves of violence and settlement expansion. And the rapport between Rabin and Arafat—the deciders of their generation—had evolved into something workable.

For all those reasons, Rabin probably stood a better chance of forging a durable reconciliation between Israelis and Palestinians than any leader before or since. That we'll never know how close he would have come is one of the exasperating consequences of the assassination.

KILLING A KING

Prologue

Yitzhak Rabin woke up before seven the morning of November 4, 1995, with an eye infection. He had plans to play tennis, hold several work meetings at his north Tel Aviv apartment, and then attend a peace rally that night at Kings of Israel Square. But the infection, which made his eye swollen and bloodshot, gave him a chance to reassess. Rabin felt ambivalent about the rally; it seemed to him like the kind of event some Bolshevik regime might organize, busing in paid apparatchiks and having them wave banners approved by the Party. He agreed to it mostly because his political opponents, with a few large and rowdy protests, had managed to create the impression that most of the country opposed his now second peace deal with Yasser Arafat. The demonstrators had held up doctored images showing Rabin draped in a kaffiyeh—the checkered black-and-white scarf worn by Arafat—and worse, Rabin in a Nazi uniform. But the prime minister feared that few people would show up at the square. Instead of refuting the perception of his political weakness, the rally could end up reinforcing it. Rabin himself wasn't exactly sure whether it was just a perception or the hard reality now.

He moved to the den, picked up the phone, and called off his tennis match. At seventy-three, Rabin still played several sets every Saturday, walking to a country club in the neighborhood and puffing on Parliament Longs between the games. He planned to phone Shlomo Lahat next, the former mayor of Tel Aviv and the organizer of the rally that night. The two had served together in the army and over-lapped as members of the general staff—the Israeli equivalent of the joint chiefs. But before he dialed, Leah, Rabin's wife of forty-seven years, called to him from elsewhere in the apartment, saying she'd tracked down an ophthalmologist who was now on the way. For the prime minister, of course he would make a house call on the Jewish Sabbath. And unless the doctor discovered something serious, Rabin would have no excuse but to attend the rally.

Around the same time, a few miles north, Yigal Amir was getting out of bed at his parents' home in Herzliya. A twenty-five-year-old law student, short and handsome, Amir also had plans for that Satur-day. He would pray at the Orthodox synagogue in the neighborhood, eat lunch with his parents and brothers and sisters—eight children in all—and head to Tel Aviv in the evening. Amir put on jeans and a dark-colored T-shirt. He lifted his 9mm Beretta from the nightstand next to his bed and tucked it in the back of his pants—he took the gun everywhere. His older brother, Hagai, with whom he shared a room, was a step behind him. Hagai palmed a velvet bag containing his tallit—the shawl with knotted fringes that religiously observant Jews wrap themselves in during prayers every day—and the two stepped out onto the pavement.

Somewhere between the house and the synagogue, on one of the leafy streets of middle-class Herzliya, Amir told his brother he would try to kill Rabin at the rally that night. It didn't come as a surprise, and Hagai did not recoil. The two had been talking about ways to assassinate the prime minister for more than two years, since Rabin's first peace deal with Arafat. With the bedroom door closed on the second floor of the house on Borochov Street, the brothers would toss out ideas, including an especially outlandish one: to inject nitroglyc-erin into the water pipes of Rabin's apartment building. The elaborate schemes belonged to Hagai. Two years older than Amir and a physics student at the Jewish settlement of Ariel, Hagai was a tinkerer. In the shed behind the house, he liked taking apart old appliances and reassembling them. But Amir kept coming back to the one simple plan that felt right: stalking Rabin and shooting him with his Beretta.

Now, on the street, Hagai revived an idea he had raised in an earlier conversation: acquiring a rifle and shooting Rabin from a safe distance. Hagai had trained as an infantry sniper during his army service and won first place in a competition at one of his stints in the reserves. He told Amir that even if he could close in on Rabin and fire his handgun, the prime minister's bodyguards were well trained and would shoot back. It would be a suicide mission. Though the two brothers were determined to kill Rabin, Hagai was unwilling to sacrifice himself doing it. Amir had his own misgivings, even on that Saturday morning. But he told himself he would get as close as he could to Rabin—and then let God guide him.

At the synagogue, Amir paged to the Torah portion of the week, Lech-Lecha, which recounts God's command to Abraham to leave his home and go to Canaan, where he would become the father of a great nation. In effect, it is the biblical moment when God promises the real estate that is now Israel (and the West Bank and Gaza and parts of Jordan) to the Jews. With the discordant voices of men praying all around him, mumbling or chanting softly, Amir thought to himself how fitting it would be for a prime minister who willfully surrendered parts of Israel to meet his death at the very time the Bible reminds Jews that the land in question is their birthright.

--- The Green Line demarcating the 1949 armistice agreement between Israel and its neighbors.

LEBANON

GOLAN HEIGHTS

HAIFA

TIBERIAS

ISRAEL

MEDITERRANEAN SEA

WEST BANK

NETANYA

SHAVEI SHOMRON
NABLUS
ARIEL

HERZLIYA

TEL AVIV

RAMALLAH

JORDAN

BIR NABALA

ASHDOD

MAALEH ADUMIM

JERUSALEM

ASHKELON

GAZA

BETHLEHEM

KIRYAT ARBA
HEBRON

BEERSHEVA

EGYPT

EILAT

CHAPTER 1

Flight of a Skeptic

"All right. All right. But no kissing."

—YITZHAK RABIN

The moment of Yitzhak Rabin's conversion occurred sometime between nine o'clock and midnight on Friday, September 10, 1993. During those three hours, he sat in the den of his Tel Aviv apartment on 5 Rav Ashi Street and pondered whether to fly to Washington over the weekend or send his foreign minister in his place. He met with an adviser and took a phone call from Warren Christopher, the US secretary of state. Throughout the evening, he sipped from a glass of whiskey doused with enough soda to render the mixture almost colorless. The hefty television set on which Rabin liked to watch soccer games and tennis matches was turned low. Israel's state-run channel aired a Spanish drama that night, *Raise Ravens*.

According to the calendar on his desk, Rabin had been the prime minister of Israel for nearly fourteen months. It was the second time he held the job, his first term having ended largely in ignominy sixteen years earlier. By his own admission, he had lacked in both age and experience, having served in politics less than six months when he entered office. Now he was seventy-one, stood five feet six and a half inches tall, and had wisps of white hair that he combed straight back, exposing a half dome of freckled forehead and scalp. He wore tailored suits, making him better dressed than most Israeli politicians. But he remained loyal to an old pair of black leather shoes that Rabin, in many ways still a creature of his first career as a military officer, took the time to polish almost every day.

Three weeks earlier, Israeli negotiators had clinched an agreement with the Palestine Liberation Organization after months of secret talks in the Norwegian capital of Oslo. Though only the outline of a peace accord, the twelve-page document had the audacity and ambition of a history-making deal. It ended the state of belligerency between Israel and the PLO, promised to upend a quarter century of Israeli policy toward Palestinians in the West Bank and Gaza Strip, and created an opening for resolving the broader Arab-Israeli conflict. President Clinton had invited the two sides to the White House for a signing ceremony on September 13.

And yet, though the agreement was his own doing, Rabin remained uneasy.

In part, it was the wavering of a man who had spent much of his early life shooting at the people he was now reconciling with, defending Israelis against their bloody attacks and thwarting their nationalist aspirations. Born in Jerusalem in 1922, Rabin joined one of Mandatory Palestine's Jewish armed groups soon after high school—the storied Palmach strike force. He fought in some of the most critical battles of the war for Israel's independence in 1948, in one notorious action overseeing the expulsion of thousands of Palestinians from their hometown Lydda. Then he signed on for more service, climbing the ranks of the officers corps until he commanded the entire army at age forty-two. It was Rabin who led Israel's astonishing six-day assault against a coalition of Arab armies in 1967—the very war that brought the West Bank and Gaza under Israel's control. It was also Rabin who, as defense minister in the late 1980s, ordered an aggressive crackdown against Palestinians agitating for independence in these territories, sometimes violently. Their rebellion would come to be known as the first intifada, meaning literally "shaking off" in Arabic.

The Oslo Accord promised Palestinians a measure of self-rule in parts of the West Bank and Gaza Strip. It implied, at least, that they might one day make their own state there. It also provided a foothold in these territories for Yasser Arafat, the head of the PLO and the man Israelis reviled more than any other enemy for a string of dreadful attacks against civilians his group perpetrated mostly in the 1970s and '80s. For Israelis who viewed the West Bank and Gaza as theirs by biblical promise—including religious and right-wing Jews who had settled there over the years—the deal amounted to an abomination. But Rabin had no religious sentiment at all (one US official would describe him as the most secular Israeli he had ever met) and little regard for the settlers. To him, the agreement mainly presented a security challenge, no small issue given that security marked the core of his identity as a politician. It also entailed direct interaction with Arafat—starting at the White House ceremony, if Rabin chose to go. Just the thought of it caused him to cringe.

There was also a political dimension to Rabin's discomfort. The negotiations that led to the agreement had been the undertaking of people close to the foreign minister, Shimon Peres. For decades, the two men—Rabin and Peres—cultivated not just a political rivalry in their Labor Party but a personal enmity like no other in Israeli politics. With a fervor that often seemed incomprehensible to people around them, they simply detested each other. Rabin took control of the Oslo process at an early stage, appointing his own envoy to the talks and directing Peres, who supervised the process from his perch at the Foreign Ministry in Jerusalem. It became the venture of both men together, with Rabin in the lead. And yet, its genesis as the unauthorized dialogue of Peres's protégés with PLO representatives sometimes appeared to taint it for Rabin. Whenever American officials asked him about the secret talks—among the few who knew they existed—he would respond with a characteristic downward wave of the hand to indicate nothing would come of them.

Even after negotiators sealed the Oslo Accord in mid-August, Rabin allowed himself a dismissive aside from time to time. When a family friend, the journalist Aliza Wallach, asked him over Friday-night dinner some days later which PLO figure led the Palestinian negotiating team in Oslo, Rabin responded derisively. "Some Abu

Ali," he said—a colloquialism in Hebrew meaning roughly "some nobody." It was in fact Ahmed Korei, the PLO's finance chief who went by the nickname Abu Ala.

With all these conflicting impulses on his mind, Rabin began his workday that Friday morning, September 10, by reading a letter he received from Arafat. During the length of his term, Rabin actually served simultaneously in two positions, as both prime minister and defense minister. He would begin his workweek in the capital, Jerusalem, in one of a row of gray office buildings that housed the government ministries. For three nights each week he and his wife, Leah, dwelled at the prime minister's stately residence in the upscale Rehavia neighborhood. On Wednesdays, they would make the hour-long drive to Tel Aviv, where Rabin conducted the country's affairs from the sprawling compound of the Defense Ministry. They slept in their own apartment for the remainder of the week.

But on this Friday, he drove to Jerusalem to receive the Norwegian foreign minister, Johan Jørgen Holst, who had arrived directly from Arafat's headquarters in Tunis. The letter Holst delivered from Arafat would serve as an appendix to the Oslo Accord. Addressed to Rabin as Mr. Prime Minister, it ran seven paragraphs long and included flourishes about the "new era in the history of the Middle East" and a "new epoch of peaceful coexistence." Its main point was to convey the PLO's recognition of Israel's right to exist "in peace and security" and its renunciation of the "use of terrorism and other violence." For a group whose 1964 charter declared the existence of Israel as "illegal and null and void," it was a remarkable text.

Rabin read it several times and then drafted his response. It contained just one paragraph and included neither the niceties nor the lofty language that Arafat had deployed. Israel had decided to "recognize the PLO as the representative of the Palestinian people," he wrote. At the bottom of the page, he withheld a valediction. Rabin signed the letter during a short news conference later in the morning, flanked by Holst and Peres and using a simple ballpoint pen. Then he convened a group of advisers to discuss the White House ceremony.

His chief of staff, Eitan Haber, had spent some part of the past week canvassing politicians and public figures, including the cele-

brated writer Amos Oz, on whether Rabin should attend the ceremony himself or send Peres in his stead. He had also been reviewing
opinion polls that showed strong support for the deal from the political center, where his boss felt most comfortable, and of course from
the peace advocates on the left side of the divide. A former journalist who sported an ear-to-ear comb-over and often looked sleep-
deprived, Haber oversaw the prime minister's schedule and wrote his
speeches—which meant he had the delicate job of trying to know
Rabin's thoughts almost as well as Rabin did. There, at the meeting, he stressed that the agreement carried huge risks and noted that
right-wingers, rabbis, and West Bank settlers had been protesting outside the prime minister's office for much of the week. Their chanting
could be heard from the sidewalk below even as he spoke.

Sending Peres would work as a kind of hedge, Haber argued. If the
deal succeeded, there would be other ceremonies for the prime minister to attend. And if it failed, Rabin could pin it on his daydreaming
foreign minister. "We can blame Peres," Haber said. Rabin sided with
his chief of staff and adjourned the meeting.

But at home later, with his family, he had second thoughts.
Friday-night dinners at the Rabin home followed a ritual. They began
promptly at eight o'clock, usually involved some political talk, and
ended in time for Rabin to watch the nine o'clock newscast. The
regulars included Rabin's daughter, Dalia; her husband, Avi; and her
children, Noa and Jonathan. Rabin's son, Yuval, had been living with
his family in North Carolina, and made only occasional visits.

By Israeli standards, the apartment where they gathered on the top
floor of the eight-story building on Rav Ashi suggested privilege but
not extravagance. It had recently been renovated and included two
bedrooms, a den, and a second, smaller kitchen on the roof, where the
couple hosted dinner parties for up to thirty people. But when it was
just family, they ate in the dining area on the main floor and skipped
the formalities. So much so that Rabin, who liked to sleep on Friday
afternoons, would sometimes come to the table in his robe and slip-
pers. Still, punctuality was essential; if someone failed to show up by a
few minutes after eight, he would check his watch and become restless.

For many months, Rabin had told no one in the family about the talks with the PLO except Leah. The secrecy reminded Dalia of the outbreak of the Six-Day War twenty-six years earlier. Her parents had sent her to school that Monday without telling her that Israeli planes would be striking Egypt later in the morning, though Rabin had decided himself on the launch time for the offensive. It taught her not to expect privileges as the daughter of the chief of staff and later the prime minister.

But now that the agreement with the PLO had been disclosed, she inquired gently why Rabin had decided against traveling to Washington. Shouldn't he be giving it the full weight of his position by representing Israel himself at the White House? Dalia had rarely questioned her father's judgment. To her, he was a rarity in Israeli politics, methodical in every undertaking and honest through and through, but also woefully untalented at self-promotion—a liability that had cost him over the years. Her father was an introvert. He hated the political drudgery of cultivating journalists or charming donors. Rabin's idea of small talk often involved his own analytical exegeses, brilliant in their insight, but delivered in a halting monotone.

Leah, who knew that Rabin felt ambivalent about shaking Arafat's hand, had been withholding her own opinion all week. Now she added her voice. By staying home, wouldn't he be letting Peres take all the credit?

The questions stirred the issue again for Rabin and at the end of dinner he left the table to phone Shimon Sheves, the director of his office and perhaps his closest adviser. At the meeting earlier in the day, Sheves had been the one man in the room to argue against Haber's position. The two—the powerbrokers in Rabin's office—held different titles but their spheres overlapped and they often competed for their boss's attention. Sheves ran Rabin's election campaign and handled many of the prime minister's political dealings, often with a stridency that rankled other aides and cabinet ministers. He was younger than the other staff members and the only one to sport a beard, which he kept meticulously trimmed. "Where are you?" Rabin inquired. Sheves sensed that his boss needed company and said he would come right over.

But before he arrived, the phone rang in Rabin's den and Clinton's secretary of state, Warren Christopher, was patched through. Rabin had managed in a conversation with Clinton earlier in the week to deflect pressure over the question of representation at the ceremony. Now, somehow, it felt more difficult to resist Christopher's courteous prodding. The secretary pointed out that Arafat had overcome criticism the previous day and mustered a nine-to-three majority in his executive committee in favor of the deal—an act of real leadership. Washington stood ready to host Arafat at the White House, a complicated maneuver given the PLO's status as a terrorist organization under US law. But only if Rabin came as well.

By the time he hung up the phone, Rabin had edged substantially closer to changing his mind. His conversation with Sheves carried him the rest of the way. The adviser pointed out that Rabin had staked his premiership on the Oslo Accord. Its failure would be his failure, even if he stayed away from the signing ceremony. To make the deal work, he would have to set aside his reluctance and genuinely own it. The two men spent the last hour of that Friday drinking whiskey and discussing sports—they were both compulsive soccer fans. When Rabin finally went to bed after midnight, he told Leah they would be flying to Washington on Sunday.

But first he would have to face down a major political crisis.

———————————

BY SEVEN THIRTY the next morning, Rabin had convened Sheves and Haber at his apartment, along with two other advisers—his military secretary, Maj. Gen. Danny Yatom, and the director of the Mossad intelligence agency, Shabtai Shavit. Now that Rabin was traveling to Washington, Yatom and Shavit would have a long list of security arrangements to tend to quickly. And since the Israeli delegation would be larger than planned, Haber needed to book more rooms at the Mayflower Hotel in Washington, coordinate scheduling with the White House, and look after many other aspects of the trip. Rabin's advisers were accustomed to working on the Jewish Sabbath—few of them were religiously observant. But an excursion abroad for an

Israeli leader on such short notice was almost unprecedented. The prime minister's plane was to depart the following afternoon, with the White House ceremony scheduled for Monday at eleven o'clock.

But the first order of business was to inform Peres that Rabin had changed his mind. The two leaders, Rabin and Peres, had forged a kind of armistice during the months of the Oslo process, both recognizing the political risk they had undertaken by conducting secret talks with Israel's most loathed enemy. It included a commitment by each man to keep the other well informed. Still, the level of distrust and suspicion remained exceedingly high. One government spokesman had come to think of them in this period as two old sumo wrestlers locked in a perpetual grip, each trying to defeat the other but also propping each other up.

Haber delivered the notice by phone to Peres's chief of staff shortly after eight in the morning. Then he called a reporter from Israel Radio, the country's public broadcasting network, to give him the news—a move he would soon regret. The network ran a series of radio stations that together owned a huge share of the listenership across the country. At the top of every hour, the stations all sounded a series of beeps, the cue that a short news bulletin would follow, originally modeled on BBC broadcasts. Haber assumed the news item would go out at nine o'clock, giving Peres's aide an hour to inform his boss.

Instead, the radio announced it in a special bulletin at eight thirty and Peres, who was about to sit down at his official residence with two of the country's most esteemed journalists, happened to have the radio on. He fumed. The interview with Nahum Barnea and Shimon Shiffer of the newspaper *Yedioth Ahronoth* was meant to highlight Peres's role in the negotiations and his achievement as a statesman. A producer for the NBC *Today* show waited for his own turn in a production truck parked outside. But inside, the journalists found Peres gloomy and short-tempered—and, at nine in the morning, well into his second round of French brandy. Peres offered each of the two journalists a glass as well, but soon asked them to step outside so he could make a call. They would hear one end of the conversation later on the tape recorder they'd left in the room. "That man ruined my life! He has been persecuting me for sixteen years!" Peres hollered at Giora Eini, a lawyer who had mediated disputes between Rabin and Peres over the years. "It's either me or Rabin, otherwise I'm staying home."

Peres also called the writer Amos Oz, his friend of many years, and told him he would resign. The foreign minister liked the company of novelists and poets and regarded himself a man of letters. It was just one of the ways he and Rabin differed. Peres had grown up in Poland and though he immigrated to Palestine at age eleven, he never fully lost his shtetl accent—a millstone in a society that consciously tried to erase the diaspora culture from its Jewish immigrants. Rabin, by contrast, was a *sabra*, a native son at a historical moment when such a status paid especially high dividends.

Their separate career paths brought them in contact early on but also shaped their rivalry. In those years, the smartest and most capable young members of the Jewish community in Palestine entered either the military or government service, as is often the case in emerging societies. Peres chose politics. He became a protégé of David Ben-Gurion, later Israel's first prime minister; helped procure arms for the Jewish army in the run-up to the War of Independence; and eventually brokered the deal for the French nuclear reactor that made Israel an atomic power (albeit undeclared). By age twenty-nine, he had come to run the Defense Ministry, the country's largest and most complicated government agency.

Still, Peres never risked his life on the battlefield, a blemish in a young country that worshipped its generals. To Rabin, he was an apparatchik. He might have heard the sound of gunfire, went the old joke, but only through the telephone.

The antagonism simmered for years, until it boiled over in 1974 during an internal election in the Labor Party. By then, Peres had been a member of parliament for fifteen years, while Rabin had been in politics for just a few months. Rabin had left the military in 1968 to serve as Israel's ambassador to Washington, returned to Israel in late 1973, and joined the government as a junior cabinet minister. Yet when the party's central committee members convened to choose a new leader in the aftermath of the devastating Yom Kippur War, they favored Rabin over Peres—a considerable slight to a man who had clawed his way up the political hierarchy over decades. The fact that Rabin had been abroad in the run-up to the war and thus untainted by its failures went a long way to explaining his victory. But the media's gushing about Rabin as Israel's first native-born prime minister compounded the indignity for Peres.

To preserve party unity, Rabin made Peres his defense minister. But he quickly regretted it, complaining to associates that Peres constantly leaked sensitive information to the press and undermined him at every turn. Among other things, Peres sided with a band of Jewish settlers in the West Bank who had squatted at Sebastia, near the Palestinian city of Nablus, forcing Rabin to provide them with provisional housing. The settlement movement was relatively small at the time and the victory gave it a significant boost. Rabin felt sure Peres had done it primarily to challenge his authority.

Three years into his term, Rabin resigned his post when a journalist discovered that his wife maintained a few thousand dollars in a bank account in Washington well after his ambassadorship ended—a violation of Israel's strict foreign currency laws. For years, Rabin suspected that Peres or one of his minions had leaked the story. Leadership of the party now swung to Peres.

To people who interacted with both men at the time, the differences between them seemed almost chemical. Peres impressed people with his big ideas—the nuclear program of the 1950s and '60s, and much later a blueprint for a New Middle East. Rabin almost never waxed on about lofty initiatives but could bore into the details of a project—a military operation, for instance—until nothing was left to chance. Peres had a Francophile side, wore double-breasted suits and honed elegant aphorisms that he sprang on people as if spontaneously. Rabin preferred the culture of Washington, where his ambassadorship included schooling in the art of realpolitik from the experts, Nixon and Kissinger. Both men smoked cigarettes and drank whiskey but Rabin had the larger appetite for tobacco. He regularly burned through two packs of Parliament Longs in a day and had yellow stains on the insides of his index and middle fingers to show for it.

By the 1980s, the rivalry had caused huge damage to the Labor Party. Rabin published a memoir full of vitriol against Peres, including a designation that would stick with him for the rest of his political life: "indefatigable schemer." The book's ghostwriter, Dov Goldstein, coined the phrase after long conversations with Rabin. When Rabin encountered it in a draft, he congratulated Goldstein for hitting the mark so deftly. "He called me in the evening and said, 'Tell me, Dovaleh [Goldstein's nickname], what was your rank in the army?'" Goldstein recalled later. "I told him I was a sergeant. . . . He said, 'In that case, make a note to yourself. This is the first time in history that a major general salutes a sergeant over the phone.'"

Peres, who would go on to lose successive election campaigns, vented about Rabin in regular meetings he convened with five of the country's top journalists. The "quintet," as Peres referred to them, included Dan Margalit, of the newspaper *Ha'aretz*, who broke the story of Leah's US bank account, and David Landau, editor of the *Jerusalem Post*. Peres hosted them in his home, where they watched the news together, talked politics, smoked, and drank. Though the journalists knew all the ugly details of the rivalry, the rough edge of Peres's tongue continually surprised them. One recurring theme was Rabin's habit of taking credit for Peres's accomplishments—as Peres saw it— including the brilliant Israeli hostage rescue in Entebbe, Uganda, in 1976. Peres insisted the idea was all his.

Now, on that Saturday morning seventeen years after Entebbe, Peres once again felt his nemesis was making claims on an achievement he regarded as his own. He ushered the two journalists out of his apartment and began writing a resignation letter. Meanwhile, Eini, the mediator, swung into action. He called Rabin to tell him about the crisis and get his permission to begin a kind of shuttle diplomacy.

In one of the many little ironies of their dysfunctional relationship, Peres and Rabin actually lived in the same neighborhood, just three blocks apart, in similar-style buildings. When his services were needed, Eini would park his car on Rav Ashi and walk back and forth between the two apartments offering bridging proposals, often in writing. If he needed to make a private call, perhaps to consult with another party member, he would stop at a phone booth situated midway between the two buildings. His appearance in the neighborhood signaled to journalists that the elders were fighting again. With his long frizzy hair, wire-rim glasses, and Frank Zappa mustache, Eini looked like a member of a '70s rock band but in a suit.

This time, however, Peres had been spending the day in Jerusalem, at the official residence of the foreign minister. Eini did most of the work by phone.

To the mediator it was clear that Rabin could not allow Peres to resign. At such a pivotal moment, it would tarnish the peace deal. But the two men had been competing for so long, both found it hard to view this collective achievement—the product of Peres's chronically wide lens and Rabin's rigorous focus on the details—as anything but a zero-sum game. When Rabin defeated Peres in the Labor primaries the previous year and won the general election, he had been determined to exclude him from any significant decision-making role. Only under pressure from party members did he relent and make him foreign minister.

For Peres, the need for public approval had grown with each electoral defeat—in the estimate of even his close supporters, to a compulsive degree. It was in fact Peres's deputy, Yossi Beilin, who had initiated the contacts with the PLO. Beilin kept it a secret even from Peres until the sides had held two successful meetings and crafted the first draft of an agreement. If anyone should have complained about stolen recognition, it was Beilin. But Peres felt he had earned the credit by pressing Rabin at key moments. "I told him, if you go this way, you won't have a better colleague than me. If you won't go this way, you'll have no greater opponent," he recounted two decades later.

One way or another, by evening Eini managed to broker an agreement that had something for everyone. Both men would go to Washington. Both would stand on stage at the White House alongside Arafat and the PLO's second-in-command, Mahmoud Abbas. The two deputies, Peres and Abbas, would sign the accord.

With advisers and guests on both sides, the delegation to Washington suddenly grew to more than one hundred people. Haber would have to tell Rabin's own daughter, Dalia, that there would be no room for her on the plane. Hours before takeoff he called her again to say a seat was now available but only if she could get to the airport quickly—and pay for the flight. She obliged on both counts.

ON HIS TRIPS abroad, Rabin flew in an old Boeing 707, a four-engine plane that streaked so much black soot across the sky, some countries would eventually ban it from their airspace. The Israeli Air Force used the plane to refuel its fighter jets in midair when it wasn't servicing the prime minister. But with a day's notice, a ground crew could reconfigure it as a luxury airliner—though only in the loosest definition of the term. Mostly it involved inserting several first-class seats in the midsection of the plane and bolting two cots to the floor for Rabin and Leah. In the front part of the cabin, Peres, his staff members, and guests sat in economy seats on one side of the aisle while Rabin's entourage filled the other side. Journalists and bodyguards sat in the back.

Rabin boarded in the late afternoon on Sunday, took his seat, and promptly asked one of the crew members for a glass of beer. The plane's flight attendants and pilots were all air force officers, among the most rigorously vetted servicemen in the military. Then Rabin lit a cigarette and sat back as the aluminum frame of the old airliner vibrated through taxi and takeoff.

From the air, the country looked tiny and vulnerable, with most of its urban clusters pressed up against a sloping shoreline. In reality, its security position had been improving for some years. The collapse of the Soviet Union and the smashing of Iraq's army by US forces in the 1991 Gulf War had created big strategic advantages for Israel. With no superpower to back Israel's enemies and with Iraq neutralized for now, the old Israeli fear of invasion by a coalition of Arab states seemed less relevant than ever.

Other forces were redefining the country economically and culturally.

Until the late 1980s, Israelis had little access to the big brands and trends that shaped other parts of the West. The country had no indoor shopping mall and just one television channel. Whatever movie aired on television Friday night was often the topic of conversation over the weekend. But a gradual deregulating of the economy opened Israel to outside influences and allowed for things like cable television in 1990. A basic package came with MTV and CNN, two huge cultural influences that had already been American staples for a decade. The easing of the Arab economic boycott against Israel the following year contributed to the process. Suddenly Israelis could buy Pepsi Cola and drive cars made by Honda and Toyota—companies that had dominated world markets but shunned Israel.

The year 1993 marked a turning point in the transition. Even before Israel announced the Oslo deal, McDonald's signed its first franchise agreement with an Israeli businessman. Other fast-food chains followed. A second terrestrial television channel went live that year and later formed a news division, the first to compete with the state-run newscasts. Big-name music performers who had previously bypassed Israel put the country on their tour schedule that summer, including Madonna and Guns N' Roses. The biggest pop star of all, Michael Jackson, was embroiled in a sex scandal over his sleepovers with underage boys in 1993. Yet when he came to Tel Aviv in the fall, 70,000 Israelis gathered to see him.

The Oslo process would accelerate these changes. But it would also affect Israel in darker ways. As Rabin's plane left Israeli airspace, the country experienced the first convulsion of a peace deal that was already rousing extremists on both sides.

In the southern town of Ashkelon, a Palestinian from Gaza, Ahmad Atala, boarded a commuter bus around six in the evening, pulled the pin from a grenade he brought on board, and lobbed it down the aisle. Earlier in the day, the Islamic resistance group Hamas had issued a statement calling the Oslo deal a disgrace and a sellout and urging Palestinians to oppose it. The group, which rejected any compromise with Israel, would devote itself in the coming years to scuttling the reconciliation. Atala had at least a loose connection to Hamas, along with an abiding rage over an Israeli shooting spree three years earlier that left seven Palestinians dead. He wore a shirt imprinted with the words "Black Sunday," a reference to the incident, which took place at a bus stop south of Tel Aviv.

Somehow, the grenade failed to explode. To salvage the operation,

Atala turned to the driver and stabbed him several times in the torso, causing him to lose control of the wheel. As the bus weaved back and forth across the lanes, a twenty-year-old corporal sitting near the front had the presence of mind to press a magazine into his military-issue rifle, pull back the charging handle, and shoot Atala in the chest. The Palestinian and the bus driver, Yehiel Carmi, would be the first fatalities of the Oslo era—dead even before the deal was signed.

The news reached Rabin midflight and instantly made plain to him the profound vulnerability of the agreement. Lone extremists, Palestinian or Israeli, could easily undermine what the two sides would now devote much of their energy to achieving—a new relationship between them, a sense of security for Israelis, and greater freedom for Palestinians. The episode would replay itself again and again in the coming years, to devastating effect. Rabin instructed Yatom, his military secretary, to seal off the West Bank and Gaza for the time being. The measure would keep out other potential militants but also prevent more than 100,000 Palestinians who worked in Israel from reaching their jobs. These extended "closures" would come to characterize the Oslo deal as well, prompting many Palestinians to wonder whether the agreement made their lives better or worse.

After a stop in Amsterdam—the 707 burned too much fuel to fly directly from Israel to Washington—Rabin spent most of the night either in his seat or on the cot, across the aisle from his wife. Leah had a clear role as the wife of Rabin the army general and later Rabin the ambassador and prime minister. At big gatherings she would take charge of the mingling, drawing the social pressure away from her husband. The two had married forty-five years earlier, during a break between battles in the War of Independence. But because Rabin had been absorbed in combat much of the time, he had a friend handle the wedding preparations, including booking the venue and the rabbi. On the day of the ceremony, Rabin was so shy that the rabbi thought it was the friend who was marrying Leah.

Peres, by contrast, kept moving around the cabin talking to anyone who remained awake. The insomniacs included Dalia Yairi, whose husband had died trying to rescue hostages held by PLO guerrillas eighteen years earlier. Rabin and Peres had allotted three seats on the plane to family members of terror victims. Their presence at the ceremony would signal that even Israelis who suffered deeply and directly from the conflict were ready to set aside the enmity. It would also help shield the decision makers from accusations that embracing the architect of these attacks amounted to a betrayal of the victims. Yairi was Rabin's choice. She hosted a popular radio show and knew him going back two decades.

Yairi's husband, Uzi, had been on leave from the army when a PLO team landed at a Tel Aviv beach in rubber dinghies in March of 1975 and took hostages at the Savoy Hotel. The guerrillas hoped to trade the captives for Palestinians held in Israeli jails. Years earlier, Uzi had commanded the military's top antiterrorism unit, Sayeret Matkal. As the standoff entered the night, he persuaded his old comrades in the unit to let him join the assault team. But the raid on the hotel the following morning went badly. Uzi and two fellow soldiers died, along with eight hostages. The team killed seven of the eight Palestinian guerrillas.

For Yairi, the plane ride brought back the anguish of that morning but it also infused her with giddy energy. On her radio show, she had gently mocked Peres during the preceding year over his dreamy pronouncements about the coming of a New Middle East. Now he teased her back, insisting the fantasy was materializing. From Yairi's vantage point on the plane, the two teams seemed to play symbiotic roles. She saw them as the dreamers and the doers. And while tensions were palpable, members of the two camps were now mixing across the aisle and telling jokes. Only one person in the front section aired any skepticism aloud. Danny Rothschild, a major general who served as the liaison between the government and the military rulers of the West Bank and Gaza, pointed out that Palestinians lacked governing institutions—the very kind that Jews had built before their independence. "We're only at the beginning. It's too early to celebrate," he said. The remark struck one of the passengers on the Peres side as a bit of chutzpah. After all, Palestinians lacked institutions because Israeli authorities in the West Bank and Gaza had prevented them from organizing for the preceding twenty-six years.

Oddly, the two people who had played perhaps the biggest role *in*

Oslo were absent from the plane. When Beilin launched the secret channel, he sent Yair Hirschfeld and Ron Pundak to do the actual giving and taking. Hirschfeld was an academic with ties to Palestinians, and Pundak had been a journalist and a former intelligence officer. The Foreign Ministry's director general, Uri Savir, would eventually take charge of the negotiation but Hirschfeld and Pundak formed the first rapport with the PLO delegation and attended every session until the deal was clinched seven months later. Still, when preparations were being made for the signing, Peres informed the two men that there would be no room for them on the plane and no seats available at the ceremony in Washington.

The foreign minister had made clear he wanted to share the spotlight with as few of the project's collaborators as possible. "You don't invite the midwife to the bris," he told people in his office. Somehow, this man of grand visions could engage in the pettiest of calculations, Pundak thought at the time. But he would not be thwarted. With a few phone calls, Pundak secured two seats at the ceremony from the batch allotted to American Jewish leaders. And he persuaded a German foundation to buy the round-trip air tickets for Hirschfeld and himself.

In the rear of the plane, the journalists waited for scraps of information to make their way back to them. Nahum Barnea, the columnist for *Yedioth Ahronoth* who had interviewed Peres at his official residence the previous day, had accompanied Rabin on several trips abroad. He liked to stay up after the other journalists fell asleep, in case the prime minister strolled back looking to share a smoke. In those moments, Rabin could be a generous talker. He didn't schmooze with journalists, but he might spend an hour peeling back the layers of a certain political dilemma, leaving the reporter with enough material for a strong front-page story. Barnea, whose witty columns often reflected the national mood, had mostly praise for the Oslo Accord. But he felt that Israelis would only embrace a slow, cautious advance. He summed it up with one sentence in a column published earlier that day: "Yes to the agreement, no to the euphoria."

Most of the reporters on board had been covering the senior echelons of government for years. They numbered among Israel's most well-connected journalists. Yet for all their sources, not one of them detected over the preceding seven months that the biggest Israeli story in decades was unfolding in Norway. The failure had caused some embarrassment for journalists and editors—Israeli officials were, after all, notorious leakers. But it pleased Rabin, who had kept the secret even from his inner circle. He told Sheves about the talks only at the point when he wanted opinion polls conducted to gauge how Israelis would respond to a deal with the PLO. Haber had been on a private trip abroad when news of the deal broke in August. It caught him by surprise.

The one newspaperman who came close to sniffing out the story was a reporter for the broadsheet *Ha'aretz* who did not cover the prime minister's office at all. Yerah Tal wrote mostly about political parties and spent at least one day a week at Labor headquarters in Tel Aviv, chatting up party functionaries. He was in the building one day in July when a source told him that Israel and the PLO had been staging a series of high-level meetings overseas. The source provided no other details, and when Tal got back to the newsroom, his editor voiced skepticism. So did the more senior journalists at the paper, including Ze'ev Schiff, whose military contacts were said to run so deep that army generals regularly called *him* for information.

Still, *Ha'aretz* published a front-page piece on July 12, 1993, under the headline: "Jerusalem Conducted Secret Negotiations with the PLO Leadership." The story got most of the details wrong, describing the venue of the talks as "an Arab country," and their focus as "Jerusalem and the borders of a possible autonomy zone." Tal's second source for the story, a PLO official, had no knowledge of the negotiation under way in Oslo but had been privy to other contacts between Israelis and PLO members. On the phone with Tal from Cairo, he confirmed the wrong back channel. For Rabin and Peres, who feared any publicity would wreck the negotiation, the errors in the story amounted to a lucky break. They allowed Peres's office to issue a more-or-less honest denial, ensuring no other newspaper would follow up.

After almost fourteen hours in transit, the 707 touched down at Andrews Air Force Base in darkness early Monday, September 13, 1993. The temperature was already seventy degrees and humid outside, typical late-summer weather for Washington. It would climb to nearly ninety degrees by the start of the ceremony later that morning.

———————

HABER HAD RESERVED nearly forty rooms at the Mayflower Hotel, a landmark in downtown Washington about five blocks north of the White House. Built in 1925 and adorned in gold trim, the hotel had been dubbed by President Harry Truman the "second best address" in Washington—second, of course, to 1600 Pennsylvania Avenue. By the time the Israeli delegation arrived, throngs of people were pouring out of the Farragut North Metro stop near the entrance to the hotel, on their way to work. Rabin crossed the lobby and rode the elevator to his suite. Haber, who had already written Rabin's speech, phoned Clinton's Middle East adviser, Martin Indyk, to settle a few last details. The weekend had been filled with drama. The next few hours before the signing would be as well.

When Rabin decided to make the trip to Washington, Haber conveyed to the White House a request that Arafat refrain from wearing his iconic military uniform and sidearm to the ceremony. To Arafat these were the symbols of a lifelong struggle for Palestinian independence, but Israelis associated them with PLO terrorism. Rabin wanted his countrymen to begin perceiving Arafat differently.

Haber also sought to ensure that Arafat would not greet Rabin in the manner of Arab tradition: a kiss on each cheek and sometimes one on the forehead as well. Rabin had resolved to make peace with Israel's enemies, but he was no hugger. He certainly did not want to feel Arafat's whiskers pressing against his face. "All right. All right. But no kissing," he had told Clinton by phone over the weekend when the president pressed for a handshake onstage. Seeing to the requests required some creative maneuvering by the White House staff. Clinton, who had been in office for nine months by this point, felt determined to make Rabin comfortable.

The relationship between the two men began awkwardly a year earlier. Rabin had just started his term as prime minister and was visiting the United States for meetings with President George H. W. Bush. Clinton asked to sit down with him as well. The former Arkansas governor was in the final stage of a tough election battle against Bush and hoped a photo with the Israeli leader would help his campaign. Rabin tried to put him off. He hated the idea of being a factor in the US election. But Clinton kept pressing.

When they did get together on August 12 at the Madison Hotel, along with the vice-presidential candidate, Al Gore, and staff members on all sides, the opening niceties gave way to a series of uncomfortable silences. Rabin felt wary of Democrats, a vestige of his run-ins with Jimmy Carter during his first term as prime minister. And though Clinton on good days could fill a room with his charm, the two men were just extraordinarily dissimilar—Rabin a regimented old soldier, and Clinton a freewheeling baby boomer and former Rhodes scholar.

Sheves, who had known Gore and his aides from a stint years earlier on a leadership program in Washington, felt the meeting drifting toward disaster. He whispered to Gore that Clinton should raise the issue of American military aid. Israel had been the biggest recipient of US defense funding since the 1970s. Perhaps Clinton could commit himself as president to sustaining the nearly $2 billion aid package, Sheves offered. Gore scribbled a few words on a scrap of paper and passed it to Clinton, who, on reading it, launched into a speech about America's commitment to Israel's security. It seemed to work—Sheves noticed Rabin perking up.

At their next meeting in March, Clinton was already president and hoping, like many of his predecessors, to help bring peace to the Middle East. The Oslo talks had been under way by then but Rabin kept the details to himself. Still, Clinton sensed a determination on Rabin's part to forge a deal with either Syria or the Palestinians—though not both at the same time. He also felt drawn to Rabin's directness and honesty, the gruff exterior notwithstanding. Clinton would say later about the meeting that Rabin "was sort of sizing me up, and I already knew he was bigger than life."

To head off any awkwardness between Arafat and Rabin, Indyk solicited the help of Bandar bin Sultan, a Saudi prince who had been serving as ambassador to the United States for a decade. An influential figure in Washington, Bandar had cultivated close ties with American elites, including members of the Bush family. He also had connections to most Arab leaders and knew Arafat personally. Indyk asked Bandar to brief Arafat about both the "no kissing rule," as people in the White House were now calling it, and the matter of his attire. While Arafat was still en route to Washington, Bandar ordered several suits delivered to his hotel room.

With three hours left before the ceremony, the two issues—tiny representations of the sensitivities Israelis and Palestinians would have to overcome—were now occupying the president and his staff. At a meeting in the Oval Office, Clinton's national security adviser, Anthony Lake, said he knew a way to thwart the traditional Arab embrace. It involved extending the right arm for a handshake while simultaneously planting the left hand firmly on the approaching person's forearm. Done right, the maneuver would prevent the person from leaning in for a kiss. Clinton practiced it several times with his national security adviser, at one point raising his knee toward Lake's groin to demonstrate his backup plan. If he could keep Arafat from kissing him onstage, Clinton thought, the old guerrilla leader would not try to kiss Rabin.

Back at Andrews Air Force Base, television journalists had set up mobile units to broadcast Arafat's arrival live on television. The United States had shunned Arafat since his rise to prominence in the 1960s. Now he grinned widely as he walked off the plane and onto the Andrews tarmac, America's gateway for visiting dignitaries. Among the benefits Arafat had hoped to reap from the Oslo deal was access to the administration in Washington—and here it was. He shook hands with Edward Djerejian, the assistant secretary of state for Near Eastern affairs, and then spotted Bandar in the reception line. "Andrews, Bandar. We're at Andrews!" he spoke into his ear. The two men rode together to the hotel.

Bandar talked Arafat out of a plan to hand Clinton his gun during the ceremony, a theatrical gesture meant to signify his turn away from the armed struggle. The symbolism, at least, seemed apt to Bandar, but the Secret Service would never let him close to the White House with a sidearm. (Clinton, on hearing the plan, quipped that if

Arafat gave him a gun onstage, he would shoot him with it.) But he couldn't talk him into a suit. When Arafat tried on one of the jackets, his advisers chuckled. They had never seen him in anything but military green. Arafat was still sore with them for forcing him to leave his wife, Suha, behind in Tunis. The tension between his aides and his wife had climbed steadily since their wedding three years earlier.

Feeling stage-managed and a little humiliated, Arafat returned to his standard garb but left off the medals and insignias he often displayed on his chest. Without them, the outfit was technically just a safari suit. Then he put on his kaffiyeh and headed out.

But Rabin knew a military uniform when he saw one. In his room at the Mayflower, he caught a glimpse of Arafat on television leaving his hotel for the White House and yelled for Haber. Rabin had freckles and fair skin—he was what Israelis called a *gingi*, a Hebrew variation on the British term for "redhead." When his anger rose, as it did now, his face flushed brightly. Haber got Indyk on the phone and told him—to Indyk's horror—that Rabin was sulking in his room and would not be coming. By now, hundreds of dignitaries had gathered on the South Lawn of the White House, including former presidents Bush and Carter and several former secretaries of state. To Indyk's relief, the crisis lasted just a few minutes—Rabin quickly withdrew the threat. But the episode foreshadowed difficulties in the rapport between Rabin and Arafat. It would take time to build.

With the two delegations now at the White House, the full significance of the event began to set in. A year earlier, Israel still had a law barring its citizens from just meeting with PLO members. A few weeks earlier, the Oslo process was undisclosed and uncertain. Now Rabin and Arafat stood on either side of Clinton in the Blue Room, an Israeli general and a Palestinian guerrilla leader about to take the stage together. Arafat reached across Clinton to shake Rabin's hand, but the Israeli leader kept his arms crossed behind his back and motioned outside, where the crowd was waiting.

Nearly three thousand people had gathered on the South Lawn, including ambassadors of Arab countries officially at war with Israel. Rabin's son, Yuval, had driven five hours from Raleigh, North Carolina, and was seated many rows back, along with his sister, Dalia.

He had not had a chance to talk to his father before the ceremony. Yairi, who had time for a brief rest in the hotel, took a seat near the front, close enough to read the facial expressions of the seven men onstage, including Peres and Rabin, Arafat and Abbas, Secretary of State Christopher and the Russian foreign minister, Andrey Kozyrev. From the raised platform, these men looked out over a mass of mostly gray heads and dark suits—and beyond, at the white obelisk of the Washington Monument towering over the National Mall.

In the coming years, signing ceremonies and Middle East peace conferences would take place with some regularity. Eventually, they would come to serve as reminders that peace itself remained elusive. But at this first event, the sheer enormity of the moment, the unscripted interactions, the nervous asides, all generated currents of electricity. Until their encounter in the White House, the two protagonists had never met, which meant the audience, on the lawn and at home via television, was seeing *in real time* the body language of icy hostility slowly thawing. Even the speeches, predictably lofty and infused with biblical quotations, had a mesmerizing quality—less for the words and more for the astonishing context.

The signing itself took place around a long wooden table dragged out from one of the White House offices—the same table Israeli and Egyptian leaders had used to seal their peace treaty in 1979. Peres sat down first, putting his name to two copies of the agreement, which included cross outs and notations in pen, changes made during the course of the morning to resolve last-minute disputes. He signed in two places on each copy of the agreement, big sloping signatures both in English and in Hebrew. Then he tucked the pen in his inside pocket. Abbas signed next and when he rose from the table, he shook hands with each of the men on stage, including Rabin and Peres. It was the first direct interaction between a Palestinian and Israelis at the ceremony and it caused people in the audience to stand and applaud.

But the real drama occurred a few minutes later, after Christopher and Kozyrev added their names to the agreement as witnesses. Clinton, who had rehearsed for this moment, shook hands with Rabin to his right and Arafat to his left, then spread his arms wide to nudge the two men together. Arafat's extended hand, almost mannequin-like in its pallor, hung in the air for an instant before Rabin reached out to clutch it. At the moment of contact, a collective gasp went up from the crowd, followed by loud cheering. Then Rabin turned to Peres and said quietly in Hebrew: "Your turn now."

Yairi, who could see the ambivalence on Rabin's face, thought of the handshake as a reluctant groom's *I do* at a wedding. Whatever misgivings existed before, the public act itself would help enforce the commitment. Nabil Shaath, one of Arafat's advisers, also thought of nuptials as he looked on from the lawn. When Clinton came over to him later, he tiptoed to whisper into his ear: "Don't worry, Mr. President, you haven't lost an Israeli daughter, you gained a Palestinian son." Barnea, who would suffer a searing personal tragedy with the unfolding of the Oslo Accord, wrote the next day: "[Rabin's] awkwardness left a mark on the grass but it won't go into the history pages. It will disappear and what will be left, for better or for worse, is the dramatic photo of the handshake between two enemies."

With the ceremony now over, Clinton took Rabin to the Oval Office to discuss the next steps. The agreement Peres and Abbas just signed contained significant gaps and flaws. It established the principle of Palestinian control over the Gaza Strip and one of seven cities in the West Bank, Jericho. But it put off negotiations on the full scope of their governing authority. It also set as a goal Palestinian autonomy in the occupied territories—without addressing the matter of Jewish settlements and how their relentless sprawl would affect the process. All the broad issues, including whether Israel would one day agree to a Palestinian state, were left to later, on the assumption that the trust built over this interim period would make the final negotiations easier. Beilin, the deputy foreign minister who launched Oslo, would come to view this as the agreement's fatal flaw. It would give time for opponents of the process on both sides to poison it with violence—undermining trust all around.

Alone with the president now, Rabin sipped ice water and explained how he had come to accept the PLO as a peace partner. The Palestinian uprising in the West Bank and Gaza had convinced him Israel could no longer put off a decision on the fate of more than two million Palestinians in the West Bank and Gaza. If it chose to keep the territories, Israel would lose its Jewish majority and become an apartheid regime, he said, invoking a term few Israelis dared utter in their own context at the time. Though Israel preferred to negotiate with Palestinians from inside the West Bank and Gaza—as it had done since the Madrid conference in 1991—it was clear to Rabin that the local leaders consulted with Arafat by phone in Tunis on even the tiniest issues. He knew so because Israeli intelligence agencies had intercepted their conversations and given Rabin the transcripts. There was simply no alternative to negotiating with Arafat.

Whether Rabin would eventually agree to the creation of a Palestinian state, he did not say. In interviews over the preceding week, he emphasized that the agreement allowed for Palestinian autonomy, not more. But his decision to deal with the PLO, a group that had devoted itself entirely to bringing about Palestinian independence for more than thirty years, meant statehood was undisputedly on the table. As Haber would point out some two decades later, no one internalized this better than Rabin. "I can tell you that no doubt he understood immediately that signing such an accord . . . in the end it will [lead to] a Palestinian state."

With just a few hours left before the Israelis were to leave Washington, the delegation members attended a lunch with their Palestinian counterparts, hosted by the State Department. Rabin and Arafat stayed back at the White House. Among the invited guests was Henry Kissinger, who had served as secretary of state in the Nixon and Ford administrations and spent much time in the Middle East brokering armistice agreements after the 1973 war. Turning to Beilin at one point, Kissinger alluded to former Israeli prime minister Golda Meir, who said in an oft-quoted newspaper interview in 1969 that there was no such thing as a Palestinian people. "If Golda was alive, she would have erected gallows for you and hanged you," Kissinger told Beilin. It was an odd remark for such a festive moment. But it would resonate with Beilin in the coming months as Israeli hardliners began referring to the architects of Oslo as traitors deserving of the death penalty.

By evening, Rabin was back on the 707, less than eighteen hours after touching down at Andrews. Rosh Hashanah, the Jewish New Year's holiday, was two days off and Rabin—unbeknownst to most people on the plane—had another country to visit on the way home. In an itinerary change coordinated hastily over the weekend, the Israelis would stop over in Morocco as the guests of King Hassan II. Morocco had no relations with Israel, and while the king maintained secret contacts with some Israeli leaders over the years—Rabin actually toured Rabat in 1976 wearing a wig and glasses—a public visit was unprecedented. It signaled to Israelis that resolving their conflict with the Palestinians would give them access to much of the Arab world. Hassan hosted Rabin at his palace and then gave the Israelis a tour of a Casablanca mosque built in his name—an imposing shrine overlooking the Atlantic Ocean, designed to accommodate more than 100,000 worshippers. In a guest book at the site, Rabin wrote in English: "This is the most impressive mosque in the world." Peres, certainly the more eloquent of the two, wrote: "Peace and faith go hand in hand."

The small world that Israelis had been accustomed to inhabiting was expanding quickly, a welcome change for people who had long craved acceptance in the region. An opinion poll published in Israel's *Yedioth Ahronoth* newspaper after Rabin returned showed a large majority of Jewish Israelis—61 percent—supported the agreement. But the opponents included some formidable figures, among them Benjamin Netanyahu, a rising politician whose verbal polish had helped vault him to leadership of the right-wing Likud Party. They also included the brothers Yigal and Hagai Amir, religious fundamentalists, recent veterans of infantry units in the Israeli Army, and amassers of ammunition and explosives.

CHAPTER 2

To Fathom God's Will

"Hit them hard, hit here, push there. Destroy stuff."

—BOAZ NAGAR

By the time the Israeli delegation landed, a wraithlike still-ness enveloped Israel, the kind that precedes religious holi-days and imposes itself on the observant and nonobservant, Jews and non-Jews alike. Shops and restaurants closed early for Rosh Hashanah, public transportation stopped running, and traffic on the highways became sparse. The military order preventing Palestinians from crossing into Israel remained in effect.

Three more funerals were held for victims of Palestinian violence while Rabin was away, soldiers caught in a Hamas ambush in the Gaza Strip. Still, the agreement signed in Washington suffused Rosh Hashanah with hopeful anticipation—not just for a new year but a new era. Newspapers printed for the holiday, with more sections than on any other day of the year, included pages and pages of speculation about the potential dividends of the peace deal. The daily *Ma'ariv* ran a large map showing roads Israel might soon build from its main cities to the capitals of Jordan, Syria, and Lebanon. *Yedioth Ahronoth* published a section in its business pages titled "Peace and Your Pocket:

Investments, Prices, Real Estate, Markets, Restaurants." Rabin had told reporters on the way home that he spoke by phone to other Arab and Muslim leaders who might soon forge ties with Israel. A headline on his return announced that the Foreign Ministry was hoping to recruit more Arabic-speakers for possible postings in the region.

Other issues occupied Israelis as well. The country would soon be marking twenty years since the Yom Kippur War, a surprise assault by Syria and Egypt that killed thousands and, for a few critical hours, appeared to threaten Israel's very existence. In a front-page story, *Yedioth Ahronoth* published long excerpts of a new book by the man who'd served as the head of military intelligence during the war, Eli Zeira. His assessment at the time that war was improbable accounted for the government's disastrous decision not to call up army reservists ahead of the invasion. Also on the front page was a prison-cell interview with a convict nicknamed Ofnobank, a serial bank robber whose motorcycle getaways had made him something of a folk hero to Israelis. In one of the inside sections, a feature story described the changing sexual norms of Israelis. For women, the ideal male was no longer the coarsely textured hard charger but the sensitive type with a strong feminine side. Yet somehow, Israeli women felt simultaneously drawn to and contemptuous of this new man.

Jewish New Year is not the carousing party night that December 31 is for Americans. Israelis tend to spend the evening with family. And so as the sun dipped into the Mediterranean, Rabin and Leah headed across town to the home of daughter Dalia's in-laws. The idea that the prime minister faced some new danger to his life for entering into a peace process with Arafat would not seriously dawn on the people around him for some time to come. Instead of summoning his driver, Rabin was in the habit of driving himself to private events on the weekends, protected by just a small security detail.

Yigal Amir read the newspapers that day with a sense of scorn for the optimism they exuded. He was also spending the holiday with family, including seven brothers and sisters. At twenty-three, he had recently moved back to his parents' two-story home at 56 Borochov Street in Herzliya, having completed five years of army service and seminary study in a program geared to observant Jews. A civilian again, he was now working odd jobs and growing out his black curly hair. He planned to continue living with his parents once he started law school in a few weeks, which in the Israeli university system—more akin to Europe's than the American one—was open to undergraduates.

Amir was short and thin and had the kind of dusky complexion that identified him to other Israelis as Teimani—of Yemeni extraction. Among a certain segment of Ashkenazim—those Jews of European origin who regarded themselves as the country's cultural elite—the skin tone suggested inferiority, a stereotype that Amir took great pleasure in disproving. In school and in the army, he showed himself to be smarter and tougher than most of his peers. An IQ test administered years later placed him in the upper tier of intellectual aptitude; he scored 144 on the verbal section. His dark eyes and broad smile, which could be either warm or menacing, made him alluring to women.

Two days earlier, Amir watched the televised handshake between Rabin and Arafat. He decided instantly that the Oslo deal was not just a calamity for Israel but an act of treason by Rabin, the land he would be handing over to the Palestinians having been promised by God to the Jews. Amir had been a supporter of Moledet, an ultranationalist party whose leader, Rehavam Ze'evi, advocated a kind of self-deportation for Palestinians—with Israel providing both negative and positive inducements. Among Israeli political figures, only the late Meir Kahane, the American-born rabbi and agitator who preached a xenophobic hatred toward Arabs, articulated more extreme positions. Amir favored Kahane but a judicial panel had ruled his Kach Party too nakedly racist to compete in elections.

Amir's political extremism arose from a somewhat unusual upbringing: an ultra-Orthodox education but also a day-to-day exposure to the material world of secular Israelis.

His father, Shlomo, had emigrated with his family from Yemen in 1942 and attended a Haredi yeshiva in Bnei Brak, "Haredi" being the Hebrew term for the most devout and "god-fearing"—the literal definition of the term—among the Jews. Shlomo dressed in dark suits and wide-brimmed hats, the outfit of the ultra-Orthodox, and worked as a religious scribe, copying by hand Torah scrolls and other religious texts in ornamented calligraphy. The home where Amir grew up had the trappings of religious piety, including portraits of rabbis on the walls and Talmudic volumes lining the shelves of an old bookcase in the living room.

But the neighborhood itself, Neve Amal in Herzliya, was comprised mostly of nonobservant Jews. Shlomo had purchased the home for a good price in 1964, when it consisted of just two rooms on a single floor. He moved in at the end of the Six-Day War with his bride, Geulah Shirion, whose family had also emigrated from Yemen. Gradually, they expanded it outward and upward. Elsewhere in the country, ultra-Orthodox Jews tended to cloister themselves in homogenous neighborhoods. The Amirs, on their tree-lined block, with a small market at one end and a grassy playground at the other, were an anomaly.

From his father and from the Haredi grade school he attended, Amir soaked up the strictest version of Jewish orthodoxy, including a provision that every word of the Torah is divined truth. But he also absorbed influences from the neighborhood. Geulah ran a day-care center in the backyard of the home, opening her door to children mostly of secular families—and the cultural winds that blew in with them. Books that made their way to the house included the novels of the German author Karl May, whose stories about life in America's Old West appealed to Amir. At some point, Geulah allowed television in the house—an appliance frowned upon in ultra-Orthodox communities—including a set in Amir's room. He and Hagai, the eldest among the siblings, liked to watch thrillers and westerns borrowed from a video rental shop in the neighborhood.

The secular influence could, in theory, have moderated Amir's worldview. Certainly it influenced his outward appearance. Amir dressed in jeans and T-shirts, with the ritual fringes that observant Jews wear under the shirt, known as *tzitziot,* tucked into his pants instead of protruding ostentatiously. But far from tempering Amir's political outlook, it produced an internal discord that seemed to radicalize him, in the view of a clinical psychologist who would evaluate him some years later. "There's a strong conflict inside him between the longing for sensual and emotional satisfaction and his commitment to a religious and ideological way of life—an ideology that demands sacrificing all material pleasures," the psychologist Gabriel Weil would write after spending several hours with Amir over two days. "He feels a sense of guilt about the longing."

The dissonance would increase in Amir's teen years. At age eleven, he pressed his parents to send him to a secondary school in Tel Aviv, Israel's secular heartland. The school belonged to the Haredi education system but offered a broader curriculum than just Torah and Talmud. Crucially, it prepared students for university instead of a life in the yeshiva. Shlomo and Geulah balked at the idea. Getting to school would require their seventh-grader to travel on a public bus for almost an hour each way. But Amir was nothing if not willful. He locked himself in his room and announced he would not emerge until his parents relented. The standoff lasted a day and a night, an eternity for Geulah, who spent the time talking first herself and then Shlomo into giving the school a try. By morning, Amir had prevailed.

The high school Amir went on to attend in Tel Aviv, HaYishuv HaHadash, had a snooty prestige to it and brought Amir into contact with the children of Orthodox nobility. A student several grades ahead of Amir would become the chief rabbi of Israel, the country's highest religious authority. Geulah recalled years later that the principal of the boarding school initially snubbed her son, perhaps because of his skin tone, but came to respect his solid command of scripture. When Amir graduated four years later, he declined the service exemption available to most Haredis and signed up for the army.

It was now 1988, the first full year of the Palestinian uprising. In the Gaza Strip, where Amir spent long stretches, Palestinian youths would gather in huge numbers to taunt soldiers and throw stones. Though the level of violence would remain relatively low in this first "intifada" (a second insurrection years later would include dozens of suicide bombings), it affirmed for Amir the notions he'd held for years: that Arabs would kill Jews at every opportunity and that only ruthless reprisals would deter Palestinians.

Amir had volunteered for the Golani Brigade, a unit with a reputation for dealing harshly with Palestinians. In dispersing large protests, it was not uncommon for soldiers to separate individuals from the crowd and dispense harsh beatings. Private Amir, Company C, 13th Battalion, seemed to take special pleasure in it, as a member of his unit, Boaz Nagar, would later recall. "Yigal was the enforcer with a capital *E*. Hit them hard, hit here, push there. Destroy stuff. He enjoyed badgering them just for fun." The behavior drew mostly praise from Amir's officers.

There were other forms of harassment as well. Amir told friends later that on patrols in Gaza, he and his buddies liked to drive their jeeps straight at oncoming Palestinian vehicles in order to provoke a response. If a driver didn't swerve to get out of their way, the soldiers would interpret the behavior as hostile and shoot at his windshield. Most of the time, the Palestinians would pull well off the road to let the soldiers pass.

The growing brutality of soldiers serving in the West Bank and Gaza raised enough concern for the government to commission an internal study in 1989 on how the intifada was affecting troops. It concluded, perhaps not surprisingly, that soldiers often became violent at home as well and cultivated a deep hatred for Palestinians.

For Amir, the power felt invigorating. A photo from this period shows him standing on a dirt road, in front of a row of tanks. He has one arm propped on his hip and the other draped over the shoulder of a somewhat taller soldier. Both men are smiling, but Amir's expression is tighter and more controlled. His Galil assault rifle hangs across his torso and the signature brown beret of the Golani Brigade is folded into his epaulette. A clump of dark chest hair projects from his open shirt.

Amir's regular evaluations were so positive that one of Israel's intelligence agencies approached him about a mission overseas. The agency, Nativ, had been sending Israelis to the Soviet Union for short periods going back decades—to smuggle books to Zionist activists who faced government harassment, teach them Hebrew, and lift their spirits. With the Communist era now over and Jews free to leave, the mission evolved. Amir was tasked with persuading these potential emigrants to choose Israel over other destinations, including Germany and the United States. He spent several months in Riga with a second emissary, Avinoam Ezer, who came to regard him as exceptionally smart and capable. By the time they left, Amir had learned enough Russian to communicate basic ideas.

Sometime during his service Amir gravitated toward a more provocative form of fundamentalism. Whereas his Haredi upbringing taught him that God alone determined the destiny of the Jews, he now bristled at the passiveness of this approach. Instead, he embraced the idea that Jews "must learn to fathom God's Will" and act accordingly. Amir had read the line in an introduction to a book of essays by Rabbi Zvi Yehuda Kook, the spiritual leader of the settlers in the West Bank and Gaza. While Kook seemed not quite fiery enough for Amir, the author of the introduction, the far-right politician Binyamin Elon, had captured something profoundly meaningful to the young extremist. "Contrary to the secular, activist approach, which holds that history is determined by man's actions alone, and contrary to the passive [religious] approach, which holds that Divine Will is the sole instrumentality, we must learn to fathom God's Will and 'come to the help of the Lord' [Judges 5:23] and 'act with God,'" he wrote in his own essay. Elon meant the passage as an exhortation: Jews must settle the West Bank and Gaza rather than wait for God to secure their sovereignty over the territory.

But Amir read it as a broader theological doctrine, one that empowered him to judge for himself—to "fathom God's Will"—whether political leaders were honoring the Bible or violating it. Amir felt uniquely qualified to execute the doctrine. In his own view, he knew God's writ better than most Jews, even most rabbis. And he was a doer—the characteristic that defined Amir more than any other, that distinguished him from his peers in school and in the military. If a leader of Israel strayed from the core tenets of the Bible, Amir had his own notions about how to "come to the help of the Lord."

At home, these notions helped draw a line between his father's Judaism and his own. Amir had already told his brother Hagai cryptically that it might be necessary to do something about Rabin. When he repeated the words one day at the dinner table, his father responded with a line he would deliver again and again in the coming years. "Only through prayer and Torah study will the government collapse. And if it doesn't, it's not God's will," he said.

To Amir it was a meek and submissive Judaism his father was preaching, one he had already left behind.

———————

SOMETIME AFTER THE holiday, Amir and his brother set out for Shavei Shomron, a Jewish settlement surrounded by Palestinian villages in the West Bank. Hagai had finished his own army service several years earlier and had been working in trade jobs, first as an electrician and now as a metalsmith. With the money he'd saved, he bought an off-white Volkswagen Beetle, a 1976 model. He also put several thousand dollars in a savings account and bought shares in a company that quickly lost most of its value. He hadn't bothered cashing out.

The two brothers looked alike, held the same extremist positions, and confided in each other about almost everything, having shared a room since birth. But they were different in significant ways. Amir engaged easily with people, including girls, while Hagai mostly kept to himself. Hagai had watched his little brother stand up to older and bigger boys if they tried to bully him on the playground but lacked the fiery temperament to do it himself. He also lacked his brother's aptitude in school. Geulah thought of her two sons as the thinker and the tinkerer, Hagai being the one who could fix appliances in the house, who liked taking apart old radios to see how they worked.

Hagai was also less crafty. Geulah kept the boys mostly indoors or in the backyard. "You wouldn't see them just walking the streets," she would recall years later. She also kept them from participating in sports, which involved dressing immodestly and mingling with girls, whether on the team or on the sidelines. Instead, the two burned their schoolboy energy around the house. Hagai liked to sneak up on his brother and knock the book he was reading from his hand, a provocation that invariably ended in a chase and a broken window. (The neighborhood glazier, a survivor of Nazi concentration camps, made a regular portion of his living from the Amirs). But Amir almost never got punished. "Hagai would get yelled, at but Yigal was clever. He would get away with things," Geulah said. Like his brother, Hagai had also served in an infantry unit and spent time in the Gaza Strip. During a grueling five-month boot camp, he trained as a sniper, learning how to stalk a target, where to position himself, and how to breathe while shooting. He also developed an interest in explosives, reading about them in army manuals and pilfering munitions whenever he could. On isolated operating bases, it was not difficult to do. The ammunition was often stored in a tent and guarded by the soldiers themselves. If Hagai did three hours of guard duty at the tent, he might leave with a pocketful of fuses or detonators.

At home, Hagai figured out how to wire explosives to a timer and a battery. He also learned to make amateur hand grenades, with iron pipes and a propellant. By the time he left the army, his munitions stash included timers, fuses, TNT sticks, ammonal powder, and several blocks of the explosive C-4, one of which he'd received recently from a friend on active duty, Arik Schwartz. He hid the items in a few places around the house, including the attic and the shed in the backyard, where he kept his tools and did his tinkering. He also punched a hole in the wall of his room and stored the more dangerous materials in the cavity of a cinderblock. He then plastered it shut and repainted the wall to hide any trace of the opening.

Hagai meant for the materials to serve his hobby; he began collecting them long before Rabin's peace deal with Arafat. But already in the coming weeks they would figure in the plans he and his brother would draw up to undermine the deal.

Shavei Shomron lay about an hour east of Herzliya and some fifteen miles into the West Bank—a territory that Israelis had increasingly taken to calling by its biblical name, Judea and Samaria. Perched on a hill overlooking the sprawling Palestinian city of Nablus, the settlement consisted of mostly single-family homes with red-tiled roofs, an eye-catcher in the otherwise rocky monochrome of the West Bank. Its 600 or so residents included Israel Shirion, a man in his late thirties who oversaw security and maintenance at the settlement and also transported schoolchildren to and from the surrounding communities. Shirion was the younger brother of Geulah Amir and the uncle of Yigal and Hagai.

The two brothers visited him regularly at the settlement, which had a swimming pool, several synagogues, and a large contingent of young people. With its population of mostly Orthodox Jews and its rural isolation, the town exuded an almost mystical serenity on holidays and weekends.

It also radiated a pioneering militancy, its residents having lived for the first years in trailers or prefabricated structures, the men all armed with automatic rifles. Shirion had been among a group of founders who left their homes inside Israel in 1977 to spearhead the colonizing of Samaria, the biblical term corresponding to the northern half of the West Bank. Until then, Israelis had confined their settlement-building mostly to the area known as Judea south of Jerusalem—around Hebron and what Israelis called the Gush Etzion Bloc. International law expressly bars countries from colonizing territories they capture in war. But since Jewish communities had existed in both Hebron and Gush Etzion prior to Israel's independence in 1948, left-leaning Labor governments argued that construction there amounted to a "reclamation" project.

The right-wing Likud Party that replaced Labor in 1977 enacted a much more aggressive settlement policy, authorizing new communities deep in the West Bank. Israelis who would populate these new outposts were motivated not by the prospect of improving their standard of living—the incentive that would draw tens of thousands to the settlements in subsequent years. These early settlers felt Jews had a singular right to the territory and that Palestinians—1 million of them in 1967, growing to 2 million by 1993—were essentially squatters. A steady expansion had brought the settler population to 140,000 in 1993, scattered across the territory in configurations strategically designed to block Palestinian contiguity.

Nothing divided Israelis more sharply than the settlement enterprise. To supporters, the settlers were rekindling that old Zionist spirit, bolstering Israeli security by putting themselves on the front lines, and bearing the brunt of Palestinian violence. To detractors, their very presence in the West Bank and Gaza amounted to a provocation. It violated international law and gradually foreclosed on the possibility of peace between Israel and the Palestinians. The religious among the settlers, including Shirion, added a messianic element to the enterprise. For them, the incredible conquest of 1967 could only have been the work of God and a sign that the messiah—the great Jewish leader who would redeem the world from war and suffering and rebuild the ancient Jewish Temple—would soon appear. Settling Judea and Samaria, the heart of biblical Israel, was a way to hasten the coming of the messiah.

Shirion was fifteen years older than Hagai and seventeen years older than Amir. More of an older brother than an uncle, he liked to mentor the two, not always to their father's liking. When the boys were teens, he would take them to a firing zone near his home to squeeze off rounds from his handgun, an Italian-made .22 caliber and later a Glock 19. When their father counseled them to continue studying the Torah in the yeshiva instead of joining the military, Shirion told them that service in the army, preferably in a combat unit, was the real way to fulfill the Zionist ethic. After their service, he helped both young men obtain gun licenses by having them change their official residency from Herzliya to his home in Shavei Shomron. Israel had strict gun laws. Only people who could show they genuinely needed one to defend themselves received licenses. Living on a settlement surrounded by Palestinians meant almost automatic approval.

On trips to Shavei Shomron, the two kept their guns wedged in their pants. Both had purchased 9mm Berettas, the standard sidearm of the US Army at the time, from a gun shop in Herzliya. The permits they held limited the number of shells they could buy each year. But the shop owner, a former policeman, sold them as many as they wanted—in Hagai's case, a good lot. On recurring visits to the store, he bought boxes of regular rounds and hollow points in equal numbers, sharing the supply with his brother.

Hagai liked to stack the shells alternately in his fifteen-round magazine, starting and ending with a hollow point, a technique he also taught his brother. Palestinians regularly stoned Israeli cars on the road to Shavei Shomron and elsewhere in the West Bank and Gaza, but drive-by shootings were also a threat. The hollow points, which expanded on impact and tended to lodge in the body, would blast a stone thrower clear off the road. But their scooped-out tip made them less effective than regular rounds at penetrating the steel frame of a car. Hagai figured that having both shell types in the magazine prepared him for any threat.

Sometime during the visit, or perhaps a bit later, Amir outlined to Hagai what he had in mind. Rabin would be putting settlers in jeopardy by ceding parts of the West Bank to the Palestinians. To counter the plan, the two would recruit young men for a militia that would carry out harsh reprisals in response to any attack on Israelis—shootings and bombings but also broader action like the downing of power lines in Palestinian areas. The spiraling violence would surely rupture the peace process. Amir would focus on students at Bar-Ilan University, where his semester would begin in a few weeks. Hagai's role was to target students at the college in Ariel, one of the West Bank's largest settlements. He had already registered for prep courses there, intending to major in physics.

The two discussed the criteria for membership in their militia. The recruits would have to be graduates of combat units in the army, comfortable with both guns and explosives. They would need to show a zealous commitment to the settlement project in Judea and Samaria and to ousting the Rabin government with its leftist agenda. Hagai's stash of munitions would serve as a start. More would have to be collected.

If the idea seemed outlandish, it certainly did not faze Hagai. There were precedents for what Amir was suggesting. A decade earlier, a band of settlers had carried out a string of terrorist attacks against Palestinians, including a shooting spree on a college campus and bombings targeting the mayors of Nablus and Ramallah. Israel's internal security agency, Shabak (a Hebrew acronym that stands for General Security Service), thwarted the group's most ambitious plan: to blow up the venerated Muslim shrine known as the Dome of the Rock in Jerusalem so that Judaism's ancient temple could be rebuilt on its ruins. Though the plot could well have ignited a regional war, most of the militia members received presidential pardons after serving short prison terms.

Amir regarded the Jewish Underground, as the media dubbed the group, a model for his militia. But he also had the grandiosity to think of himself in historical terms—as a link in a chain of Jewish rebellion and zealotry, from the Maccabees, who revolted against the Seleucid Empire in the second century BC, to the Jewish armed groups that operated in Palestine before Israel's independence. He and Hagai had both read *The Revolt*, a kind of manual for guerrilla warfare written by Menachem Begin, who headed the pro-independence Irgun Zvai Leumi (or Irgun, for short) in the 1940s and later became Israel's prime minister. The group distinguished itself by carrying out devastating attacks against both Palestinian civilians and British administrators of Palestine, including the 1946 bombing of Jerusalem's King David Hotel that killed ninety-one people. Amir viewed the Rabin government much the way Begin regarded the British Mandate and the Maccabees saw the Seleucids: as intruders, purveyors of a foreign culture and a threat to Jewish existence. It mattered not that Rabin himself was Jewish, the hero of 1967, and the elected prime minister of Israel.

With the conciliation process between Israelis and Palestinians only just getting under way, the Amir brothers made a commitment to each other: they would risk spending years in jail in order to prevent Rabin from surrendering parts of Eretz Israel—the Jewish homeland—to Arafat. Hagai drew the line there, telling his brother he would not die for the cause.

———

IN THE FOLLOWING weeks, every day seemed to bring some nugget of news that suggested Israel had altered its troubled trajectory with the signing in Washington. Jordan's King Hussein agreed to a common agenda for peace talks with Israel after decades of quiet contacts. Two African nations, Gabon and Mauritius, established ties with Israel— not exactly a diplomatic triumph but noteworthy enough to be heralded on the front page of Israeli newspapers.

Rabin brought his deal with Arafat to lawmakers on September 23 and won their endorsement by a comfortable margin, 61 to 50. In an embarrassment to Benjamin Netanyahu, three members of his Likud Party abstained instead of opposing the agreement. Netanyahu had taken control of Likud just six months earlier and struggled to impose discipline. But Rabin had problems of his own. One of his coalition partners, the ultra-Orthodox Shas Party, failed to support the deal, forcing him to rely on the votes of Arab-Israeli parliament members to clinch an absolute majority in the 120-member legislature known as the Knesset. Opponents of the agreement would seize on this to discredit the approval process, advancing the unsavory argument that Jewish votes alone should count when broad national issues are at stake. Netanyahu told reporters after the parliamentary session that Rabin's coalition "stood on chicken legs."

More distressing for Rabin was the surge in attacks on Israelis by Hamas and Islamic Jihad—a smaller Palestinian group that had also vowed to resist the peace deal. The violence included a fatal stabbing on September 24 and an attempted car bombing a week later that went awry. But it was the brutal killing of two Israeli hikers in a scenic gorge in the West Bank on October 9 that prompted many Israelis to begin questioning whether the core transaction of the deal—security for territory—was even realistic. A squad of Palestinians shot the two young men, slit their throats, and then bludgeoned them with rocks as other hikers looked on from ridges high above the canyon. The killers had no ties to Arafat's PLO, and Arafat himself was still in Tunis. It would take him another nine months to relocate to Gaza and deploy his forces. But Israelis had watched the dramatic handshake in Washington and expected immediate results. That internal Palestinian divisions might hamper the deal seemed to be an afterthought.

Amir started classes at Bar-Ilan days after the double murder; the mood on campus was palpably glum. The university he had chosen was the academic bastion of the Israeli right, including the Orthodox establishment and the settler movement. Most senior faculty members regarded the Oslo deal as a terrible turn for Israel and a potential disaster for the settlements—where some of them lived. The few professors who supported the agreement did so quietly, to avoid trouble with their tenure boards.

The religious stream of the Zionist movement had founded Bar-Ilan in the 1950s as an alternative to the prestigious—and very much secular—Hebrew University in Jerusalem. Its board of governors usually included the country's top rabbis and Orthodox politicians. Though the campus was open to all applicants, the criteria for acceptance favored graduates of religious schools, a policy that guaranteed a largely religious student body. Bar-Ilan was the only university in Israel to include Jewish studies in its required curriculum.

The Six-Day War marked a turning point for the university. The religious stream of Zionism had long associated the return to biblical Israel with the coming of the messiah. Now that Israel had restored its rule in Judea and Samaria, the messianic age had clearly arrived, a premise that stirred both excitement and extremism on campus. In 1980, a campus rabbi published an article in one of the university's student journals predicting an inevitable holy war for the "annihilation of Amalek," a clan described in the Old Testament as an enemy to the Jews. The remark was widely understood as a call for ethnic cleansing against the Palestinians or, worse, genocide. The university eventually fired the rabbi but the air of extremism remained strong on campus. In a book years later, an Israeli legal scholar referred to the rabbi as the "evil in the heart of Bar-Ilan."

Already in the first weeks of the school year, activists formed a group to oppose the Oslo deal—Students for Security. Amir spotted their booth at the entrance to campus one day and stopped to give it a look. The students had hung posters on the booth and around campus depicting Rabin shaking hands with Arafat while handing him a gun or Rabin clad in a kaffiyeh, Arafat-style. But the people Amir encountered seemed tepid, not quite the stalwarts he hoped to enlist for his militia. Still, he put his name to a petition on the table calling for Rabin to step down and volunteered to join the rotation of activists manning the booth.

Among the students, one did stand out, a blue-eyed firebrand with a slight stutter named Avishai Raviv. In their first conversation, Amir learned that Raviv had been active in Kahane's Kach movement as a youngster, then joined a combat unit hoping to see action but suffered a leg wound when a fellow soldier discharged his gun accidentally. He liked rolling up his pant leg to show people the scar. With a physical-disability discharge, Raviv cycled through a series of extremist groups, including a quasi-apocalyptic one dedicated to rebuilding the Jewish Temple in Jerusalem. Recently, he had founded the Jewish Nationalist Organization, a group with sharply anti-Arab positions that went by the acronym EYAL. Pleasant-looking but rough around the edges, Raviv had caught the attention of the media as an agitator who craved attention and controversy.

Raviv boasted to Amir that he'd been investigated for a series of alleged crimes, including running a training camp for Kach-affiliated youngsters and assaulting a left-wing Knesset member. Yet somehow he managed to avoid prison—so many times that some people on the right wondered what pull he had with the police or the Justice Department. Though he seemed to have no paying job, Raviv owned a car and a cell phone, both of which he put to use in the organizing of rallies—of a kind that even some fellow rightists found gratuitously provocative. He rarely showed up for class.

Amir made a mental note to talk to Raviv about the militia. He also told himself not to let school get in the way of the plans he made with Hagai. First-year students in his program carried a heavy load of courses, including Jewish law, the penal code, contracts, and constitutional law—*konstee*, as people in the department referred to it. But since professors almost never took attendance, Amir figured out quickly that he could skip most lectures and study from the notes of more diligent students. One of them was Amit Hampel, whom he'd met through a mutual friend in Tel Aviv years earlier. Amir noticed that Hampel showed up to class every day and had almost perfect handwriting—neither too sloping nor too tightly packed. Hampel took notice of Amir as well—ambling into class from time to time, muttering something sarcastic, and ducking out before the end of the lecture. He agreed to let Amir pick up his notes before tests and photocopy them at a shop near his home in Tel Aviv.

The arrangement allowed Amir to spend his time organizing weekly rallies on campus and studying Talmud at Bar-Ilan's seminary, known informally as the *kolel*. A long stucco building square in the middle of the university, the *kolel* played no official role in the student curriculum. But it functioned as a gathering place for men to pray and conduct study sessions with rabbis. Many of the young men at the *kolel* were law students like Amir, and most viewed the Oslo Accord not just as a political misstep but a sin against God. As the semester progressed, Amir would return to the same questions in the study sessions—all revolving around situations where Jews endangered other Jews. What preventative action would Jewish law countenance?

Somehow, the inquiries did not strike the rabbis as odd. They perceived them as Amir's attempt to understand the present reality through the lens of scripture; as a natural blending of religion and everyday life. But while other students probed in similar directions, Amir stood out for his sheer fervor. Rabbis and students at the seminary came to view him as stubborn and obsessive.

By early winter, the Students for Security were staging rallies against the Oslo Accord every week outside campus, drawing several hundred people to a spot along one of Israel's busiest highways and waving signs at passing cars. The pictures and slogans became increasingly aggressive, depicting Rabin with blood on his hands, comparing him to Philippe Pétain, the leader of Vichy France who collaborated with the Nazis, or declaring him a traitor outright. But the students also socialized during the outings and kept the event to thirty minutes before heading back to class—all of which irritated Amir.

One week, he and other students persuaded the group to step out onto the highway and stop traffic for several minutes. The event showed remarkable recklessness and almost ended in tragedy. The highway ran four lanes in each direction, with no stoplight for miles. The first wave of cars came at the protesters so fast that some thought they would be run over. But the action paid off. An Israel Radio reporter who happened to be attending a symposium on campus broadcast the chaotic moments live through his cell phone. Suddenly, Students for Security had name recognition.

Police detective Yoav Gazit would occasionally watch the students gather for the weekly protest from a pedestrian bridge above the highway. A fifteen-year veteran of the force, Gazit was on sabbatical in 1993, taking classes at Bar-Ilan toward a bachelor's degree in a program geared toward members of law-enforcement agencies.

Gazit had worked on a series of high-profile investigations over the years, including a corruption case against Ariel Sharon, the right-wing Knesset member. Short and stout with a warm face and a shock of black hair, he specialized in cultivating a rapport with suspects until they delivered their confessions. Most of the student protesters struck Gazit as harmless; young idealists stirred to action by a policy they opposed. But a few had lashed out at policemen on campus over crackdowns against right-wing protests around the country. In the vicious outbursts and the twinning of politics with this fanatic strain of religion, Gazit sensed trouble.

Amir had settled into a routine. He left the house in Herzliya around six on most mornings and came home after dark. Before exams, he would spend hours sitting at a plastic patio table in the front yard, marking up Hampel's notes with a highlighter. Most teachers allowed students to flip through their books and notes during the tests. Amir was scoring 80s and 90s, among the highest grades in the class.

Near the end of autumn, Amir attended the wedding of a friend in Tel Aviv, an event that would shape his thinking in the coming years. Ariel Schweitzer, a fellow student at seminary, was marrying a certain Shira Lau at one of the city's most opulent wedding halls, Gan Ha'Oranim. The wedding drew publicity because of Lau's pedigree: Her father, Israel Meir Lau, had recently been named Israel's Ashkenazi chief rabbi and was renowned for his story of survival during World War II. Separated from most of his family at age five and sent to the Buchenwald concentration camp, Lau evaded the death march at the end of the war by hiding under a heap of corpses. He emigrated to Palestine a year later and became an ordained rabbi. Not long before his daughter's wedding, Lau traveled to the Vatican for a meeting with the pope, the first of its kind in Israel's history.

Amir drove to Tel Aviv in his brother's Beetle, the four-cylinder engine wheezing along the highway. In the hall, he sat with friends from the seminary, young men in white dress shirts and black skull-caps. A sliding partition separated them from the women. Soon Amir was taking stock of the prominent figures around the room, including Knesset members and ministers in Rabin's cabinet. Then he spotted Rabin himself, sitting at a table with just one bodyguard at his side.

The sight of him flooded Amir with adrenaline. The prime minister was so close at hand and so manifestly mortal, just flesh and blood. Amir had his Beretta jammed in his belt, covered by his shirt. He contemplated walking over to Rabin and shooting him in the back of the head. Other people approached to shake hands with the prime minister. A photographer snapped pictures from across the room.

A minute elapsed and then another. Amir told himself he would come to regret passing up the opportunity. But he also felt a stitch of hesitation. Did God put him in the same room with Rabin so that he could eliminate the Israeli leader and his Oslo process? Or would Amir be imposing his own plan on God? He thought about the bullets in his magazine, the hollow points and the regular rounds. Then he turned his gaze back to Rabin and watched him leave the hall; Amir had missed his chance. But he gleaned valuable information. Rabin was hardly protected. If protests didn't stop the peace process, killing him might be a viable alternative.

At home, he related the events to Hagai. It was too early, he told his brother. He needed to build his inner readiness.

———————

THE ENCOUNTER WITH Rabin electrified Amir and he yearned to relive the experience. Hoping to get a glimpse of him again, he joined a group of people who demonstrated outside Rabin's home on Rav Ashi every Friday. The protesters would gather across the street from the building at two in the afternoon, usually numbering no more than a few dozen. Eran Fogel, a senior in high school who lived next door to Rabin, liked to count them from his eighth-story window, knowing that a demonstration of fifty or more required a police permit. They seemed to know it as well, rarely exceeding the permissible number.

Some of them had been motivated to attend by the continuing violence, which was now making headlines almost every day. In late October, Hamas gunmen posing as Jews picked up two reserve soldiers at a hitchhiking post near a settlement in the Gaza Strip. After a short ride, the Palestinian on the passenger side spun toward the backseat and shot both of them several times. A few days later, Palestinians lured a resident of the settlement Beit El near Ramallah, Haim Mizrahi, to a chicken coop where he regularly bought eggs in order to resell them to Jewish vendors and pocket the profit. The men stabbed him to death, put his body in the trunk of his car, and drove off with it. They ditched the vehicle near Ramallah and torched it, along with the body.

But the core members of the protest group were ultra-nationalists who opposed the Oslo deal from its very inception. They included Rehavam Ze'evi, a retired general who headed the Moledet Party and had served with Rabin on the military's general staff in the 1960s. Ze'evi often held up a poster of Rabin's mug with two words at the bottom: THE LIAR. Avishai Raviv, Amir's friend from Bar-Ilan, showed up from time to time in his favorite blue pullover with the Adidas logo on his chest. When camera crews came to film the event, he usually found some way to stand out.

Rabin mostly ignored the protesters, parking his car in the open-air lot alongside the building and walking to the entrance with his head down. He told reporters that the hecklers had no effect on him and certainly would not cause him to change course. When protesters spotted his car, they would launch into menacing chants, including "Rabin is a traitor," and "Rabin is a murderer," and also "Rabin is a drunk"—a reference to the rumors of his heavy drinking. In fact, Rabin had a low tolerance for alcohol. He liked wine with his meals. "Water is for horses," he would say. But heavier drinks made him drowsy. Rabin liked to joke that if Edgar Bronfman, who ran the Seagram alcoholic beverage company and gave money to Jewish causes, knew how much soda he poured into his whiskey, the Canadian philanthropist would stop supporting him.

But Leah, who heard the protesters chanting under her window all afternoon, every week, felt intimidated. When they caught sight of her either entering or leaving the building, someone would shout something menacing about the Rabins being destined to meet the same fate as Mussolini and his mistress, who were executed toward the end of World War II, or the Ceauşescus, the repressive Romanian dictator and his wife who were shot by a firing squad during the collapse of Communism in 1989. The commotion underneath her bedroom window would sometimes keep Leah from sleeping on a Friday afternoon, a coveted siesta hour for many Israelis. It could also make for some comical moments. When Rabin walked in the door one Friday, Leah broke into a chant of her own from the bedroom: "Rabin is a traitor, Rabin is a traitor." It took her husband a moment to get the joke.

But the events, like the protests outside campus, left Amir feeling restless. They gave opponents of the deal a sense of power but changed nothing. On a winter weekend, he invited several students to spend the entire Sabbath with him on Rav Ashi, from Friday afternoon to Saturday night. At the very least, he would learn something about the prime minister's comings and goings. Amir drew people mostly from the leadership of Students for Security, but he also invited Nava Holtzman, a first-year economics student who showed up occasionally to political events on campus. Amir had met Holtzman a year earlier in a chance encounter in the southern town of Mitzpe Ramon, where she was doing her National Service, a yearlong volunteer program offered to religious women in lieu of military duty. Fair-skinned and pretty, with green eyes and below-the-shoulder hair, Holtzman drew attention at Bar-Ilan. Amir spotted her on the way to class one day and urged her to come along for the weekend.

By now, at age twenty-three, Amir had had several girlfriends, including a nonreligious one he dated in high school and a young German woman he met during a trip to Europe in the summer before his army service. The German kept in touch and later visited Amir in Israel. (Geulah, who took a liking to the young woman, had hoped she would convert to Judaism and marry her son.) But he had engaged in little or no physical intimacy with any of them, in keeping with the Orthodox prohibition on sexual contact before marriage. Since Orthodox Jews tended to marry relatively young, Bar-Ilan served as a venue more for matchmaking than the time-honored college hookup.

On the appointed Friday, the group took part in the usual protest outside Rabin's building and stayed on after the regulars departed, chanting into the evening. Amir had his Beretta with him, as always.

When he was bored, he liked to let the magazine drop from the handle, pull the rounds out one by one, and then reload them. From across the street, he noticed that only two guards secured the building. He also saw that Rabin's official car was not in the parking lot—that on weekends, his driver dropped the prime minister at home and drove off. If Rabin went anywhere on a Friday night, Amir thought, he probably took his own car. He hoped to confirm the premise by seeing it for himself, but Rabin stayed home the entire evening.

Since most of the students were religious and would not drive on the Sabbath, Amir had arranged for the group to spend the night at homes within walking distance from Rav Ashi—the women in one apartment and the men in another. When they reconvened outside Rabin's building the next morning, Amir struck up a conversation with Holtzman about kabala, a form of Jewish mysticism he had studied in seminary. In the classroom, Amir had heard stories about autistic children who could relay messages from God. But he became skeptical after visiting a center for youngsters with communication disorders in Bnei Brak.

By afternoon, Amir grew tired of waiting for Rabin and so did the others. They walked to the beach, watched the sun set, and took buses home. For Amir, the preceding months felt like a failure. He envisioned a million people taking to the streets and forcing Rabin to dissolve his government. Amir divided Israelis into two camps: leftists who wanted Israel to be like every other Western country in the world, and religious idealists who were guided by the laws of God. But even the latter group, even the settlers and the right-wing politicians, seemed lackluster to him, unwilling to risk their position and status. His plan to assemble a militia had also stalled; Amir had yet to recruit a single member. The one person who seemed suitable was Avishai Raviv, but Amir had begun to think this student who never went to class, who wore a skullcap but seemed casual about his religious observance—might be an undercover agent.

Hagai fared no better in his recruiting effort. At his college in the settlement Ariel, he shared trailer number 89/1 with another student but did not bother hanging things on the wall or fixing it up in any way. The few personal belongings he brought from Herzliya—clothes, a spare magazine for his gun, and boxes of cartridges—he kept locked in a metal cabinet on his side of the room. Hagai was too shy to make friends at Ariel and too guarded to discuss the militia idea with other students. He spent much of his free time at the library, looking in chemistry books for bomb-making recipes.

Among other things, he learned that he could make a crude napalm bomb from ingredients found around the house. The concoction had two advantages over a regular petrol bomb: When the mixture stuck to a target—a person or a car—it was almost impossible to peel off. And it burned for a long time. He experimented with the solution in the backyard of the house in Herzliya.

Hagai copied other recipes into a small spiral notebook he could fit in his breast pocket, including one for gunpowder and another for nitrocellulose—a lightweight combustible explosive. On a page titled "Dynamite," he noted to himself in tight little handwriting: "Mixture is very dangerous. Make in small amounts and test before making large amounts." Lower down on the page, he wrote: "The mixture does not dissolve in water and can be submerged in water in order to cool." Other pages included instructions for making blasting gelatin and also nitroglycerine, which Hagai notated with the molecular formula $C_3H_5O_3(NO_2)_3 + 3H_2O$.

For all the complacency Amir attributed to the opponents of Oslo, the leadership body of the Jewish settlers known as the YESHA Council (YESHA being the Hebrew acronym for Judea, Samaria, and Gaza) was quietly plotting its strategy. At a meeting just weeks after the signing in Washington, members of the council discussed a range of measures, including taking over the army bases Israel would evacuate, calling on soldiers to refuse withdrawal-related orders, staging mass demonstrations around the country, and burning Palestinian orchards. When the plan leaked, the Israeli media called it a blueprint for a "Jewish intifada."

But snags in the negotiation between Israel and the Palestinians gave rightists some hope that perhaps the agreement would never be implemented—and may have dulled their zeal for immediate action. The Oslo deal had set December 1993 as the target for finalizing the details of Israel's withdrawal from Gaza and Jericho. One set of talks took place in Taba, the resort town just across the Israeli-Egyptian border. Other teams were meeting regularly in Paris to formulate an economic agreement between Israel and what would be the Palestinian Authority. When the December deadline came around, the two sides were still arguing over the status of the Gaza settlements, the size of the Jericho enclave, and the precise security arrangements in both areas. Nahum Barnea wrote in *Yedioth Ahronoth* that it wasn't just Israel fretting about whether Palestinians could assume control of the territories; the PLO itself wondered whether it had the money and wherewithal to do it.

One way or another, Amir doubted the YESHA Council's resolve. These settler representatives had gone soft, compromised by the comforts of their suburban life in the big settlements. On a Saturday afternoon, sometime after the weekend he spent on Rav Ashi, Amir asked his brother if he wanted to scout out Rabin's neighborhood. Amir had been contemplating whether he could target Rabin in or around his home. Though he hadn't decided yet whether he would try to kill the prime minister, he wanted to put Hagai's technical mind to work on the issue.

The two waited until well after sundown—the Sabbath ends only when three stars appear in the sky—and set out in Hagai's Beetle. The traffic from the suburbs into Tel Aviv could get heavy on a Saturday night, with young people pouring into the city to dance at the clubs along the beach or eat al fresco at one of the many restaurants. In the car, Amir raised the ideas he'd been mulling: planting explosives on Rav Ashi and setting them off when Rabin's car passed or, better yet, attaching a bomb to the car and triggering it remotely.

Once in the neighborhood, Hagai drove slowly past Rabin's building and then turned onto Oppenheimer, where Peres lived across from a small strip mall. He sized up the buildings on both streets, the trees and hedgerows that framed them, looking for a place a sniper could position himself. The bombing idea seemed out of the question to Hagai. The explosives he knew how to build would be bulky things, too hard to hide on the street or under the car. A more realistic plan might be for his brother to stand far from the target and fire a long-range rifle equipped with a scope, or an antitank missile. Hagai could wait for him in the car along Highway Two, the main north-south thoroughfare just down the road from Rav Ashi, for a quick getaway.

But on the ride home, Hagai listed aloud all the ways the operation could fail. Even if his brother managed to kill Rabin, his chances of surviving were slim. Hagai couldn't face the idea of having to tell his parents their favorite son—the boy his mother and father affectionately called Gali—died in a plot they hatched together. He told Amir they needed a better plan.

CHAPTER 3

A Stray Weed

"The extremists [among the settlers] are getting
stronger.... The struggle is moving towards militancy."

—YOEL BIN-NUN

The secure phone rang in Rabin's apartment at a few minutes
after six, an inauspicious start to the morning of February
25, 1994. The prime minister had returned the previous day
from a trip to Spain and Portugal, the first official visit by an Israeli
leader to each of the two countries. He had been in a reflective mood
on the way home, chatting with journalists on the plane about the
months that had passed since the signing in Washington. Countries
that had shunned Israel were now seeking a role in the peace process and inquiring about investments. The Tel Aviv Stock Exchange
had soared since September, gaining more than 80 percent in value.
Negotiations over the ground-level details of Arafat's rule in Gaza and
Jericho were finally close to conclusion. Only the violence marred the
process. Palestinians had killed twenty-one Israelis in the preceding
six months, nearly one a week—a painful toll that was steadily eroding support for peacemaking. Israeli troops had killed a similar number of Palestinians in military operations, a violent cycle Rabin hoped

Arafat could arrest once he took control of the territory. For the time being, the Palestinian leader remained in Tunis.

The secure line had two extensions in the apartment, one in the kitchen and another in the den. Predictably, the phones in both rooms were red. They linked Rabin with a small number of other top officials, including the chiefs of Mossad and Shabak. In the years Rabin had been defense minister in the 1980s and now prime minister, he came to recognize the ring as a harbinger of bad news.

He picked up the receiver and heard the raspy voice of his military secretary, Danny Yatom. He was calling from Hebron in the West Bank, a Palestinian city with a combustible set of ingredients—a religious population that identified largely with Hamas, a small but exceedingly radical settler community living in the very heart of the Arab populace, and a shrine, the Cave of the Patriarchs, that was sacred to both groups, the Muslims and the Jews. Yatom got right to the point: a Jewish settler committed a horrible massacre at the shrine earlier in the morning, he told his boss.

Friday mornings were usually reserved for meetings with defense officials, including a weekly forum Rabin convened with the heads of the intelligence agencies and the chief of staff. It was his favorite part of the week. Though a quarter century had elapsed since Rabin shed his military uniform, he still found himself more comfortable with soldiers than politicians—and more trusting of them. Only Yatom took notes at these meetings and nothing ever leaked.

On this Friday, Hebron scrambled Rabin's agenda and instantly plunged his eighteen-month-old administration into crisis.

Though the city was only about fifty miles southeast of Tel Aviv, it could not have been more different from the freewheeling Israeli metropolis on the Mediterranean. Gray and cold, with a population of 130,000 Palestinians, Hebron was the largest city in the West Bank, an urban clutter of winding streets and stone bazaars laid out over a series of rocky hills. It boasted a university, two hospitals, and two rundown hotels but, in keeping with the conservative spirit of the city, not a single movie theater. The shrine, a towering Herodian structure set in the center of Hebron, was its showpiece—and also its curse, a pilgrimage site fought over for thousands of years.

The shrine derived its sanctity from the Book of Genesis, which recounts how Abraham bought the cave from a certain Ephron the Hittite (for "four hundred shekels of silver") as a burial site for his wife, Sarah. Eventually, Abraham is interred alongside his wife and later other Hebrew patriarchs and matriarchs are buried there as well—Isaac, Jacob, Rebecca, and Leah. Over the centuries, the appeal of this Old Testament narrative to all three monotheistic religions made the cave a trophy for competing empires. It served as a Jewish shrine under Herod the Great, who surrounded it with huge stone walls, a basilica in the Byzantine era, and a mosque after the invasion of the Muslims. The Crusaders made a church of the site in 1100 but it reverted to a mosque when Saladin conquered the area in 1188.

By the early twentieth century the Cave of the Patriarchs and the city around it were one more flashpoint for the rivaling Jewish and Arab nationalist movements. In 1929, Palestinians killed scores of Jews there in a rampage fueled by false rumors that Jews were killing Arabs in Jerusalem. The massacre effectively ended centuries of Jewish presence in the city. Thirty-eight years later, when Israel's victory in the Six-Day War brought the West Bank under Israeli rule and unleashed a messianic fervor among religious Jews, the first place these Jews pushed to colonize was Hebron. They formed a settlement adjacent to the city in the late 1960s known as Kiryat Arba and a settler community inside Hebron itself in 1979.

Yatom had boarded a helicopter for the city as soon as he got word of the shooting. At the site, he received a briefing from military commanders and relayed the information to Rabin. The Israeli who committed the massacre, Baruch Goldstein, entered the shrine around five in the morning dressed in the army uniform he kept as a reservist and carrying a military-issue assault rifle. At the top of the stairs, he pushed past the worship area designated for Jews and entered the Ibrahimi Mosque (Ibrahim being the Arabic name for Abraham), where hundreds of Palestinians engaged in morning prayers. Friday marked the midpoint of Ramadan, a month of daytime fasting and praying. It was also Purim, the day Jews commemorate having been saved from extermination in the ancient Persian Empire.

As the worshippers knelt and bowed to touch their foreheads to the carpet, a practice known in Arabic as *sujud*, Goldstein fired more than a hundred rounds from behind the crowd, spraying bullets from side to side. Throngs of people rushed the doors of the mosque, creating a bottleneck; Goldstein fired on them as well. Only after he emptied three magazines was there a pause in the shooting. While he tried to load a fourth one in his gun, one of the Palestinians struck him with a fire extinguisher and then others rushed the shooter and beat him to death. In less than two minutes, he'd managed to kill twenty-nine Palestinians and wound more than one hundred. Among the dead were eight teenagers.

The bodies were gone by the time Yatom entered the hall but the spent shells still lay scattered across the carpet. During a thirty-year military career that included a rotation as commander of Sayeret Matkal, Yatom had seen his share of carnage. The sight in the mosque rivaled the horrors he'd witnessed in battle: streaks of blood in almost every corner of the chamber, the great marble pillars of the mosque chipped and pocked, lights on the chandeliers shot out. The bag Goldstein had carried into the mosque still had a handgun in it and three fully loaded magazines. He'd brought seven in all.

Goldstein had been a thirty-eight-year-old reserve army captain and the doctor of Kiryat Arba, which by 1994 had several thousand residents. Raised in an Orthodox home in New York, he'd been active in Meir Kahane's Jewish Defense League, a far-right group whose members engaged in both activism and vigilantism against perceived enemies of Jews or Israel. The FBI would eventually outlaw it as a terrorist organization.

He immigrated to Israel after finishing medical school in 1981, changed his name from Benjamin to Baruch, and soon came to the attention of Shabak, the internal security service that focused mostly on Palestinian insurgents but had a separate department to deal with Jewish radicals. During his military service, and later as a doctor in Kiryat Arba, Goldstein refused to treat Arabs, a position that almost got him court-martialed. While running for Kiryat Arba's local council in 1992 as a representative of Kahane's Kach Party, he advocated "transferring these hostile Arabs across the border." He told a journalist that Palestinians strove to inflict a second holocaust on the Jews of

Israel and that "treasonous politicians were preventing the army from operating effectively against them."

The police had detained Goldstein several times over the years for minor offenses—knocking over a bookcase full of Korans at the Cave of the Patriarchs and circulating leaflets calling for attacks against Palestinians after Kahane was assassinated in New York (by an Egyptian American). But in the months after the signing of the Oslo deal he seemed to have come unhinged. Several of the Hamas attacks that followed the signing in Washington occurred in the Hebron area, triggering angry and sometimes violent outbursts by settlers against Palestinian bystanders. Goldstein, as the resident doctor, would often rush to the scene of these attacks to treat the wounded. The army valued his efforts so highly that a regional commander recommended promoting him to the rank of reserve major. "If there's any officer worthy of being promoted in the Judea, Samaria and Gaza area, it is without a doubt, Dr. Baruch Goldstein," the commander wrote just five weeks before the massacre.

Two shooting incidents in particular might have pushed him over the edge. In early November, Palestinians sprayed the car of an Orthodox rabbi much revered by the settlers, Haim Druckman, in a drive-by shooting near Hebron. A bullet struck Druckman in the arm, wounding him moderately. But his driver, Efraim Ayoubi, was hit in the chest and by the time Goldstein arrived, was barely breathing. Another Kiryat Arba settler who rushed to the scene, Eliezer Waldman, recalled years later watching Goldstein try for long minutes to resuscitate Ayoubi and then grow angry when he realized the man would not survive. "He just threw his medical bag to the ground and stormed off."

A month later, Palestinians shot dead a father and son outside Kiryat Arba, Mordechai and Shalom Lapid. The Lapid family, with fourteen children, had been a pillar of the settler community. The funeral procession the following day drew thousands of people, including Goldstein, who joined others in a menacing chant for vengeance against Palestinians.

Rabin summoned his cabinet ministers to Tel Aviv for an emergency meeting, hoping to prevent events from cycling out of control. Already, Palestinians across the West Bank were protesting the massacre, throwing stones at soldiers and drawing fire. The day's casualty toll would steadily climb. Arab citizens of Israel were also venting their anger, protesting around Jaffa and in a part of northern Israel where Arab towns are clustered, known as the Triangle. As the hours passed, the pressure on Arafat to respond firmly against Israel mounted. In Tunis, he announced he was suspending the Gaza-Jericho negotiations. Rabin's realization back in September that a lone extremist could subvert the entire process with a single act of sensational carnage was materializing even before the agreement could be implemented.

At the cabinet meeting, security officials described to the attendees—some twenty of them, seated around a large wooden table—what they knew about Goldstein. Shabak had worked hard to cultivate informants in the settlements after it exposed the plot by Jewish extremists in the 1980s to blow up the Dome of the Rock in Jerusalem. They had been running several in Kiryat Arba. But nothing in the file the agency had on Goldstein suggested he was capable of something this extreme. Jacob Perry, who had headed Shabak since 1988, told the cabinet ministers Goldstein appeared to have plotted the massacre alone. But others in the agency, including the man in charge of tracking Jewish extremists, Hezi Kalo, suspected that he received at least tacit approval from rabbis before setting out to kill Palestinians. Though most religious settlers were law-abiding, a running concern for Shabak was that certain rabbis held more sway with the ideological core of the community than the state itself with its laws and institutions—that their theological rulings stood above the decisions of the democratically elected government. The Rabin government's willingness to cede land to the Palestinians had put these two competing authorities, the state and the rabbis (at least a segment of them), on a collision course.

The massacre presented an opportunity to address this Kulturkampf, though it wasn't clear to people around the table whether Rabin recognized the extent of the challenge it posed to the country's civilian authority. His Labor Party and the people it represented—secular, largely Ashkenazi liberals—had been hegemonic through most of his lifetime. Rabin, the scion of Palmach and the army's chief of staff during the 1967 war, was the very embodiment of Israeliness. That the settlement movement, with its redemption fixations and its rabbinical authorities, was anything more than a fringe phenomenon seemed difficult for Rabin to grasp. And yet, for years now, the tide had been shifting in their favor.

With the hours ticking down until the start of the Sabbath, the ministers made two decisions. The first was to initiate the legal procedure for outlawing Kach and its offshoot, Kahane Chai. Both groups espoused racist ideologies and preached violence against the Palestinians. Banning them would make it easier to go after their top activists, several of whom lived in Hebron and Kiryat Arba. They also decided to form a commission of inquiry to probe the circumstances of the massacre, including how Goldstein managed to get past the soldiers at the entrance to the Cave of the Patriarchs and whether new arrangements for sharing the shrine were necessary. Rabin opposed a commission. He felt its very formation would imply that the government shared the blame for the massacre. But around the table, he was outnumbered.

At some point the cabinet ministers took up a more ambitious idea: evacuating the settlers from Hebron. Some five hundred Jews lived in several enclaves of Hebron's city center—the radical fringe of the settler population. They tangled regularly with Palestinians in the city and with Israeli soldiers as well. The army regularly stationed three battalions in Hebron to safeguard the Jews—meaning soldiers outnumbered settlers by at least two to one—a huge toll on the military. How they had come to live in the city was the story of the settler enterprise itself: They squatted there illegally and eventually won retroactive approval from authorities. Even dovish governments had a habit of yielding to the settlers, often on the heels of a Palestinian terrorist attack.

The Oslo Accord did not require Rabin to evacuate a single settlement. The fate of the 140 or so Jewish communities scattered across the West Bank and Gaza would be determined in the final negotiations between the two sides, which were set to begin in 1996. But Rabin did commit to handing Arafat control of all Palestinian cities in the

West Bank in the second stage of the agreement, including Hebron. The fact that Jews lived in the heart of the city would complicate the endeavor. The massacre, which revealed to Israelis more starkly than ever the fanatic undergrowth of the settlement enterprise, seemed to offer an opportunity to dismantle the Hebron communities.

The ministers debated the idea for much of the afternoon without arriving at a decision. Hours later, Rabin raised the issue with a smaller group he convened at the Defense Ministry—Perry, Yatom, and the army's chief of staff, Ehud Barak. But all three worried that a large-scale eviction would prompt violent confrontations with the settlers of Hebron. Perry, the Shabak chief, offered an alternative: evacuating Tel Rumeida, a single enclave isolated from the rest of the Jewish clusters in the city and home to some twenty settlers. The eviction would signal to Jewish radicals that violence, far from halting the handover of territory to Palestinians, would actually accelerate it. And it would be a message to Palestinians that Rabin intended to deal harshly with the extremists—just as he expected Arafat to do with Hamas.

Rabin seemed to like the idea. In the earlier meeting he referred to Goldstein as "Jewish Hamas." Now he left participants with the impression that he would order the evacuation the next day.

―――――――――

BY SATURDAY MORNING, February 26, the full scope of the previous day's bloodshed became clear. In addition to the slaughter at the shrine, Israeli troops had opened fire on protesters across the West Bank and Gaza, killing fourteen people and bringing the death toll to forty-three. It was the worst single-day carnage in years. The army imposed its usual closure on the territories to prevent revenge attacks and also added a curfew to the mix, confining more than 2 million Palestinians to their homes for most hours of the day and night. With anger running high in the West Bank and Gaza, Israeli authorities felt the restrictions were the only way to prevent an explosion. But to Palestinians, they compounded the injustice. The victims of the massacre were now being punished for the massacre. The curfew did not apply to settlers in the territories, including Hebron, where Jews walked around the city center freely, armed with Uzis and other automatic weapons. Palestinians could only watch from their windows and seethe.

More about Goldstein had also come to light. In the months leading up the shooting, Palestinians had complained to Israeli authorities several times about a tall bearded man named Baruch harassing worshippers at the Cave of the Patriarchs. On one occasion he poured acid on the carpets of the Ibrahimi Mosque. Police buried the complaints. Though Israeli authorities responded aggressively to any suspicion against Palestinians, they were notably slow about investigating settlers. The phenomenon had been criticized repeatedly in Israel's own government reports. One written by Deputy Attorney General Yehudit Karp and published in 1984 cited the "ambivalence" of Israeli police officers who did not view settler violence against Palestinians as criminal in the "common definition" of the term. Karp examined seventy Palestinian complaints of attacks by settlers for the report. In fifty-three of the cases, the government took no action.

Two days before the shooting, Goldstein called his insurance agent and asked to double his life insurance policy. The night before, he penned a letter to his family—he had an Israeli-born wife and four children—saying in part that he prayed God would grant him "full redemption." American journalists writing about Goldstein emphasized the role Americans played in the settlement enterprise, not only in Hebron but throughout the West Bank and Gaza. Though settlers made up fewer than 3 percent of Israelis, 10 percent of the settlers were American-born. The Long Island daily, *Newsday*, captured the phenomenon with a mordant headline: "America's 'Gift' to Israel."

Rabin read the reports about Goldstein with a sense of revulsion. He had been nursing a toothache for some days, taking antibiotics but avoiding the dentist. The pain now fused his anger at the settlers. As if the massacre weren't appalling enough, some residents of Hebron and Kiryat Arba were now defending Goldstein, claiming his actions somehow thwarted an imminent attack on the Jews of Hebron. They based the assertion on rumors that Palestinians had been storing armaments at the shrine. Even the local council of Kiryat Arba, which included both religious and nonreligious Jews, refused to condemn the shooting. Many other right-wingers did speak out against it. But few if any entertained the possibility that Goldstein reflected a broader trend toward violence in the radical settlements. He was a lone fanatic, what Israelis referred to as an *esev shoteh*, a stray weed.

Rabin had an icy relationship with the settlers going back decades. The conquests of the Six-Day War had inspired a kind of rapture even among members of the Labor Party, a secular version of the messianism that infected religious Israelis. Officially, the Labor-led government stood ready to trade the territories for peace treaties with the Arab states. But some prominent Laborites, including Rabin's former Palmach commander, Yigal Allon, quietly encouraged Israelis to settle beyond the "green line" that marked the border before the war—and not just in areas they deemed vital for Israel's security. Eliezer Waldman, a prominent rabbi, recalled approaching Allon for help when the latter was a cabinet minister in 1968 and getting what could only be interpreted as implied consent. "He said, 'You're waiting for permission from the government? That's not how Zionism works.'" Waldman and his wife checked into a Palestinian-owned hotel in Hebron, along with two other families, and refused to leave until the government promised to create a settlement just outside the city. Allon helped get the measure passed, giving birth to Kiryat Arba—where Baruch Goldstein would eventually make his home.

Rabin seemed to be immune to this territorial fixation (except with regards to Jerusalem's Old City, with the Jewish shrine in its heart, the Western Wall). He had no trouble arguing that Israel needed parts of the West Bank for security, but Rabin regarded the notion that every inch of the territory was sacred as obnoxious and reckless. It threatened to turn Israel into a second Lebanon, where competing religious groups fought one another relentlessly, nearly destroying the country. In the memoir he published in 1979, Rabin wrote that the settlers had undermined Israel's long-term well-being by deliberately planting themselves in Palestinian-populated areas. He described them as a "cancer in the body of Israeli democracy."

The settlers came to see Rabin as a dangerous opponent, a political figure with no religious or romantic attachment to the territory they saw as sacred. Their fears about him materialized when, as prime minister in 1992, Rabin froze government housing projects in the settlements. The move would signal to the Palestinians that he intended to negotiate more earnestly than his Likud Party predecessor, Yitzhak Shamir. But it also conveyed Rabin's determination to change Israel's priorities—from security and settlements to infrastructure inside Israel and to education. Spending on education doubled during his first year in office. Previous governments had enticed Israelis to move to the settlements with tax breaks and lower-interest mortgages, incentives that helped swell the communities with people who sought a better standard of living, not some ideological fulfillment. Now the settlers complained that Rabin was hanging them out to dry.

To placate the settlers, Rabin appointed his deputy defense minister, Mordechai "Motta" Gur, as an informal liaison to the YESHA Council. A retired general, Gur had commanded the division that conquered Jerusalem's Old City during the Six-Day War. The settlers viewed him as an ally in the otherwise hostile Labor Party and trusted him to notify them before the government took any significant steps regarding the West Bank and Gaza. Rabin also maintained a direct dialogue with some of the more pragmatic settler leaders. One of them, Yoel Bin-Nun, took it upon himself to explain the settler position in long, handwritten letters he sent Rabin every month or two beginning in 1992 and in occasional meetings with the prime minister. Bin-Nun had been one of the founders of the settlement Ofra and a member of the YESHA Council. A former paratrooper, he served under Gur in the battle for Jerusalem in 1967.

His letters during the first year of Rabin's term were short and friendly enough. Bin-Nun wanted Rabin to invite the National Religious Party, a parliamentary faction that represented the mainstream of the settler movement, to join his coalition. Though he acknowledged deep ideological divisions between Labor and the NRP, Bin-Nun thought the two parties could cooperate at least until the moment negotiations with the Palestinians or Syria produced a breakthrough—a moment he doubted would come. When that endeavor failed, Bin-Nun tried to persuade Rabin to annex the main settlement blocs to Israel and to accept the position that Jordan was the real homeland of the Palestinians. "The PLO, in its current situation, might be the only group that can take control in Amman at this critical hour and stop the rise of Islam," he wrote Rabin on September 9, 1992, suggesting that King Hussein was losing ground to Jordan's Muslim Brotherhood.

Bin-Nun also tried to defuse tensions between Rabin and the settlers, a near-impossible undertaking. Even before the Oslo Accord, settlers had taken to protesting outside Rabin's office in Jerusalem. One of his cabinet ministers, Uzi Baram, recalled years later Rabin hearing their chants during a particular cabinet meeting, walking over to the window, and growing red with anger. More often, though, he would dismiss their rants with a downward flip of the hand.

The Oslo Accord with Arafat raised the hostility to new heights. After it was signed in Washington, Gur went to the home of YESHA Council leader Israel Harel in the settlement Ofra and got an earful. The YESHA Council had become so influential in the preceding decade that its leaders could not imagine a prime minister making sweeping decisions without consulting them first. Gur tried to reassure them by pointing out that the interim agreement did not include the uprooting of a single settlement. But this old ally of the settlers had lost his credibility. Rabin had kept the secret of Oslo from him as well.

Bin-Nun, who attended the meeting, felt betrayed by Rabin. But he also felt a need to preserve his line to Rabin in hope of minimizing the damage from the Oslo deal. Bin-Nun saw himself and the other members of the YESHA Council as moderates who had risked their own standing in the settler community by advocating dialogue with Rabin. Now he worried that he and his cohorts would lose ground to the hardliners, including the Hebronites. "In this whole process, the extremists are getting stronger, the ones who warned all along not to trust this government," he wrote Rabin in a six-page, handwritten letter dated September 29, just sixteen days after the signing in Washington. "In a short time, if there's no dramatic change, I will no longer be able to influence people towards moderation the way I have for years because everyone knows that nothing will come of our quiet contacts and cooperation with you. . . . The struggle is moving towards militancy and I'm not sure we'll be able to control it."

The warning was certainly prescient, as the Goldstein massacre would demonstrate. The Oslo deal fired up the militants on both sides. But it was also self-serving. Rabin was Israel's democratically elected leader. He had won the election on a promise to forge peace deals between Israel and its neighbors, including the Palestinians. The settlers, by contrast, had put only a few lawmakers in parliament; a hardline list led by the Hebron rabbi Moshe Levinger drew fewer than 4,000 votes. Bin-Nun's argument struck Rabin as a kind of extortion bid: meet the YESHA Council's demands or contend with the violence of the extremists. As with most of Bin-Nun's letters, he read this one personally (Bin-Nun had written at the top: "Personal—Urgent!") but did not respond.

Bin-Nun continued to write Rabin regularly over the next two years. A letter five days after the six-page one argued that Arafat's Fatah group had not really dropped its policy of armed struggle as promised and that its operatives in the West Bank and Gaza were working together with Hamas militants to attack Israelis. As evidence, he included photos of graffiti he spotted in Beit Hanina, a Palestinian neighborhood in East Jerusalem, where someone had scrawled: "Fatah and Hamas, together till victory."

But while he prodded Rabin to listen more attentively to the settlers, Bin-Nun also took part in YESHA Council meetings where settler leaders plotted ways to grind down his legitimacy. In one of them sometime after the signing in Washington, the council invited psychologists and public-relations executives to strategize how to discredit Rabin personally and force him to resign. Bin-Nun recalled the discussions years later with some embarrassment. "[The idea] was to break Rabin, those around him, his legitimacy, his image. There was an orderly discussion about attacking Rabin alone. If both [Rabin and Peres] were attacked, the campaign would become diffused and Rabin would get off because public opinion would blame Peres." The council members decided, among other things, to dispatch hecklers whenever Rabin appeared at a public event.

One such event took place at Bar-Ilan University, where in the fall of 1993, Rabin received an honorary doctorate. The university had chosen the recipients months in advance, well before the Oslo negotiations had come to light. They included Margaret Thatcher, the former British prime minister, and Robert Jay Lifton, an American psychiatrist and scholar of the Holocaust and the psychology of genocide. Rabin was to be the main speaker but when he stepped up to the podium dressed in the traditional black cap and gown, protesters in the audience stood and jeered. One of the hecklers managed to tap into the public address system and cause a loud buzz whenever the prime minister leaned in to speak. Rabin waited silently while guards pulled the protesters out.

By late 1993, Rabin had had enough of the settlers. The YESHA Council was pushing for a meeting to make its case for a partial lifting of the settlement freeze—enough to accommodate what it defined as "natural growth" in its communities. But Rabin now felt the chasm was too wide to bridge, a clash over the very character of Israel. Haber, whose job as chief of staff included smoothing the wrinkles with various constituencies, pushed Rabin to meet the settlers and concede something small—agree to form a committee, say, that would study their demands. But Rabin had virtually no skills in diplomacy—he couldn't hide his contempt. An argument erupted as soon as the settler leaders sat down.

"He couldn't pretend he's now friends with these people," recalled Uri Dromi, who served as director of the Government Press Office at the time. "He felt they were undermining everything we're trying to build."

With all that as the backdrop, the massacre at the shrine now struck Rabin as the biggest wrecking ball his opponents had launched at the peace process yet. Goldstein wanted revenge for the bloodshed he'd seen in the preceding months. But he also aimed for something bigger—a prayer-hall slaughter so horrific that it would ignite the Arab street and turn Palestinians away from the peace deal. Hamas would surely respond in kind, souring Israelis on the process. The nihilists on both sides had a common agenda.

Rabin recognized the danger. And yet he found himself wavering about the evacuation of Tel Rumeida. Yossi Beilin, who thought the decision was all but finalized Friday night, listened to the radio throughout the weekend expecting to hear the announcement that soldiers had begun dismantling the enclave. It never came.

———————

A STEADY RAIN fell on both sides of the green line over the following days, helping diffuse the protests in the West Bank and Gaza but not the tension. Goldstein's family sought to bury the body in Hebron's old Jewish cemetery on a hill surrounded by Palestinian homes, a move that would surely have provoked more friction and violence. When the army refused, settlers in Kiryat Arba cleared a section at the end of a park in their town, named, aptly, for Meir Kahane.

The funeral drew more than a thousand people, including Kach activists now fleeing arrest warrants. Baruch Marzel, who led Kach and lived in Tel Rumeida, eulogized Goldstein as "a saint, a great man who had the courage to carry out a heroic act." Another Kach activist, Avigdor Eskin, promised to name his newborn son after the killer. Incredibly, some people held signs demanding revenge for *Goldstein's* death. His family had the gravestone chiseled with the words "He gave his life for the nation of Israel, its people and its land," and also a line from the Book of Psalms: "Clean hands and a pure heart." With little else in the park but gravel and shrub, the stone tomb protruded from the earth like a shrine.

Rabin spoke to Arafat by phone in Tunis, laying out the measures his cabinet had enacted. In addition to outlawing Kach and Kahane Chai and starting to arrest top members of the groups, authorities had decided to ban some fifteen hard-core settlers from the West Bank and Gaza for now and to confiscate weapons from another twenty people. Rabin also informed the Palestinian leader that he would be releasing hundreds of Palestinians from prison in the coming days, a gesture that had already been agreed upon in the talks and not yet implemented.

But Arafat stood by his decision to suspend the negotiations. Though he kept the conversation polite—the two men had already met face-to-face several times since the signing in Washington—he told Rabin the measures seemed minor for such a horrific event. "Hollow and superficial," is how he described them to a journalist later. Arafat pressed Rabin to move the hundreds of settlers from Hebron itself to Kiryat Arba less than a mile away. He also wanted an international force deployed in the city.

Whether or not to evacuate some Hebron settlers now became entwined with the very fate of the peace process. Rabin would ponder the question for weeks, with legal advisers and military officers giving him a range of opinions. The generals who ran the military, the body that would be charged with carrying out the evacuation, mostly opposed it. Dismantling Tel Rumeida alone would require several battalions in addition to the three stationed there routinely, they informed Rabin. The settlers would resist, perhaps violently. When troops evacuated the last remaining Israelis from Sinai in 1982 under a peace accord with Egypt, right-wing activists had dropped sandbags and burning tires at soldiers from rooftops, in images that Israelis found difficult to stomach. Some extremists— mostly Kach people who had moved to Sinai in the weeks leading up to the withdrawal—threatened to blow themselves up if soldiers tried to pull them out.

The specter of an armed confrontation in Hebron worried Rabin. It also stirred dark memories of the *Altalena* affair forty-six years earlier, a violent clash between soldiers under Rabin's command and members of the right-wing paramilitary group known as the Irgun. The *Altalena* was a cargo vessel the Irgun had purchased to ship tons of weapons and ammunition from France to Israel in the weeks following independence in 1948. Though Irgun leader Menachem Begin had offered to give much of the weaponry to the newly formed Israel Defense Forces— while keeping some for Irgun battalions—Ben-Gurion had already resolved to bring all the fighting groups under a single jurisdiction. The weapons ship seemed to undermine that objective. As the *Altalena* drew close to Tel Aviv's coastline, soldiers fired on it and took control of the cargo, leaving sixteen people dead. To historians, the affair marked a critical point in the provisional government's assertion of sovereignty. But it also poisoned relations between left and right for decades to come.

Rabin's role in the ordeal had come about by chance. He had been visiting government headquarters when the ship came in and was ordered to the beach. Though he brushed off accusations over the years that he'd been responsible for the shedding of Jewish blood, it seemed to friends that the affair left a scar. "I think the *Altalena* case haunted him," recalled Amos Eiran, who had worked with Rabin at the Israeli embassy in Washington in the late 1960s. The two remained friends—and tennis partners—for decades.

Whether Rabin would face legal hurdles in seeking to dismantle Tel Rumeida was also a question. Settlers had established a presence in Hebron in 1979 with the same wildcat tactics that worked elsewhere in the West Bank, squatting in a building known as Beit Hadassah that served decades earlier as a clinic for Jews. The Israeli government at the time was initially opposed to a Jewish enclave in the city but gave its approval following a Palestinian shooting attack in Hebron. Over the years, the settlers were allowed to take over other buildings once owned by Jews and expand steadily.

The consultations in Rabin's office ate up several hours of each day, including his birthday, March 1. He turned seventy-two in the thick of the crisis. Lawyers told Rabin that the settlers would surely challenge any evacuation order with a petition to Israel's High Court of Justice. Though the government would cite its security needs to justify the measure, some lawyers thought the case might be difficult to win. Goldstein, after all, had lived in Kiryat Arba, not Tel Rumeida. And if the government was arguing that it could no longer protect Jews living in the heart of a hostile Palestinian city, that the military's resources were being drained, why was it focusing on Tel Rumeida and not all the enclaves? Even Rabin's attorney general, Michael Ben-Yair, who supported the evacuation idea, had bad news. He told Rabin the measure should rightly be submitted to parliament for approval and not just to the cabinet, a significant challenge given that Rabin controlled only a minority of the seats in the plenum.

The extended deliberation gave settler leaders and right-wing rabbis a chance to fight back. In the days after the massacre, they mounted a campaign against any change to the status quo in Hebron. The group now had no illusions about being able to sway the government. But it could certainly influence individual soldiers and officers who might be called on to evacuate settlers from their homes. Elyakim Haetzni, a lawyer and political activist who lived in Kiryat Arba, favored an approach that included both persuasion and intimidation.

A former member of parliament with the right-wing Tehiya Party, Haetzni founded the Action Center for Canceling the Autonomy Agreement soon after the signing in Washington and proceeded to issue vitriolic attacks against Rabin and the agreement. It was Haetzni who had first likened Rabin to Philippe Pétain. His slogans appeared on signs and bumper stickers throughout the country. Weeks before Goldstein mowed down Palestinians in Hebron, Haetzni published an article in the settler journal *Nekuda* calling for nothing short of an insurrection against the Rabin government. "A people whose government committed an act of national treason, collaborated with a terrorist enemy to steal the heart of his homeland . . . must be ready to fight. And in this war as in every other war, there are risks and casualties," he wrote. His article also included a warning to Israeli soldiers. "An IDF soldier, though Jewish, who would pull us, our wives, our children and grandchildren from our houses and make us refugees—will, in our view, be conducting a pogrom. We shall look upon him as a violent thug acting like a Cossack."

Two weeks after the massacre, Haetzni held a news conference to push the message further. In a hall teeming with journalists, he screened a half-hour film his Action Center had produced about a fictional battalion commander named Ron Segev struggling with the dilemma of evicting settlers from their homes. In the film, Segev consults with legal scholars and reads texts on conscientious objection. By the end, he decides to disobey the evacuation order, citing—among other things—the Oslo Accord's provision for an armed Palestinian police force to operate in Gaza and Jericho. "If a soldier steals a few weapons and sells them to Arabs, he's indicted," he concludes. "But if the government does the same thing on a much larger scale, people applaud." Haetzni announced that he was distributing several thousand copies of the film to soldiers.

Authorities paid little attention to Haetzni and his Action Center. Though inciting soldiers to revolt amounted to sedition and might well have been grounds for an indictment, it was not clear whether he had much of a following. Even in the settler milieu, he was an outlier—deeply ideological and politically extreme but not religious. His pronouncements lacked the weight of ecclesiastic authority.

But three rabbis whose opinions did matter to settlers quickly followed up with a religious ruling—one that troubled Rabin deeply. Their edict, framed as an answer to a question from a soldier, declared that it was "forbidden for a Jew to take part in any activity which aids in the evacuation [of Judea, Samaria, Gaza and the Golan]." The rabbis, Moshe-Zvi Neria, Shaul Yisraeli, and Avraham Shapira, cited the writings of the twelfth-century Torah scholar Maimonides, who said: "Even if the King orders you to violate the laws of the Torah, it is forbidden to obey."

The ruling, posted in religious neighborhoods across the country, had no precedent. In the contest between religious and secular authorities, the army, an almost sacred institution for Israelis, had generally been spared. Now, respected rabbis were telling soldiers to ignore their chain of command and obey a different authority, a nightmare scenario for any military. The three rabbis were easily the most influential figures of the national religious camp—the term that took in not just settlers but a broad swath of observant Israelis. Shapira had been Israel's chief Ashkenazi rabbi for a decade. If only a fraction of religious soldiers heeded the call, the army faced deep trouble. Though Israel's combat units (which would be called on to evacuate settlers) and officer corps were traditionally filled by secular Israelis, the demographics of the army had been changing for some years. By the early 1990s, the so-called knitted skullcap soldiers were ascending in these units—a trend that would accelerate in the years to come.

By now, Rabin's determination to confront the settlers was eroding. An expert on political extremism in Israel, Ehud Sprinzak, drafted a memorandum for the government that predicted a "high likelihood of violent confrontations with the settlers and possible Jewish fatalities" if any attempt were made to remove Jews from Hebron. Bin-Nun, the settler who corresponded with Rabin, suggested a compromise of sorts in a letter dated March 25. He asked Rabin to allocate more territory to the settlers in order to create contiguity among the Jewish enclaves of Hebron—alongside a decision to dismantle Tel Rumeida. But Bin-Nun conceded that even with that far-reaching gesture, other members of the YESHA Council would likely reject any evacuation order. "Because these ideas are unacceptable to my colleagues, I would ask that you keep them between us," he wrote. To Rabin it was a non-starter. He had concluded long ago that allowing Jews to settle in Hebron had been a terrible mistake. Entrenching the community further—in the aftermath of a massacre a settler perpetrated against Palestinians, no less—struck him as downright perverse.

And yet, he could not bring himself to order an evacuation. In late March, Rabin dispatched Gur to Israel's chief rabbis with the message that the Hebron settlers would not be removed. It was an admission of defeat. A month earlier the public had been outraged by Goldstein's brutality, but the prospect of internecine violence seemed to work in the settlers' favor. Polls now showed most Israelis opposed an evacuation. In one conducted by *Yedioth Ahronoth*, 18 percent of respondents—nearly one in five Israelis—thought soldiers should put the rulings of their rabbis ahead of the orders of their commanders. Fifty-two percent rejected the notion that legal measures should be taken against the three rabbis who issued the insubordination decree. Ben-Yair, the attorney general, would come to regret not ordering a police investigation against the rabbis. But at the time, he worried that religious Israelis would find the sight of three octogenarian rabbis in the dock just too upsetting. Two of the rabbis would die within eighteen months of the decree.

The Council of the Chief Rabbinate "registered with great satisfaction" the fact that the settlers would stay put. In a letter to the prime minister, the council wrote: "It is therefore clear that the question of military orders to evacuate settlers or settlements—which are against Jewish law—is not on the agenda and the army must be taken out of the political debate."

Rabin saw the episode as a temporary retreat. A full peace agreement with the Palestinians would require the evacuation of settlers in huge numbers—not dozens but tens of thousands. In the weeks after the massacre, he concluded that it would be better to wage one big battle than several small ones. With the legal challenges and the political ordeal it entailed, evicting twenty people from Hebron could well have taken months. Rabin thought it would ultimately distract the government from more important things—like completing the Gaza-Jericho agreement and striking a peace deal with Jordan, which now seemed within reach.

For the extremists, the victory felt significant. It confirmed that the entire settler leadership would mobilize to block even the tiniest withdrawal. Rabbis could disrupt the army's chain of command by invoking Jewish law as an authority that stood above the decisions of the elected government. If those things weren't troubling enough, it also underscored how a lone gunman could bring the peace process to a crashing halt with just an automatic rifle and a few magazines. There was a lesson here for opponents of the process on both sides.

———

AT THE START of April, the crisis finally seemed to ebb. The cabinet ministers and advisers to Rabin who opposed confronting the settlers, including Haber, breathed a sigh of relief. Even the advocates of eviction were happy to forget the ordeal and move on. Arafat, who had prevented his negotiators from meeting Israelis for more than a month, finally relented, dispatching them to Cairo to make what both sides now felt were the final security arrangements ahead of Israel's withdrawal from Gaza and Jericho and their transfer to Palestinian hands. If the teams could lock up an agreement within weeks, Arafat would relocate his headquarters to Gaza by summer. The months of violence had dimmed the enthusiasm on both sides, but the long-awaited commencement of Palestinian self-rule would be so momentous, perhaps it could erase some of the ill will.

Getting Arafat to resume the talks had involved a combination of gestures—condolences and reassurances from Rabin conveyed repeatedly by emissaries in person; Israel's agreement to a temporary international force in Hebron—unarmed and essentially devoid of any real powers but the first introduction of foreign forces to the West Bank nonetheless; and a visit to Tunis by Dennis Ross, the White

House Middle East envoy. Still eager to bond himself to the United States, Arafat viewed every meeting with senior American officials as a windfall.

Ross had been working in government on Arab-Israeli issues since the mid-1980s, but because the United States had no relations with the PLO until the Oslo Accord, American officials engaged solely with Palestinian figures in the West Bank and Gaza, not with Arafat himself. When Ross landed in Tunis, where the PLO had made its headquarters since Israel ousted Arafat from Lebanon more than a decade earlier, he was struck by the disparity between the group's revolutionary beginnings and its staid, comfortable existence. Arafat's aides all wore expensive suits and watches. They lived in villas in an upscale part of the city. In the waiting room outside Arafat's office, apparatchiks sat around watching an episode of *The Golden Girls*, an American sitcom about four elderly women sharing a home in Miami, Florida. Ross thought of the show's humor as typically Jewish, not what he expected PLO men to find amusing.

As signs of an early spring appeared in Israel, Rabin's government wrapped up other matters as well. Treasury officials struck a new wage deal with university lecturers, whose strike had disrupted classes for two months. With Israel's labor federation still wielding enormous power, strikes periodically paralyzed everything from state-run hospitals to the country's only international airport. Police finally nabbed Baruch Marzel, the Kach leader wanted since the day of the massacre. He had been hiding at the home of another settler, Yoram Skolnick, who faced trial for shooting a Palestinian militant after he'd been subdued and tied up. For weeks, the actions of others had lunged Rabin from crisis to crisis. Now he felt himself regaining control.

But the sensation was short-lived. On April 6, exactly forty days after Goldstein's killing spree, a nineteen-year-old Palestinian drove a car full of explosives from his town in the West Bank to Afula, a few miles across the border, and blew it up, killing eight people. Hamas, which trained and equipped the bomber, had waited until the end of the Muslim mourning period to take vengeance on Israel.

The bomber had stopped his light-blue Opel Ascona near a public bus and waited a few moments until a group of high school students drew near before detonating his load. With the blast, the front of the bus burst into flames and thousands of razor-sharp metal fragments sliced at the crowd. Though the event pre-dated camera phones, a bystander who happened to be carrying a camcorder captured much of the carnage on video. In quick, jerky pans, it showed a man whose head had been severed and survivors whose skin was charred and clothes burned off. One of the bodies at the scene belonged to the assailant; he had killed himself in the act of killing others.

The Afula bombing would come to be remembered as Hamas's foray into suicide attacks—as the moment the group embraced the tactic in response to Goldstein's mass murder. In truth, Hamas had launched several suicide bombers at Israeli targets over the preceding year. But while the group had confined itself mostly to assaults against soldiers and settlers in the West Bank and Gaza—attacks that usually left two or three people dead—from now on it would strike at the heart of Israel, aiming for as many civilian casualties as possible. The car bombing marked the deadliest attack by any group since 1989. Goldstein hadn't spawned the suicide phenomenon in Hamas, but his massacre motivated the group to take it to new heights.

The bombing preceded the official start of Holocaust Memorial Day in Israel by just hours. The twenty-four-hour mourning period begins with a piercing siren heard throughout Israel and a ceremony at Yad Vashem, Jerusalem's museum and memorial for the 6 million victims of Nazi genocide. In its early years, Israel struggled to find a fitting way to mark the Holocaust. The idea of commemorating the persecution of Jews ran against the ethos that Israel had fostered for itself as a country of citizen-warriors who would not be victimized under any circumstances. Only eight years after the end of World War II did Ben-Gurion's government get around to establishing an official day for marking the genocide, calling it, poignantly, Yom Hashoah Ve'hagvura, "Holocaust and the Heroism Day." It would coincide with the anniversary of the Warsaw Ghetto uprising, one of the war's few instances of large-scale Jewish resistance.

Rabin spoke at the ceremony that evening but made no mention of the bombing. At the funerals for the victims the next day, crowds chased away the one Labor Party member who tried to attend. Funerals for victims of Palestinian violence often included fiery speeches and attacks on the government. In this case, the context of the bombing—that it came in response to a massacre perpetrated by a radical settler—became predictably obscured by grief and rage.

By the time Rabin convened his cabinet in the aftermath of the violence, the tension climbed even higher. A Palestinian from Gaza somehow crossed into Israel with an automatic rifle and sprayed bullets at a bus stop near the southern town of Ashdod, killing one Israeli. In Hebron, a visit by Jesse Jackson, the American minister and civil-rights activist, turned violent. Jackson had been invited to attend a PLO event in Jerusalem but Israel canceled it as part of its policy of preventing Palestinian political activity in the city. Instead, Jackson traveled to Hebron, where he led several hundred Palestinians to the Tomb of the Patriarchs for prayer.

Israel had allowed Jews to continue praying at the shrine after the massacre in February but kept Muslims away until authorities could put a new worship regime in place—adding further insult to Palestinian injury. When soldiers now blocked the group from passing, Jackson held a prayer service there at the entrance, along with a Hamas preacher, Taysir Tamimi. To the soldiers and settlers, the scene must have looked surreal, with Jackson chanting the slogan that electrified delegates at the Democratic National Convention in Atlanta six years earlier, "Keep Hope Alive," and Palestinians echoing his words and clapping. But when Jackson got back on the bus to leave, Palestinians hurled stones at Israeli soldiers, who responded with gunfire, wounding eight of them. The clashes lasted some thirty minutes, with Palestinians at one point using Jackson's bus for cover.

Rabin now faced questions about how Palestinian assailants were managing to get through Israeli checkpoints. The closure that the army imposed on the West Bank and Gaza after the massacre had still been in effect. Under pressure to protect Israelis from additional bombings, the cabinet decided to extend the closure indefinitely. Since the measure would harm Israeli farmers and building contractors who relied on cheap Palestinian labor for their enterprise, it also decided to offer visas for large numbers of foreign workers, mainly from Eastern Europe and the Far East. The twin decisions would cost many thousands of Palestinians their livelihood—60,000 had permits to work in Israel. In the months since the signing in Washington, a perverse reality had emerged. The process that was supposed to enhance Israeli security and give Palestinians more freedom and prosperity was undermining all three.

CHAPTER 4

Din Rodef

"My own morality doesn't matter. It is determined solely according to the Torah itself."

—YIGAL AMIR

The Goldstein massacre captivated Amir and also taunted him. Amir regarded himself as a doer and others as talkers and compromisers. He once described Kahane supporters to a friend as "children." Though he respected the settlement movement, he suspected most settlers would abandon the West Bank and Gaza if the government offered them enough money to forfeit their land to the Palestinians. The problem, he often told people, was that Jews lacked the zealous devotion to the cause that Israel's Islamic enemies, Hamas and Hezbollah, demonstrated regularly. But Goldstein had not been a talker. He was not one of those self-appointed settler spokesmen who courted the media. He had taken action knowing he would likely be killed. If Amir thought sacrificing himself might be a courageous way to derail the peace train, Goldstein had beat him to it.

Amir had been studying in the *kolel* at Bar-Ilan the morning of the massacre. He heard the news on the radio, realized the significance of the event—initial reports estimated an even higher death toll—and decided to attend Goldstein's funeral over the weekend. On campus, where opinions had hardened in the preceding months, few people rushed to condemn the shooting. The rumor that Palestinians had been storing weapons at the shrine and planning to attack the Jews of Hebron had spread quickly from the settler enclaves outward, despite denials from the Israeli military. How the killing of innocents was meant to thwart this attack went unexplained. Still, the Amir brothers (and many other people) embraced the account. "It would have been ungrateful of me not to support him because he did it for all Jews," Hagai would say years later. "You don't see a lot of people willing to sacrifice their life in this country. A person who is willing to go against everyone and give his own life, that's something."

The funeral allowed Yigal Amir to take in the complexity of Kiryat Arba. The town included some of the most hardline settlers in the West Bank, but it was hardly homogenous. Goldstein had belonged to the Kahanists, a group of mostly American and Russian immigrants in the town. A core of secular right-wingers included Elyakim Haetzni, the lawyer and propagandist who made the film about the fictional battalion commander and his refusal to evict settlers from their homes. Members of the Hasidic movement Chabad made up a third group. The sect owned properties in Hebron dating back to the nineteenth century and its members made regular pilgrimages to a certain grave in Hebron's Jewish cemetery. Avishai Raviv, the radical Bar-Ilan student Amir had considered for his militia, circulated in the mass of skullcaps and beards. Raviv seemed to have several residences, one at a settlement north of Jerusalem and another in a suburb of Tel Aviv. Now he told people he was moving to Kiryat Arba.

Goldstein's wife and children, all four under the age of twelve, huddled over the grave. To leave them behind must have been a painful decision, Amir thought, yet more evidence of Goldstein's saintly devotion to the cause. But he told a friend later that he would have chosen a better target, one with lasting impact.

The spring semester brought changes to Amir's routine on campus. He had been working toward a minor in criminology but found it tedious and dropped it. Instead, Amir took up computer science, a surprising choice for him. Amir told people he had an irrational fear of computers; he found them intimidating. But he liked the idea of facing down his phobias. One of his early projects was to make a spreadsheet and input contacts. He included the names and numbers of some 350 people who attended the weekly protests on campus.

He also started dating Nava Holtzman, the pretty economics student who took part in the protest weekend outside Rabin's building on Rav Ashi Street. Holtzman would later recall a "deep emotional bond" between them, visits to Amir's home, and even a peek into Hagai's toolshed in the backyard, where he modified bullets and made timers for explosives. But the relationship suffered problems from the outset. Amir's mother found Holtzman cold and bossy and thought she was a terrible match for her son. She regarded her Gali as handsome and full of charisma, a prize for any woman. Holtzman's parents also had misgivings. "[They] were against my relationship with Yigal but not over ideology. In any event, they never even got to know him. My mother only saw him once for a few minutes," she related later.

Their qualms might have had something to do with Amir's skin tone. The Holtzmans traced their roots to Europe, making them Ashkenazi, the elite ethnic group in Israel roughly analogous to America's WASPs (white Anglo-Saxon Protestants). Amir was Mizrahi—the term for Jews who came from Arabic-speaking countries—and not just Mizrahi but Yemeni, the darkest shade on the ethnic palette. Though mixed couples were certainly part of the social tableau in Israel in the 1990s, disapproving parents formed a part of it as well. Holtzman's parents might have been especially concerned. At Bar-Ilan, religious couples in a relationship for just a few months often ended up married.

In what was now Israel's fifth decade of existence, the ethnic tension seemed at times to be waning. The grievances of Mizrahis (the term means literally "easterner" and is frequently interchanged with the word "Sephardi") were rooted in events long in the past—their mistreatment as immigrants in the early years of Israeli independence and lingering traces of discrimination. But it could also flare over contemporary issues in ways political parties were quick to exploit.

Around the time Amir and Holtzman started their relationship, an event transpired that would bring these tensions to the surface, especially for the Yemeni community.

The event revolved around the demands of a certain rabbi from the community, Uzi Meshulam, to have the disappearance of several hundred and perhaps thousands of Yemeni babies and toddlers in the 1940s and '50s investigated by a judicial commission. The story of the missing children had long been a source of anguish and suspicion for Israel's Yemeni Jews. Many in the community believed that in the chaos of their absorption in Israel, government agents stole the children and gave them to Ashkenazi families in Israel and abroad. Though never proven, the suspicion seemed to be reinforced by the government's broader mismanagement of Mizrahi immigration at the time—its high-handedness toward the immigrants, its policy of settling them in far-flung areas, and, most of all, its attitude toward the newcomers as primitives who needed to be reeducated.

In early May, following a dispute with a building contractor, Meshulam barricaded himself in his home in the town of Yehud, along with about a dozen armed followers. The rabbi had been known to police as an eccentric—he wore a large wig and had a record of disputes with neighbors. For several days, police kept troops posted around the house in a standoff reminiscent of the Waco siege in Texas a year earlier. As neighbors gathered to watch the events unfold, Meshulam's supporters buttressed the house with sandbags. When Meshulam left his home one night to negotiate with the police commissioner, officers stormed the house and killed one of the armed men inside. The rest, Meshulam included, were arrested and later sentenced to months or years in prison.

The Rabin government responded to the incident by granting Meshulam his wish—a judicial commission to investigate the fate of the missing Yemeni children. But the Amir brothers saw the raid as one more way Rabin silenced truth-tellers and shut down dissent. Amir was now going to every large antigovernment protest he could reach by bus or in Hagai's old Beetle. He complained to friends that police were cracking down brutally against right-wing protests and that the media, mobilized on behalf of the government, was playing down the scope of the dissension.

The same week as the raid on Meshulam's home, Rabin and Arafat at last finalized the Gaza-Jericho agreement. They signed the deal in a ceremony in Cairo (though only after an embarrassing last-minute dispute). The start of Palestinian self-rule first discussed in secret talks sixteen months earlier and almost derailed by violent extremists on both sides was finally going forward. Israeli troops had already begun their withdrawal from military bases they'd occupied for decades. They would be out of Jericho and most of Gaza—except for the settlement areas and some key roads—by July.

With the drawdown a reality now, Amir shifted strategies. Instead of encouraging students to protest on campus or outside Rabin's apartment building, he helped organize trips to the West Bank and Gaza. He now wanted to spend as much time as he could in the territory that Rabin, in his contempt for the Jews' biblical birthright, was willing to surrender. And he hoped other students would forge their own connection to Judea and Samaria, as many had come to refer to the territory. Though Israel had been occupying the West Bank and Gaza for more than a quarter century, Israelis who didn't live in settlements rarely ventured across the green line, except where it bisected Jerusalem. Even many right-wingers who argued Israel should never cede an inch had seen the territory only on the nightly news.

Amir and other students started with a trip to Jericho, the desert city on the road to the Dead Sea that would soon come under Palestinian control. To draw a large group, they billed the trip as a singles event with a prayer service to be conducted at the remains of a Byzantine-era synagogue in the city. Several dozen students signed up. But sleepy Jericho, with its shabby Arab bazaar and its parched landscape, offered little to connect to.

On a day off from classes, Amir joined a religious group on a trip to a shrine on the outskirts of Nablus, another Palestinian city in the West Bank. Aboard the bus, he spotted a young man he'd served with in Golani, Dror Adani. Short and lean with a wide, crocheted skullcap, Adani had made a strong impression on Amir. Though he wasn't the brawniest soldier in the unit, he had grit and stamina and liked to help others. On long, grueling hikes, he would walk behind the weaker soldiers and push them forward. Adani had also grown up in Herzliya with parents who'd emigrated from Yemen. Amir quickly sized him up: here finally, was a good candidate for the militia. On the trip, Adani introduced Amir to his sister, Rachel. Ten years his senior, she maintained an unusual lifestyle for a religious woman. Rachel was single, lived on her own in Tel Aviv, and made her living as an astrologist.

A few weeks later, Amir and Adani attended a rally together in Tel Aviv. Several groups were now sponsoring antigovernment events every week, including the YESHA Council, Netanyahu's Likud Party and a growing list of ad-hoc movements. When it was over, Amir suggested they stop at Rachel's home. Amir had dabbled in Jewish mysticism and was constantly looking for signs that God intended something special for him. Maybe he would find it in astrology.

At her apartment, Rachel provided a basic reading based on his birth date: what signs in the zodiac he was compatible with, how the coming weeks would look for him, dangers that lurked. When Amir pressed for more, she told him she could draw up a detailed chart but only once he provided his specific time of birth. He promised to come back with it.

Amir also asked her about Rabin—whether Rachel could predict his future. She told him that sometime in the past two years, she had prepared an astrological chart for a woman who worked as a typist in Rabin's office. The woman wanted to know whether she would get promoted. Based on the chart she drew up, Rachel told the typist that her connection to Rabin was strong, and that she helped foster a sense of tranquility in the office. The woman seemed pleased. Rachel also told her that Rabin was a Pisces, and that people under his sign would undergo three difficult years.

Before leaving, Amir asked Rachel if she would come on one of the weekend outings he was organizing for students in the West Bank and Gaza to lecture on mysticism and astrology. She said she would consider it.

Outside, the balmy Mediterranean summer was already well under way. June marked the official start of beach season, when lifeguards began manning the raised huts posted all along the shoreline. In Tel Aviv, even on a weekday evening, it wasn't unusual to see men and women walking back from the beach in nothing but their bathing suits, carrying folded beach chairs or bags of food. The drama and the bloodletting that Rabin's peacemaking let loose had been playing out far away from this secular metropolis. Even on days of horrific violence, the cafés in the city teemed with hipsters and old-timers, tycoons and intellectuals. The zealots and the fundamentalists lived elsewhere.

At the end of June, the judicial commission investigating the massacre at the Cave of the Patriarchs issued its findings. Most were unsurprising. Goldstein had conducted the killing spree alone without informing even his wife of his intentions. The testimony of Palestinian witnesses who said there may have been a second shooter in the prayer hall did not hold up to scrutiny. The five-man panel, headed by Supreme Court President Meir Shamgar, recommended separate prayer hours for Jews and Muslims at the shrine. Under no circumstances should both groups be inside the Cave of the Patriarchs at the same time.

The probe did turn up details that helped explain why Goldstein had no trouble getting into the hall and killing so many Palestinians. On the morning of the massacre, only five soldiers or policemen were present at their posts instead of the requisite ten. The others failed to wake up for guard duty. One of the closed-circuit cameras didn't operate and the others covered only parts of the shrine.

When the panel asked soldiers what they do when seeing settlers firing at Palestinians, their answer struck Shamgar as troubling: Most were under the impression that the rules of engagement forbade them from shooting at fellow Jews. So even if a soldier had entered the Muslim prayer hall and seen Goldstein gunning down the worshippers, it's not clear that he would have stopped the attack. Here the commission had stumbled on a paradox of Israeli rule in the West Bank and Gaza. International law mandated that Israel protect the occupied population—the Palestinians. But in reality, the soldiers were there to guard the settlers. The commission instructed the army to remind troops of their duty to protect innocents on both sides. "The law must be enforced with rigor, decisiveness and equality, against anyone who breaks it," the report said.

In their testimony to the commission, intelligence officials stressed the difficulty of thwarting an attack by a lone gunman. All the methods of intelligence gathering, including surveillance and undercover work, relied on the would-be assailant including others in his plan. "The prospect of identifying this lone gunman in advance and finding out something about the time and place he intends to stage his attack is a near impossibility," the panel wrote, summarizing the testimony of agency chiefs. The officials would find themselves making precisely the same argument to another commission in the not-too-distant future.

Referring to Goldstein, the commission wrote:

The objective he set for himself justified any and all means. The extremeness of his positions meant he recognized neither the supremacy of the law nor the total authority of the state's institution. . . . He saw himself as an emissary of the Nation of Israel, commanded to operate according to the will of the Creator. . . . He became determined, as far as we can tell, to carry out an action so horrific and excessive that it would halt the peace process, which he saw as the ultimate danger.

Had Amir read the report, he would surely have recognized himself in those lines.

———————

IF CLINCHING THE Gaza-Jericho deal had seemed to restore some energy to the peace process, events in July 1994 put it in full swing again. Arafat moved from Tunis to Gaza, setting up his headquarters at the Palestine Hotel on the beach. The peripatetic icon now had a territory to run. Rabin met openly for the first time with Jordan's King Hussein amid a push for a peace treaty by the end of the year. It would be the first between Israel and an Arab country since the historic agreement with Egypt in 1979. Even the negotiations between Israel and Syria seemed to show some promise, with President Hafez al-Assad agreeing to one-on-one talks between the Israeli and Syrian ambassadors to Washington.

The economy was looking up as well. A combination of the peacemaking and the influx of immigrants from the former Soviet Union had put Israel's GDP on track to grow by nearly 7 percent in 1994. And while the Tel Aviv Stock Exchange had fluctuated in recent months, the TA-25, the market's most important index, had climbed nearly 20 percent since the summer of 1992, when Rabin first took office. Some years before Rabin's election, Treasury officials had repealed a widely hated exit tax, making it easier for more Israelis to travel abroad. Now, as prolonged heat waves grew unbearable through the summer, they did so in record numbers.

Amir had no travel plans. With school out, he got a job as an armed guard at a summer camp run by the Jewish National Fund, a group that American Jews know for its fund-raising and tree-planting. Amir had a few thousand shekels in the bank—about a thousand dollars—some of which he was giving to a Haredi charity in small monthly installments. He might have made more money interning at a law office but the idea held no appeal. He'd put away his textbooks for the summer and was reading a novel his brother had recommended instead: Frederick Forsyth's thriller *The Day of the Jackal*.

The book is a fictional account of a right-wing group's effort to assassinate French President Charles de Gaulle over his decision to end the war in Algeria and withdraw French forces. France's colonization of Algeria differed markedly from Israel's occupation of the West Bank and Gaza—it had been under way for more than 130 years when Algeria finally gained independence in 1962. But to anyone steeped in French history, Rabin's circumstances in the 1990s would have seemed remarkably similar to de Gaulle's in the waning years of colonial rule in Algeria. Both men were war heroes who surprised their public by embracing peace programs. Both came to be seen as traitors by a segment of their countrymen—settlers and other right-wingers—for their willingness to cede territory. And both refused to take the threats against their personal safety seriously. Though the plot to kill de Gaulle as rendered in *The Day of the Jackal* is made up, the French leader survived several real assassination attempts.

Yigal Amir likely saw himself in the character of the assassin, an Englishman identified only by his code name, the Jackal. Cool and methodical, he reconnoiters Paris for the ideal spot to kill the president. A subplot revolves around his acquisition of a custom-made sniper rifle with a silencer, a section rich with the kind of technical detail that would have appealed to Hagai.

But to the extent that the French backlash against de Gaulle resonated with Amir, the comparison had its limits. Resistance to France's withdrawal from Algeria centered on issues of heritage and national pride. "Algeria is French and will remain so," was the slogan of the Organisation de l'armée secrète, the dissident paramilitary group that fought to scuttle Algerian independence.

Amir framed his fanatical resistance to an Israeli withdrawal almost entirely in religious terms and specifically in the context of God's biblical 613 commandments. He liked to describe these commandments, which ranged from dos and don'ts about prayer and idol worship to long-outdated doctrines on animal sacrifice, as his "instruction manual" for life. "My own morality doesn't matter. It is determined solely according to the Torah itself," he would eventually explain. To Amir, as to other Jewish fundamentalists, the Old Testament was literal, word-for-word truth. "The Torah is the brain. If the Torah tells you to do something that runs counter to your emotions, you do what runs counter to your emotions."

As long as the peace process sputtered, Amir allowed himself to deliberate, alone or with his brother, on the options for ensuring its failure. But now that it was in gear again, his resolve to kill Rabin grew stronger. He thought about it every day. In contemplating the religious justification for such an act, Amir focused on a Talmudic principle known as *rodef*. The concept referred to a person who pursues another person with the intent to kill him—*rodef* meaning literally "pursuer." The law of the pursuer, or *din rodef*, permitted a bystander to kill the aggressor in order to save the innocent victim. It was one of the few circumstances in which the Talmud allowed extrajudicial killing.

Amir decided that Rabin fit the definition of *rodef*—he was a pursuer—because his policies were undermining the safety of settlers in the West Bank and Gaza. In his logic, Rabin was effectively chasing them down with the intent to kill them. He also decided that Rabin was a *moser*, a person who handed over Jews to a hostile power, in this case the newly formed Palestinian Authority. In truth, of course, all the settlers remained under Israeli rule, subject solely to Israeli law, including those in Gaza, which Arafat now controlled. *Din moser* also mandated death for the offender.

If his conclusions seemed like a stretch, Amir was certainly not the only person scouring the Talmud for laws that Rabin might be violating. By now, questions about *din rodef* and *din moser* had already surfaced in the Haredi press and been discussed in religious seminaries. The majority of Israelis would remain unfamiliar with these terms for some time to come. But in the religious world they had slipped into common usage.

In yeshivas, these discussions may have had a theoretical quality to them, as if the question of *din rodef* and whether it applied to Rabin possessed some scholarly value. But Amir, true to both his character and his zealous brand of faith, interpreted them literally. If *din rodef* applied, he was permitted to kill Rabin—not just permitted but obligated to do so. The possibility of being jailed or killed had no bearing. "There's no such thing as cognitive dissonance with me. The moment my consciousness . . . reaches a certain conclusion, I have no weakness, no compulsion about doing it. And the actions go accordingly. I don't flinch from things," he would say later. "One of the guidelines of Judaism is to suppress the body and the bodily urges and the emotional needs. . . . The goal is to control entirely the emotions and not to let the emotions guide you."

In the broader landscape of right-wing opposition to Rabin, the *din rodef* phenomenon represented only a fraction of the goings on. But it captivated a certain population because of its scriptural certainty and because the rest of the right seemed to be flailing around ineffectively in trying to counter Rabin's historic advances.

Benjamin Netanyahu led the political thrust as head of the largest opposition party, Likud. "Bibi," as nearly everyone referred to him, was the brother of Yonatan Netanyahu, a national hero who died in the Entebbe rescue operation in 1976. He became a figure in his own right while serving in diplomatic posts in Washington and at the United Nations, with his fluent English and his skill for making Israel's case in clean rhetorical strikes. The exposure in the United States helped Netanyahu hurdle over some formidable Likud figures to win the party leadership in early 1993. But a year later, he still struggled to impose discipline on the notoriously unruly party.

In part it was the American aura he exuded. Netanyahu had become a favorite of the US media in the '80s, a regular guest on Ted Koppel's *Nightline* program, where his sound-bite mastery helped soften the edges on his hardline views. Larry King, the CNN talk-show host, considered Netanyahu one of his best recurring guests, especially appealing to women, an 8 on a scale of 1 to 10. "If he had a sense of humor, he'd be a ten," he told a journalist profiling Netanyahu for *Vanity Fair.*

But in Hebrew, the rhetoric came across as glib and artificial. During Netanyahu's primary campaign against Likud stalwarts, rumors swirled that he'd been having an affair and that a videotape existed of his hotel-room dalliance with the other woman. To counter possible blackmail, Netanyahu confessed publicly to the infidelity and accused an unnamed "party higher-up surrounded by underworld figures" of plotting against him. In other countries, it might have been seen as a shrewd preemptive measure. But in Israel's macho political culture, the strategy backfired. Instead of getting credit for coming clean, Netanyahu looked to many Israelis like a chump who succumbs easily to pressure. In the widely invoked Yiddish term, he was a *freier,* a sucker—one of the worst things you can be in Israeli politics.

After the Oslo deal was signed, Netanyahu struggled to formulate an alternative policy. Some members of his party thought he should tack to the center and embrace at least parts of the agreement as the new reality. Certainly, few Israelis felt an attachment to the Gaza Strip, where nearly one million Palestinians lived mostly in poverty. As Rabin drew closer to peace with Jordan in the summer of 1994, these more pragmatic voices in Likud grew louder. An agreement with Jordan would have none of the contentiousness of the deals with the Palestinians. Moshe Katzav, a popular member of Likud who would later hold the ceremonial post of president, warned that Rabin's achievements would make the right wing irrelevant. "The Likud has got to come to terms with the irrevocability of the policies undertaken by the Rabin government," Katzav said.

Instead, Netanyahu aligned himself with the hardliners, the settlers and the rabble-rousers, speaking at rallies across the country where crowds branded Rabin a traitor and a murderer, and consorting with rabbis who'd urged soldiers to disobey evacuation orders. At least once, Netanyahu gently scolded an audience for its inflammatory rhetoric. "We have an issue with political adversaries, not enemies," he said from the podium. But more often, he ignored it. Occasionally he seemed swept up in it.

Other groups coordinated their strategies either with the YESHA Council or with Mate Hamamatz, a steering committee that issued some of the harshest invective against Rabin. Zo Artzeinu launched a campaign of civil disobedience that mostly angered the public. In early 1994 the group, headed by a settler named Moshe Feiglin, announced a plan to grab land in the West Bank and quickly erect 130 new communities, doubling the number of settlements. Since Rabin had frozen settlement construction at the start of his term, the wildcat initiative would involve bypassing Israeli authorities and confronting soldiers sent to evacuate the activists. But the plan fizzled early in the process.

The failure of these initiatives to make any real impact contributed to Amir's notion that the protesters lacked resolve and discipline. Whenever policemen or soldiers broke up a protest or prevented a land grab, as they did with Zo Artzeinu's settlement-duplication campaign, Amir maintained that the government was stifling legitimate dissent. *Din rodef* required the bystander to try to stop the pursuer by "lesser means" before resorting to killing him. For Amir, these protests counted as the lesser means. In their futility, he saw mounting evidence that nothing short of killing Rabin would fulfill the decree.

At the end of the summer, Amir and Holtzman took a weeklong trip to the Sinai Desert in Egypt, their first vacation together and the longest stretch they would spend in each other's company, day and night, since the start of their relationship. Amir took along a back-pack with several shirts, a heavy jacket for the cool desert nights, a hiking hat with snaps on the sides, and an electric shaver. Since the trip involved crossing a border, he left his Beretta at home. Holtzman brought along a girlfriend who would serve informally as a chaper-one. For an unmarried religious couple to travel alone would have been unseemly.

Israel had captured Sinai in the 1967 war and then returned it to Egypt under the terms of their 1979 peace treaty. The agreement included a provision for reciprocal tourism but it took some years before Israelis felt safe enough to venture back to Sinai in large num-bers. By 1994, about 200,000 Israelis entered the peninsula every year, most by crossing the border on foot at the southern Israeli town of Eilat. On the Egyptian side, Bedouins waited with their sand-beaten cars to taxi the Israeli tourists to pristine beaches in towns along the Red Sea, including Nuweiba, Dahab, and Sharm el-Sheikh. The cross-border tourism offered Israelis quick and cheap getaways and Egyptians a small revenue stream.

Amir, Holtzman, and the friend headed south along the Red Sea but then had the driver cut west, toward St. Catherine, a town in the parched interior of the desert. Far from Sinai's beaches, St. Cather-ine offered a different attraction. It was situated at the foot of what some religious scholars thought might be Mount Sinai, the spot in the Bible where Moses, having led the Israelites out of Egypt, received the Ten Commandments from God. The Egyptians had established a tourist village at the site in the 1980s and named it for the monastery there, built in the sixth century and still active. About 4,000 Egyp-tians lived in St. Catherine.

The three Israelis spent the week hiking and camping. Holtzman would say later that Amir made occasional comments about the polit-ical situation, describing the government as illegitimate because it lacked a Jewish majority in parliament. But he seemed to fixate on Rabin less when he was with her than with his other friends. He made no mention of *din rodef.*

The Israelis hired a Bedouin guide, who led them on a hike, their food and gear strapped to the back of a camel. They stopped at a watering hole to snap pictures and relaxed in a cave while the guide prepared flat bread on an open flame. In one photo of the four of them, Amir is kneeling in the foreground while the mustachioed guide stands behind him, his dark hands resting on Amir's shoulders. Amir, whose facial hair grew dark and stubbly after just a few days, shaved in the mornings and then dusted his face with baby powder. Holtzman spent much of the trip in a white T-shirt and a loose-fitting pair of genie pants, her long brown hair hanging freely below her shoulders.

When they got back to Bar-Ilan for the first week of school in October, Holtzman broke up with Amir. She told him the emotional connection felt precarious. If Amir took it badly, he confided his feelings to no one. He told his parents that he was the one to break it off and Geulah responded with relief. She'd envisioned a marriage in which Holtzman constantly pecked at her son and made him miserable. To Hagai, Amir said he no longer wanted to date women as long as the political situation remained dire. In what must have sounded like a dramatic pronouncement, he said relationships would only cloud their judgment when it came to making life-or-death decisions and they needed to stay unattached. For Hagai, who was too shy to engage with women and found them generally inscrutable, it made little difference. "Girls are weird," he would write in a diary later. "They're impossible to understand. Whoever thinks he understands them should brace for disappointment."

In time, Amir's father would come to think of the breakup as a turning point. Had his son stayed with Holtzman and perhaps married her, the relationship might have distracted him from his vendetta against Rabin. Holtzman, for her part, started dating another second-year law student at Bar-Ilan almost immediately, a former paratrooper who attended study sessions at the *kolel* with Amir. They would be married by spring.

HIS VOW OF ABSTINENCE notwithstanding, Amir could not stifle his interest in women. One friend at school, Nili Kolman, felt he was pursuing her and distanced herself to avoid leading him on. Before pulling away, though, she visited him several times at his home in Herzliya, where Hagai worked on her car. Amir told Kolman that he'd been seeing someone but broke it off because she was shallow. In an evident dig at Holtzman, he said he was looking for a woman genuinely committed to her beliefs and not superficial. Kolman felt a certain warmth in the house and got the impression Geulah was an affectionate mother. But Amir's extremism put her off.

Amir also befriended a first-year law student named Margalit Har-Shefi, whose life would be shaped by the acquaintance. Tall and thin, with long hair she often wore in a single braid down her back, Har-Shefi grew up in the West Bank settlement Beit El, opted for a year of national service instead of enlisting in the army, and then enrolled at Bar-Ilan. At nineteen, she was younger than most law-school students and eager to fit in. In her first weeks at the university, she met Ohad Skornik, who had studied with Amir in the Kerem Be-Yavne seminary during his army service and was now a first-year law student himself. Skornik introduced her to Amir.

The three of them shared a deep disdain for Rabin and his peace process but together they made an odd triad. Skornik exuded urban superiority—having grown up in Tel Aviv—along with the self-assurance that comes with pedigree: his father was a doctor at Ichilov, the country's busiest hospital. Har-Shefi also had an illustrious lineage. Her mother was related by marriage to the Elon family, whose kin included a member of parliament, a well-regarded rabbi, and a Supreme Court justice. In the national religious world, the Elons were settler royalty.

And yet, it was Amir, shorter than both of them and the son of Yemeni immigrants, who dominated. Har-Shefi had attended an all-girls high school. In her religious community of a few thousand residents, she'd been insulated from the wider currents of Israeli society. Now she was away from home, mixing with young men and enjoying the interaction. She found Amir's capacity to be at once affable and assertive deeply appealing.

The three of them spent much of the first month of the semester planning a student weekend at Netzarim, an isolated Jewish settlement in the Gaza Strip. Built in 1972, Netzarim had foundered for years, struggling to attract newcomers to a place where coming and going required military escort. Some twenty-five religious families inhabited the settlement when the Gaza-Jericho agreement was signed—among the most ideologically committed of all the settlers. Though Israeli troops continued safeguarding the residents, Arafat's rule in Gaza had increased the feeling of isolation. Amir wanted students to connect with the settlers and offer support. And he hoped the signup sheet would provide a pool from which he might recruit people to his militia.

At one point, Amir and Har-Shefi sat alone on a patch of grass on campus. Bar-Ilan stretched out over several city blocks, with lawns and open areas sandwiched between low-slung buildings. Har-Shefi lived with a roommate on the second floor of a girls' dormitory at the university and returned to Beit El only on weekends. She often wore headphones on campus, which connected to a portable tape player she kept in her black bag. Amir, who had made several more trips to Hebron since the Goldstein funeral, turned to her and asked what she thought of the shooting spree at the Cave of the Patriarchs months earlier. It was a kind of litmus test for Amir, an issue that divided the milksops from the genuine right-wingers.

Har-Shefi thought for a moment, then said she opposed the killing of innocents. But she wasn't firm about it. The narrative that Palestinians had stored armaments at the shrine and planned a large-scale attack against Jews had become accepted wisdom among settlers, even the moderate ones. That authorities refused to acknowledge it underscored their determination to besmirch the settlers. Amir spotted an opening. Goldstein sacrificed himself to save Jews, he told her. There were plenty of instances when Israelis had to kill Arabs preemptively. Amir hammered on until Har-Shefi felt worn down by his utter certainty. From that point on, she would mimic his defense of the Hebron carnage in conversations with others.

The weekend at Netzarim drew several dozen students, including Avishai Raviv, who organized food for the trip. Dror Adani joined the group, though he was not enrolled at Bar-Ilan—he studied at a yeshiva at Kibbutz Shaalavim, about halfway between Tel Aviv and Jerusalem. Hagai came along as well but hardly spoke during the weekend. The only impression people seemed to form about him had to do with his appearance. Students kept telling him he resembled his younger brother. The group prayed together, toured in and around the settlement, heard from Netzarim members about life under siege, and departed by bus on Saturday night. To Hagai it seemed most people attended in order to meet other singles. Still, a spirited defiance hung in the air.

Sometime after that weekend, Amir started talking to Adani about the militia. The next stage in the peace process would involve a broad Israeli pullback in the West Bank and the handover of more territory to the Palestinians. Negotiating teams were already meeting to thrash out the complicated details of what would come to be known as Oslo II. After the withdrawal, Amir explained, his militia would act as a kind of strike force against the Palestinians, conducting reprisal raids whenever settlers were attacked. He told Adani about Hagai's stash of armaments and the ideas they had discussed, including downing power lines in Palestinian areas. Adani, who had been pondering on his own what could be done to stop the government, agreed to join without hesitation. Later, he would lend his army-issue Uzi to Hagai, who measured the barrel in order to fit it with a hand-crafted silencer.

At one point the conversation turned to *din rodef.* Adani told Amir he'd approached a rabbi at Shaalavim sometime in the preceding year and asked whether the decree applied to Rabin. The rabbi's response included a nuanced exegesis of the Talmud. The ceding of land to the Palestinians did indeed make Rabin a *rodef,* he said. But the law of *rodef* was only relevant to individuals, and since Rabin represented an entire constituency, there was no practical way to apply the edict. "It's not so simple," Adani now said. The yeshiva at Shaalavim had a reputation for extremism. That its rabbi was hedging seemed noteworthy to Adani. But not to Amir, who dismissed the explanation contemptuously. The rabbis were too scared to interpret the law honestly, he told his friend. They're paid by the state and fear for their jobs.

The conversation gave Amir an opportunity to talk about the discussions he'd had with Hagai on murdering Rabin. Amir had said aloud many times by now that Rabin needed to be stopped or even killed. Students at Bar-Ilan had heard the pronouncements and so had his own father. But this was the first time he'd told anyone that he and Hagai had actually discussed ways to do it—that they were plotting Rabin's murder. If the revelation surprised or disturbed Adani, he made no show of it.

Amir approached Ohad Skornik next. In conversations with Hagai, Amir had resolved to recruit only veterans of combat units. Skornik had spent his service with the desk jockeys in military intelligence, not exactly hardened fighters. But Amir and Skornik had been best friends at the seminary. The two would take long hiking trips together on their days off, sometimes with one of Amir's sisters. And Skornik's contempt for Rabin matched his own. He talked about moving to one of the settlements when he graduated from law school.

Amir made the militia pitch much the way he did with Adani, describing it as a strike force against Palestinians. Skornik knew Amir was militantly anti-Arab and that he and Hagai had a fixation with guns and other weapons. On one of their trips together, Amir brandished his Beretta and explained how the gun's double-action mechanism allowed him to both pull back the hammer and drop it with just a squeeze of the trigger. The feature made it quicker to draw and fire. Skornik would say later that he thought Amir intended the militia to be a kind of civil guard that would operate within the bounds of the law. But Amir felt certain he got his message across. To him, Skornik seemed enthusiastic.

Amir now counted four people on his mercenary roster, including himself and his brother. As a settlement protection force, the way Amir sometimes described his aim, it was a ridiculously small group. But for vigilante attacks against random Palestinians that would deepen the hostility and roil the peace process, four could well be enough. Amir considered the so-called Jewish Underground from the 1980s to be his model. The group, only somewhat larger, had managed to kill several Palestinians and nearly blow up the Dome of the Rock in Jerusalem,

Islam's third holiest shrine. In fact, Hagai worried that adding more people would raise the risk of being discovered by Shabak. He pressed his brother to keep quiet about the group.

But Amir couldn't resist divulging the secret to Har-Shefi and inviting her to join. Har-Shefi had not even served in the army but Amir thought she could be an asset nonetheless. She was, after all, the one real settler in the bunch, young and reasonably pretty. Like many other settlements, Beit El had an armory where automatic rifles were stored. Amir asked her, perhaps playfully, whether she'd be willing to flirt with the guards and then steal several rifles. Hagai liked the idea because stolen guns would be difficult to trace back to the militia. Sometime later and on a more serious note, Amir talked to Har-Shefi about buying digital timers at an electronics shop near Tel Aviv's central bus station. Hagai had already purchased several of these timers for his bomb-making experiments and wanted more. But as the militia plan grew serious, he became more cautious. Har-Shefi initially refused, then thought it over and agreed. But Amir backtracked, saying she'd be bad at haggling and would likely be overcharged.

The two, Amir and Har-Shefi, spent many hours together over the semester, alone or with others, often sitting on the floor of the student union, preparing signs for an upcoming protest. Amir was losing any inhibitions he might have had about telling people Rabin needed to die. Raviv heard him say so repeatedly and so did Skornik. On subsequent student weekends in the settlements, Amir declared it even with crowds of people gathered around. Har-Shefi seemed to find the bluster exhilarating—and Amir clearly liked the reaction it provoked. At one point, he told her outright that he intended to shoot Rabin with his Beretta.

But Har-Shefi wasn't sure whether to take him seriously. And she challenged him at times—once while visiting Rachel Adani, the astrologist in Tel Aviv. In her apartment, Amir pushed Har-Shefi to talk to Rachel about her zodiac sign and her astrological chart. At a certain moment, the conversation turned to *din rodef*, with Amir launching into a sermon about how the edict applied to Rabin and he needed to be killed. Rachel shot Amir a look and asked him if he'd lost his mind. Har-Shefi seemed skeptical as well. She said she wanted to consult the rabbi of Beit El, Shlomo Aviner, a respected figure among the settlers, and proposed that they both accept Aviner's response, no matter what it was. But Amir made no commitments.

At the settlement, Har-Shefi knocked on the door of Aviner's home one day. Beit El sat on a hill overlooking Ramallah, one of seven Palestinian cities in the West Bank. Much of the settlement was built on land Israeli authorities confiscated from individual Palestinians in the 1970s, citing security needs. Inside, Aviner led Har-Shefi to his study, where religious texts lined the shelves from floor to ceiling.

For an hour, they discussed the minutiae of *din rodef* and *din moser*. Har-Shefi told the rabbi that a certain student at Bar-Ilan was saying a death sentence hovered over Rabin because of the edicts. Was it true? Aviner said he was being approached regularly about the issue and that his response was unequivocal: Rabin was a fellow Jew and an elected leader and should not be killed for his policies. Aviner opposed the peace process vehemently but said it made Rabin neither a *rodef* nor a *moser*. Still, when Har-Shefi asked whether she should report this student to the authorities, the rabbi advised against it. He, too, was a fellow Jew and might be harmed if she involved the police.

The rumblings over *din rodef* and *din moser* were still confined to the rarefied world of Orthodox rabbis and religious seminaries. In the year since Rabin shook hands with Arafat, these terms hardly appeared in the Israeli and foreign press. But in the clerical world, where anger was constantly rising over the shrinking Jewish homeland and the attacks by Palestinians, the discourse had become ubiquitous.

Around the time Aviner explained to Har-Shefi that *din rodef* did not apply to Rabin, three prominent settler rabbis were making the most explicit case yet that it did. In a long letter full of references to the government's "collusion" with terrorists, the three asked some forty Haredi sages around the world, the "wise men of their generation," to rule on the matter, one way or another. The letter's authors included Dov Lior, the rabbi of Hebron who praised Baruch Goldstein as a holy martyr at his funeral. They framed their text as an inquiry, one they were making at the behest of "men and women from the settlements of Judea, Samaria and Gaza and the rest of the country." But it read more like an ecclesiastical putsch attempt: three religious figures trying to have the elected government of Israel repudiated and its members condemned to death, no less.

Much of the letter concerned the rise in terrorist attacks against Israelis and specifically against the settlers since the signing of the of the Oslo deal. No mention was made of the Goldstein massacre or its role in escalating the violence. Rabin and his cabinet ministers were depicted as reckless leaders who put Israelis in danger by reaching an agreement with the PLO. "What is the rule about this bad government? Can they be regarded as accomplices to acts of murder committed by terrorists, since in their plans they are responsible for the strengthening and arming of these terrorists?" the rabbis wrote.

They addressed the matter of *din moser* in another series of questions toward the end of the letter. "Should they be tried according to Jewish law? And, if proven guilty as accomplices to murder, what should their sentence be? If they are, indeed . . . punishable in court, is it the obligation of every individual to bring them to trial in a court of justice, or, for lack of an alternative, in an ordinary secular court? Is it not the obligation of the community's leaders to warn the head of the government and his ministers that if they keep pursuing the agreement . . . they will be subject . . . to the Halakhic [Jewish legal] ruling of *din moser*, as ones who surrender the life and property of Jews to the gentiles?"

All three rabbis signed the letter—Eliezer Melamed, Daniel Shilo, and Dov Lior. They included a phone and fax number the sages could use to reply. How or even whether the sages responded is not clear. But to people who regarded the three as spiritual authorities, the letter itself affirmed the Rabin government's apostate status and the importance of toppling it by whatever means necessary. Shilo would confirm years later that the questions were largely rhetorical and that the rabbis were hoping with the letter to draw the Haredi community into the circle of resistance against Rabin.

Amir was already entrenched in that circle. But the ongoing rabbinical fixation with *din rodef* and *din moser* emboldened him. "If I did not get the backing and I had not been representing many more people, I would not have acted," he would say.

When a copy of the letter reached the hands of Yoel Bin-Nun, the relatively moderate settler rabbi who had maintained a regular correspondence with Rabin, it filled him with dread. Later he warned Rabin in one of his handwritten letters that reasonable right-wingers had lost control of the struggle. "The extremists are mocking us. They gave up long ago on the army and the government and all the institutions and built their own spiritual path outside the state institutions. Now it's happening to the moderates and the tide is strong," he wrote.

"More and more people are liable to operate out of desperation and it could endanger all of us."

CHAPTER 5

He Told Us the Truth

"At the beginning, it was such a hatred that you can't even imagine."

—EITAN HABER

From his desk at the prime minister's office in Jerusalem, Rabin called out to his military secretary in the next room. "Get Arafat on the line." Danny Yatom, who had been operating in crisis mode since that morning, October 11, 1994, recognized the agitation in his boss's voice. This would not be an amicable call.

Earlier in the day, Hamas had released an abduction video showing a shackled Israeli soldier seated in front of an armed man in a ski mask. The group had grabbed Cpl. Nachshon Wachsman from a hitchhiking station midway between Jerusalem and Tel Aviv and was threatening to kill him unless Israel released some two hundred Palestinian prisoners. Rabin, who in crises could burn through a pack of cigarettes in the course of a long meeting, watched the video in a conference room adjoining his office, along with his military and intelligence chiefs. The security establishment had a drill for these situations: Analysts would begin studying the video for clues while intelligence operatives probed their Palestinian informants—of which Israel was rumored to have thousands. But Rabin also wanted to lean on Arafat. Hamas had delivered the videotape to the Gaza office of the Reuters news agency. Gaza was Arafat's domain.

Rabin had been holding regular conversations with Arafat for more than a year now, but the calls usually required some cumbersome arranging. Aides from both sides would discuss the talking points in advance and set a time for the call. Someone had to track down an interpreter, who would listen in on the line. The two leaders communicated in English but Arafat's comprehension sometimes faltered.

With the Hamas ultimatum ticking down, the call this time went through quickly. The captors had given Israeli authorities until Friday at nine p.m. to meet their demands. It was now Tuesday. Rabin opened by asking Arafat what he knew about the event. For months, the Israeli leader had been pressing him to crack down on Hamas and Islamic Jihad, strip the militants of their weapons, and jail their political leaders. Arafat always gave the same response: he had his own way of dealing with the groups, a Levantine blend of coercing and co-opting that would bring the Islamists to heel without setting off a civil war. Certainly, he knew something about asserting power. The torchbearer of the Palestinian liberation movement had been out-maneuvering political opponents for three decades.

But Hamas kept killing Israelis. Just two days earlier, a gunman from the group fired into a crowd at a Jerusalem promenade, wounding dozens of people, two of them fatally. Much of the time, Rabin suspected that Arafat lacked the necessary leadership or resolve or worse—that he quietly condoned the violence. Now on the phone, he demanded a sweeping operation to find Wachsman's captors. But Arafat had inquired with his security chiefs and was sure the Israeli soldier was being held in the West Bank, where Israel still maintained full control. "I checked and he's not in Gaza," he said. Arafat repeated the line several times until Rabin lost his temper. "I will burn Gaza to the ground if you don't find him. I will destroy every home," he hollered into the receiver.

From the awkward handshake at the White House thirteen months earlier, the sediment of the relationship had never quite settled. Rabin embraced the idea that Israel's rule over the Palestinians needed to end and that Arafat should wield genuine authority, at least until Palestinians could muster an election. But he also viewed Arafat as Israel's auxiliary in the fight against Islamic militancy—a subcontractor who could operate with fewer constraints. In a television interview a few months after signing the Oslo deal, Rabin reassured viewers that Arafat would be able to fight terrorism without being hampered by B'Tselem and Bagatz. B'Tselem was an Israeli human-rights group that reported regularly on Israeli abuses in the West Bank and Gaza. Bagatz, an acronym for the Israeli High Court of Justice, had occasionally set curbs on the government's antiterrorism policies, including its jailing of Palestinians without trial. To Rabin, each Palestinian attack after Oslo felt like an infringement of the agreement's core transaction.

Arafat saw it differently. He and Rabin had a common enemy in Hamas, that much was clear. The Islamic group had been in existence for just seven years and already it had its own power base in the West Bank and Gaza, a charity network that catered to many thousands of Palestinians, and the backing of religious authorities. Hamas projected discipline and political integrity compared to Arafat's PLO, which had grown fat on the patronage of Arab regimes. The Hamas military wing, Izz ad-Din al-Qassam, had accumulated weapons and bomb-making know-how and posed a challenge to the sovereignty of the new Palestinian Authority. And yet Arafat refused to see himself as Israel's enforcer against the Islamists.

And Arafat had his own grievances against Rabin—chiefly around what he saw as Israel's creeping entrenchment in the West Bank and Gaza. Rabin had imposed a freeze on most housing construction but allowed some settlements to grow, including those in and around East Jerusalem. For Arafat, any expansion came at the expense of the state he expected to get at the end of the Oslo process. In places where the freeze *was* imposed, the settlers sometimes found ways to cheat. At Elon Moreh, for example, settlers hired several hundred Palestinian laborers to pour dozens of new foundations over the course of a weekend before Rabin's moratorium went into effect. Though observant Jews are not allowed to ask non-Jews to work on the Sabbath, settler rabbis granted special dispensation for the campaign. The result was a new neighborhood at Elon Moreh.

Arafat's administration tracked the data on housing starts in the settlements. In Rabin's first two years in office, the figure dropped by 79 percent, an encouraging sign. But Palestinian leaders also noted the network of roads Rabin was building from Israel to the settlements, a huge and expensive undertaking that seemed to suggest Israel was digging in. In Rabin's thinking, the roads were a stopgap. Until the final status of the territory was determined, they would allow settlers to bypass Palestinian towns that would come under Arafat's rule and get to their homes more safely. Rabin conceded to his advisers that many of the roads would end up on the Palestinian side of the border when a permanent agreement was reached. But the sight of so many Israeli bulldozers grinding up the territory just didn't square with a process that was supposed to lead to Palestinian sovereignty.

Only much later would the unintended consequence of these roads become evident. They would transform many settlements from isolated colonies to bedroom communities easily accessible from Israel's main cities. The roads and the cheap housing at the settlements would make them appealing to everyday Israelis and not just ideologues, powering their expansion for years to come.

All these factors hampered the relationship between Rabin and Arafat. But there was something else as well—a palpable lack of chemistry and trust that deepened in the first year of their partnership over a series of difficult interactions. "At the beginning, it was such a hatred that you can't even imagine," Eitan Haber, Rabin's chief of staff, recalled.

The most damaging of these occurred in May, at the ceremony in Cairo for the Gaza-Jericho agreement. Onstage, flanked by the US secretary of state and the Russian foreign minister, Arafat balked at signing one of the maps appended to the accord, suspecting Israeli negotiators had somehow tricked him into accepting less than what the sides had decided. The standoff on live television lasted nearly an hour and turned the event into a fiasco. Arafat's own advisers eventually brought him around, but the drama left Rabin feeling embarrassed and angry.

A few days later, during a speech at a Johannesburg mosque, Arafat urged an audience to join the "jihad to liberate Jerusalem." The

Palestinian leader was attending the inauguration of South African president Nelson Mandela, another former revolutionary who had reconciled with his enemies. But unlike Mandela, Arafat seemed to have a tough time shedding the persona of his old guerrilla days. When a recording of Arafat's speech reached Israel, Rabin threatened to pull out of the peace process. Arafat explained later that he meant a jihad for peace.

Even Arafat's festive arrival in Gaza in July, an event that marked the official start of Palestinian self-rule, was marred by discord. Hours after he and his men crossed from Sinai in a convoy of Mercedes cars, Rabin discovered that his entourage included former militants Israel had expressly barred from the territory. After a night of heated exchanges between Israeli and Palestinian negotiators by phone, Arafat was forced to send them back to Egypt. "Rabin was very angry that his trust was breached. . . . It was a very difficult evening," recalled Nabil Shaath, one of the Palestinian officials involved in the conversations back and forth.

The animosity between the two leaders was apparent to everyone involved in the peace process. It became even more glaring as Rabin edged closer to a peace agreement with Jordan's King Hussein in the late summer. To Israelis, Hussein had some deeply appealing qualities that Arafat lacked—a regal gentility, a gift for eloquent speechmaking, and a willingness to embrace the emotive side of reconciliation. Though Jordan had fought in two wars against Israel, the relationship between the countries lacked the toxic legacy of either occupation or terrorism. In their months of negotiations, Hussein and Rabin developed a rapport that seemed exceptional by any standard of diplomacy. Haber, who often participated in their meetings, thought that the two leaders had come to trust each other more than they trusted their own staff members and confidants. "No doubt about it, Rabin and Hussein fell in love."

In mid-September, Rabin sat in his office and reviewed the data on Palestinian attacks over the preceding twelve months. The first year of peacemaking had been more violent than any of the intifada years. Sixty Israelis were killed, compared to forty-one in the preceding period. Most were civilians. In every category, from bombings and stabbings to hand-grenade and Molotov-cocktail attacks, the numbers had spiked. Rabin could hardly blame Arafat. Most of the casualties preceded his arrival in Gaza. And even Israel's pervasive and proficient security agencies had never been able to shut down the violence altogether. At a meeting with the Palestinian leader at the Erez border crossing between Israel and Gaza in late September, Rabin conveyed how critical it was to stop the cascade. The attacks were turning Israelis against the peace process and vindicating the hardliners. When Rabin left the meeting, he felt he'd gotten through to Arafat. The two leaders were finally understanding each other.

And then Wachsman went missing—touching off the most wrenching two-week period of Rabin's term.

The nineteen-year-old soldier had been serving in the army for about a year, having followed his two brothers to the Golani Brigade. Short and slight, Wachsman got through the rigorous infantry training by sheer force of will. His unit had just completed a rotation in southern Lebanon, where Israel maintained a security zone to protect itself from rocket attacks. On Sunday, October 9, Wachsman got a ride with a friend from a base in northern Israel to a junction near Ben-Gurion Airport. When he climbed out of the Subaru, he told his army pal he would travel by bus the rest of the way to a friend's house in Ramle or else hitchhike, whichever was quicker. In the late-afternoon traffic rush, someone was sure to pick him up. Wachsman was holding an M16 assault rifle and a plastic bag full of clothes. He had a weeklong leave coming to him, which he intended to spend with his parents in Jerusalem.

As soon as he raised his hand to hitch a ride, a red van pulled over with four men inside. Wachsman bent over and peered through the open window on the passenger's side. He noticed the driver was wearing a crocheted skullcap much like his own, and so were the others. A Jewish prayer book lay on the dashboard and Hasidic music chimed from the speakers. Wachsman squeezed into the backseat and balanced his rifle between his legs.

The men in the van belonged to a Hamas cell from the Jerusalem area. They'd purchased the skullcaps the week before and rented the vehicle that morning. Hamas militants had abducted four other soldiers in the preceding year in a similar manner but in those incidents, they killed their captives soon after grabbing them. Wachsman actually knew two of the victims—they'd grown up in Ramot, the same Jerusalem neighborhood where he lived. One of them was his upstairs neighbor. Now the group had a new strategy. Israel had been releasing members of Arafat's Fatah movement from prison as part of the Oslo deal. Hamas wanted its own men freed as well.

On the road, the men overpowered Wachsman quickly. One passenger grabbed him by the neck and pushed his head toward his knees while another lunged for his gun. Wachsman fumbled for the charging handle trying to load a round in the chamber, but one of the militants swung at his hand with a hammer. Once he lost his gun, he stopped resisting altogether. As the van sped toward Jerusalem, the men tied up their captive and lowered a hood over his head. From the darkness, he heard one of the Palestinians say in accented Hebrew: "Don't worry. . . . We just want to trade you for our people in prison."

The cell had prepared a safe house in Bir Nabala, a Palestinian town just north of Jerusalem and well into the West Bank—which Israel continued to control. Inside the two-story home, surrounded by fruit trees and a low wall, the Hamas men went straight to work. In a room on the second floor they filmed two videotapes, one showing a masked man holding Wachsman's ID card and offering to exchange the soldier for 200 Palestinian prisoners, including the wheelchair-bound spiritual leader of the group, Ahmed Yassin. The second one featured Wachsman himself, looking into the camera nervously and pleading for his life. "If my parents are watching, I'm fine for now. I hope to return to you if Rabin decides to free their prisoners."

From Bir Nabala, the Wachsman home was less than two miles to the south. When her son didn't get home Sunday night, Esther Wachsman, an English teacher who had grown up in New York and moved to Israel in her twenties, feared the worst. It was unlike him to change plans without calling. Esther had somehow endured the military service of her two older sons. Both volunteered for combat roles, following a trend among religious youngsters. She had a pact with the boys: if they were posted someplace remote and couldn't call home, she would try not to worry. But if she knew they had access to a phone and weren't calling, then the anxiety would set in. Late in the evening, Esther dialed a number she had for the army and reported that her son was missing. The woman on the other end of the line seemed unconcerned. Soldiers were always heading off to Eilat during leave without telling their parents, she said. The beach town on the Red Sea was swarming with tourists in bikinis.

The following morning, one of the captors took the two videotapes and headed to the Gaza Strip. Israel had been restricting Palestinian travel between the West Bank and Gaza, which involved crossing through Israeli territory. But the twenty-eight-year-old Hamas man, Jihad Yarmur, lived in East Jerusalem and, as such, carried an Israeli identity card that allowed him to move around freely. At the Erez crossing, he showed the Israeli soldiers his blue ID and entered Gaza.

The transition was dramatic. The sparsely populated area on the Israeli side included communities with single-family homes and lush fields. Across the border, most people lived in squalor, with nearly a million Palestinians crammed into a five-mile-wide strip along the shoreline. Many were descendants of refugees who had fled their homes in 1948. They now resided in tightly arranged tenements made of exposed cinder block and administered by the United Nations.

And yet Gaza was changing. The peace deal had drawn investors from around the Arab world and Arafat's new administration was handing out jobs—hiring civil servants and policemen. During the intifada years, the cultural scene went dormant. Now, suddenly, it had come to life. Arab performers put Gaza on their destination list, including the Lebanese singer Fawzi Yazbek, who did two shows at the Palestine Hotel in September 1994. A seventeen-member Egyptian circus came to town around the same time. On the anniversary of the Oslo deal, the Nasser movie theater in Gaza City opened its doors for the first film screening in seven years. Eight hundred people showed up, each paying about a dollar to see *Dragon: The Bruce Lee Story*. The owner of the theater, Mohammed Saleh, apologized to the crowd for selecting a movie that was already a year old but said newer ones were too expensive.

Yarmur spent Monday night in Gaza City and delivered the video-tapes to the Reuters office there the next day. The Hamas men had chosen to get the material out through Reuters because one of them had a brother who worked as a photographer for the agency. More important, the venue served their ruse. With the abduction videos emerging from Gaza, Israeli security agencies would assume Wachsman was being held there and not in the West Bank. So would Rabin.

BY TUESDAY AFTERNOON Israel Television obtained a copy of the tapes from Reuters. The news division sent a duplicate to the Wachsman home, along with a cameraman who filmed the family watching their son's abduction video on the television set in their basement. It was now two days since Wachsman went missing. Esther had been assuming he was dead. For all the dreadfulness of watching her son speak to her from his captivity, she felt immense relief at the evidence that he was, in fact, alive. A few hours later, Israel Television broadcast the video on its nightly newscast—along with footage of the family at home. From that moment on, the fate of Cpl. Nachshon Wachsman riveted the country.

With the ultimatum three days away, Rabin convened top security officials again Tuesday evening, including Army Chief Ehud Barak and members of the general staff. Rabin puffed on Parliaments throughout the meeting, turning his end of the large conference table into a smoky haze. The participants included people who had played a role in some of Israel's most daring antiterrorism raids. Barak had helped plan the rescue of hijacking victims at Entebbe in 1976. Three years before that, he wandered the streets of Beirut dressed as a woman in an operation against top PLO guerrillas. But without intelligence on Wachsman's whereabouts, none of the men at the table had ideas to offer. Haber looked around in disbelief. A few loathsome kidnappers had reduced the smartest military brains in the country to a helpless heap, he thought.

Once again, the vulnerability of the peace deal vexed Rabin. The preceding year had changed the country incontrovertibly. Israelis and Palestinians had forged relationships and partnerships previously unthinkable. Israel and Jordan would be signing a full-fledged peace accord later in the month, an agreement made possible by the reconciliation with the Palestinians. Rabin and Arafat were candidates for the Nobel Peace Prize, with an announcement expected in the coming days. Yet the Wachsman ordeal showed once more how easy it was for opponents of peacemaking to push the process to a breaking point. If the soldier proved to be in Gaza and Arafat failed to find him, the pressure on Rabin to suspend negotiations would be enormous. What was the point of partnering with Arafat if he could not exert authority over the territory he now controlled?

Rabin pressed the men around the table for options. At one point the conversation turned to the question of negotiating with Hamas. The slow-motion drama of hostage ordeals often made them more excruciating than shooting or bombing attacks. In a country with mandatory conscription, many Israelis were at that very moment envisioning their brothers or sons in Wachsman's predicament. But Rabin also had to look beyond Wachsman. Yassin, the Hamas spiritual leader, was serving a life sentence for ordering attacks on Israelis. Allowing the group to force his release would invite more abductions. Rabin listened to the arguments for and against but took no position himself.

By the following morning, Shabak operatives had picked up a clue that Hamas might be holding Wachsman in the city of Khan Yunis in southern Gaza. Shabak prided itself on having informers in almost every town in the West Bank and Gaza. Its analysts had spent years compiling lists of the most influential people in each area and identifying their vulnerabilities. Since Israel controlled virtually every aspect of daily life for Palestinians, any request to military authorities, for a driver's license, perhaps, or permission to be hospitalized in Israel, might be used as leverage in the recruiting process. Early on Wednesday, an informer had pointed Shabak to a specific house in Khan Yunis where the cell might be holding Wachsman.

But Khan Yunis was the hometown of Mohammed Dahlan, who ran the emerging Palestinian intelligence service known as Preventive Security. Dahlan had his own network of agents and informers, many of them fellow Fatah activists he knew from the years he organized resistance against Israel's occupation in Gaza. Dahlan could be a tough negotiator and already had a reputation for financial corruption. But Israelis had grown comfortable with him as a partner on security matters, in part thanks to the Hebrew he taught himself while imprisoned by Israel. Now, in phone calls back and forth between Gaza and Jerusalem, Dahlan reported that Wachsman was definitely not in Khan Yunis. By midmorning Shabak's own information confirmed it.

While Shabak ran down other clues, an Islamic scholar the government occasionally consulted suggested that perhaps Yassin himself could defuse the crisis. Yassin detested the Oslo process, viewing it as an alliance of heathens—Israel and the PLO—forged expressly to destroy Hamas. But Islam had laws about protecting prisoners. And members of Hamas held up Yassin as a religious authority. He would certainly not call on the Hamas men to release Wachsman, but he might instruct them to keep him alive.

For the interview, Rabin's media advisers suggested Danny Levy, a reporter with Israel Television's Arabic language service. Israeli prison authorities rarely granted interviews with inmates, but in this case they processed the request quickly. By early afternoon, Levy and his camera crew were allowed through the gates of the Kfar Yona prison east of Netanya and into Yassin's cell.

To Levy's delight, Yassin said just the right things. "Keeping him alive could serve our purposes, so he must be kept alive," he told the journalist in Arabic. "I advise them to respect him, protect him and not to kill him. They should protect him and not threaten his life." Levy left the prison thinking that he'd saved Wachsman's life.

But when the interview was broadcast later in the day, security officials debated whether it would have the desired effect. For one thing, there was no guarantee the Hamas men who abducted Wachsman would even see it. Safe houses were often basement hideaways with no electricity. And there was also the question of how the interview would be perceived. Carmi Gillon, who had been filling in as head of Shabak for some weeks now, was sure the captors would think it was staged or coerced. "There's not a single Hamas person who would have considered the remarks authentic," Gillon would say years later.

By now, more than a hundred journalists had gathered outside the

Wachsman home in Ramot, including the correspondents of the *New York Times* and the *Washington Post*. The neighborhood lay just inside the West Bank, effectively a settlement populated mostly by religious Jews. But it was built on land Israel annexed after the 1967 war and districted as part of the new, expanded Jerusalem.

Inside, the house had become a makeshift command center, with people constantly coming and going, some foreign to the Wachsmans, others familiar. The army had sent a psychologist to be with the family, which included Esther Wachsman's Israeli-born husband, Yehuda, and their six sons. Other soldiers manned a dedicated phone line the army installed in the den along with a recording device, in case the captors called. Academics specializing in Islamic studies sat with the family and offered advice. Some were phoning Muslim clerics around the Arab world, asking them to call on the captors not to harm Wachsman. At Yehuda's request, a rabbi was going from room to room to check the *mezuzot*—the ritual cases that religiously observant Jews affix to their doorposts with a prayer rolled up inside. A defective parchment might bring bad luck.

At one point the phone rang in the den and Rabin came on the line. He had called to assure Esther and Yehuda that he would do whatever he could to free their son. But in the back and forth, he also let on that he did not intend to trade Hamas prisoners for Wachsman. As defense minister in the 1980s, Rabin had approved two staggeringly lopsided prisoner swaps under heavy pressure from the parents of the captive soldiers. He hoped to head off demands from the Wachsmans by explaining his position directly. Yehuda pleaded with Rabin to just hint publicly that he was willing to negotiate. Even if he did not intend to strike a deal, at least he could buy time. With all those journalists camped in front of the house, Yehuda considered stepping outside and making the bogus announcement himself. But Rabin alluded to other initiatives under way and said Yehuda would only harm the chances of freeing his son.

When the conversation ended, Esther decided on a different approach. She stepped outside her front door and told journalists that President Clinton should get involved. Though Esther's children were born and raised in Israel, they all inherited their mother's American citizenship. The United States had an obligation to protect its nationals, she said to the cameras. Back in her living room, she dialed the White House. To her surprise, a Clinton staffer eventually phoned back and put the president on the line. Until a few days earlier, she'd been an ordinary high school English teacher; now she was talking to the president of the United States. Esther asked Clinton to press Rabin. Yes, Israel had a policy of not negotiating with terrorists. But prime ministers had applied it selectively over the years. Clinton promised to do what he could.

The hours passed with no news and no relief. It had been an unusually hot day for autumn in Jerusalem but by the late afternoon a soft breeze wafted through the house. Esther envisioned her son lying in a dungeon somewhere in Gaza, more than sixty miles away. In fact, he was just across the valley from Ramot, tied to a bed on the second floor of the home in Bir Nabala, his eyes covered with a red kaffiyeh.

In the evening, with forty-eight hours remaining until the deadline expired, a call came from Ahmed Tibi, an Arab-Israeli member of parliament. Tibi was sitting with Arafat in Gaza and wanted to put the Palestinian leader on the line. Esther had been ambivalent about the Oslo Accord when it was signed a year earlier. She hadn't voted for Rabin and did not believe Arafat genuinely intended to make peace with Israel. But now, on the phone, he was promising to help. Arafat told her he'd ordered his security chiefs to find her son and get him home safely. Though it had been more than a year since Israel and the PLO signed their mutual recognition agreement, it was unusual for Arafat to be speaking to an ordinary Israeli—one who did not represent either the government or the military. Esther thought he sounded sincere.

Morning came with no breakthrough. The security chiefs still believed Hamas was holding Wachsman in Gaza, but one top Shabak official, Gideon Ezra, decided to check the names of people who rented cars in Jerusalem over the preceding week. The cell would likely have used either a rental or a stolen car for the abduction. Astonishingly, no one had thought to check with the car companies.

Getting the lists and combing through them took hours but by the afternoon, one name stood out: Jihad Yarmur. The East Jerusalem resident had rented a car on Sunday morning and paid his bill in cash. He returned the car on Tuesday, four days before the rental contract expired. Shabak had no file on Yarmur but did have information about one of his brothers. He was a known Hamas activist. For the first time since the abduction, investigators finally had a lead. Police officers picked up Yarmur at his home in the neighborhood of Beit Hanina, just a mile south of Bir Nabala, and brought him to a detention center for questioning.

Shabak interrogations could be corporal affairs. Over the years, investigators routinely beat Palestinian detainees, occasionally to death. After two major Shabak scandals in the 1980s, a government commission banned some interrogation methods but allowed investigators to exert "moderate physical pressure" on suspects—including shaking them violently and keeping them tied up in stress positions for hours. To Israeli and international rights groups, these "special procedures" still amounted to torture. But under the new regulations, investigators had to obtain permission from Shabak officials high up the chain of command before getting physical with suspects.

As the interrogation got under way, Gillon phoned the state prosecutor, Dorit Beinish, to notify her that he would be allowing investigators to deploy the special procedures. Still new to the job, Gillon wanted cover for what could prove to be a controversial decision. There was, as yet, no evidence linking Yarmur to the abduction. But in the initial questioning, he seemed to be hiding something the interrogators already knew—that he'd rented a car on Sunday. And with the ultimatum expiring in less than twenty-four hours, Shabak had to get to the truth quickly. Beinish thought it over quietly for several moments while Gillon held the phone to his ear. Yes, she finally said, she would back his decision.

Meanwhile, at the plaza of the Western Wall, tens of thousands gathered to pray for Wachsman's safety, the worshippers pressed up against one another in the cool Jerusalem night. And in the interrogation room less than a mile west of there, investigators worked on Yarmur.

At six the following morning Gillon entered a meeting of the army's top brass at the Defense Ministry in Tel Aviv with no news to

report. The interrogation had gone on all night and was still in progress. But while the meeting wound on, a secretary pulled the Shabak
chief out of the room for a call from Ezra, in Jerusalem. Yarmur had
finally opened up, describing the abduction in detail and providing
the location of the safe house. The cell was holding Wachsman in Bir
Nabala, not Gaza, Ezra reported. Arafat had been telling the truth.

Gillon went straight to Rabin's office, with Barak a step behind
him. Soon Rabin's entire security team crammed into his room,
including the heads of Mossad and military intelligence. Rabin grilled
Gillon about the interrogation, dwelling on almost every detail. Yarmur had last been at the house in Bir Nabala on Tuesday. He provided
a description of the interior and the names of the men inside—two
Hamas militants from East Jerusalem and one from Gaza. The men
had automatic rifles and possibly explosives. Wachsman, he said, had
been alive and well earlier in the week. Yarmur had communicated
with him in Hebrew.

Yatom, Rabin's military secretary, watched his boss take in the information. Even before the prime minister spoke, Yatom knew where the
conversation was heading. Rabin had felt an agonizing powerlessness
throughout the week. Now that the intelligence had come through,
he would want action. "It was utterly clear that we would carry out a
military operation at the moment a military operation was feasible,"
Yatom recalled years later. "Not one person objected to it."

Rabin instructed several of the participants, including Barak and
Gillon, to head immediately to Bir Nabala to case the house. They
left the Defense Ministry separately, to avoid arousing the suspicion
of journalists who had been stalking the compound for news about
Wachsman. Rabin also ordered the country's two top antiterrorism
units to begin preparing for an operation. He would leave it to Barak
to choose between the two—the military's Sayeret Matkal and the
police unit known by the acronym Yamam.

Throughout the morning, officers from both units reconnoitered
quietly in Bir Nabala. Of the two, Matkal was the better-known
unit (in English, the general staff reconnaissance unit), having led the
Entebbe mission and a series of other rescues and assassinations. To
prepare for operations, Matkal liked to fashion life-size models of the

structure they were targeting—a building or a plane—and use it to drill dozens of times. But the deadline was now less than twelve hours away. The teams would draw up their assault plans based on very little—the details obtained from Yarmur and their own hasty survey of the house.

———————

WHILE THE PREPARATIONS for a raid got under way, members of the Nobel Peace Prize committee gathered in front of journalists in Oslo to announce their decision. The timing could not have been more awkward. A Shabak reconnaissance team had set up a hidden camera and trained it on the Hamas safe house, with the images transmitted directly to the Defense Ministry in Tel Aviv. The two broadcasts, one from Oslo, the other from Bir Nabala, captured the paradox of the moment. Together, they represented the main event and the sideshow of the thirteen-month peace process—though it wasn't always clear which was which. Rabin and his aides could now see the two-story home where Wachsman had spent the past five days. Though nothing moved on the screen except for the occasional fluttering of leaves, Haber was mesmerized by the image.

The Nobel panel had deliberated for days. Not since 1973, when the committee awarded the peace prize to Henry Kissinger for negotiating a US withdrawal from Vietnam, had the arguments been so heated. One panelist, the conservative Norwegian politician Kåre Kristiansen, objected to honoring Arafat in light of his terrorist past. He resigned from the committee before the announcement. Others thought it was important to let Peres share the award. Not doing so would surely have aggravated the relationship between him and Rabin, a rivalry the Norwegians knew all about.

Finally, the panel decided to award the prize to all three men—Rabin, Peres, and Arafat. To avoid any perceived slights, the chairman of the committee announced the names alphabetically. "By concluding the Oslo agreements and subsequently following up on them, Arafat, Peres and Rabin have made substantial contributions to a historic process through which peace and cooperation can replace war and hate," Francis Sejersted told the reporters in Oslo.

Rabin might normally have gathered his advisers and family members for a toast. Instead, he issued a statement congratulating Arafat and Peres and warning the Palestinian leader against letting Hamas get the upper hand. "Today, the Palestinians face the moment of truth: if they do not defeat the enemies of peace, the enemies of peace will defeat them." Rabin also inserted a line meant to lull the captors into believing Israel still thought Wachsman was in Gaza. "At this time, Israel Defense Forces soldier Nachshon Wachsman is in a Hamas cell in Gaza; his plight is our plight."

By midday, both Sayeret Matkal and Yamam had drawn up their assault plans. Barak reviewed the two proposals, then handed the mission to Matkal. The choice surprised no one. Barak had served in Matkal early in his career and so had several other people who now held senior posts in the government and the military. The camaraderie among alumni of the unit, which included Yatom and Netanyahu, marked the closest thing Israel had to an old-boys' network.

Matkal also had a tactical advantage. Just three months earlier, members of the unit had raided a home in Lebanon, grabbing the Muslim guerrilla leader Mustafa Dirani from his bed and whisking him to Israel. Officials believed Dirani had information on the whereabouts of an Israeli airman missing since 1986. The operation involved travel by helicopter and a complicated extraction, elements that the raid in Bir Nabala would not require. But the unit had spent much time rehearsing a procedure that would now be essential: a slow, stealthy approach to a house in hostile terrain.

The action now proceeded on three fronts: Matkal members drilling for the operation in a staging area near Jerusalem, other soldiers keeping a constant watch on the house in Bir Nabala, and Rabin holding long meetings with his security team in his Tel Aviv office. As head of Shabak, Gillon sat in on the meetings with Rabin. He would recall later pondering whether the captors would make good on their threat to kill Wachsman—and concluding that indeed they would. Holding a hostage was an exhausting ordeal, difficult to sustain for more than a few days. The Hamas men would have had little sleep since Sunday and might well be running out of food and supplies. And Hamas had a track record: it had abducted and killed four soldiers in the preceding year.

At the Wachsman home in Ramot, the setting sun just after five brought matters to a standstill. Journalists still lingered at the front door, waiting for the ultimatum to expire. But inside, the Wachsmans shifted to their Sabbath routine, shutting off radio and television and—even now, with their son in captivity—unplugging the phone. "We have a rule that when the Sabbath begins, you enter a different stratosphere. You let the Almighty run the affairs," Yehuda Wachsman would say later. Rabin had not informed the family about Yarmur's arrest or the pending operation. Instead, he appointed a major general to wait in his car not far from the house in Ramot, ready to notify the Wachsmans about the outcome of the raid one way or another.

After dark, a surveillance team in Bir Nabala spotted a Mercedes approaching the house and a man entering. When he left twenty minutes later, soldiers let him get some distance from the neighborhood and then pulled him over. In a quick interrogation at the scene, the man admitted serving as an assistant to the cell. He had brought a tray of *knafeh*—a Middle Eastern cheese pastry—and other food for the captors and the hostage. The man confirmed seeing Wachsman on the second floor of the house, in a room with blankets draped over the windows—valuable information. The soldiers radioed the details to members of the Matkal team, who by this time had quietly taken up positions around the house. With the confirmation that Wachsman was alive, the operation was a go.

———————

THE FORCE, NOW divided in two, stormed the house at 7:45 p.m., an hour and fifteen minutes before the deadline. The plan called for the two teams to blast their way in through separate entrances, with one group engaging the Hamas men inside while the other raced upstairs to free Wachsman. But the operation went badly from the outset. One team headed by Capt. Nir Poraz came under fire immediately on entering the house. Poraz died instantly, and several of his men sustained bullet wounds.

The second team, meanwhile, had trouble forcing its way in. By the time Capt. Lior Lotan and his fighters entered the house and sprinted upstairs, the two remaining Hamas men had barricaded themselves in the room with Wachsman. Lotan tried to shoot his way into the room but the heavy door would not open. From the other side, he heard one of the Hamas men threatening to kill Wachsman if the soldiers didn't leave. He also heard gunfire. Minutes passed while Lotan tried to blast the door off its hinges. The Matkal fighters had counted on their ability to surprise and overwhelm the cell. Now, as the setbacks multiplied, Lotan heard the man inside saying he'd killed Wachsman and was not afraid to die. Finally, Lotan's force charged through the door and killed the two Hamas men. But Wachsman was already dead. The operation to save one soldier had cost the lives of two.

Barak, who followed the events from a staging area near Bir Nabala, phoned Rabin to report that the raid had failed. Yatom had been with the Israeli leader all evening. In the hour leading up to the operation, he watched his boss pace back and forth in his office. Now, as the phone conversation dragged on, Yatom could read the news on Rabin's face. "I understood from his expression that something went wrong." That Wachsman died was bad enough. Poraz, the twenty-three-year-old captain who commanded the raid and died in its initial moments, was just a few weeks from completing his military service. Poraz's father had also been killed in action, his plane shot down over Sinai during the 1973 war.

The rest of the ordeal unspooled over a grueling weekend. Late in the evening, Rabin held a press conference to explain his decision to order the raid. "It is our obligation not to surrender to a terrorist ultimatum but to fight against terrorism with all of the attendant pain and suffering," he said. The following day, he paid a visit to the Poraz family. As army chief and later defense minister, Rabin had made plenty of condolence calls over the years but this one felt especially excruciating. Poraz's mother had tried to prevent her son from serving in a combat unit but eventually relented. Now, she lashed out at Rabin for sending him on a mission that was doomed to fail. "They had a very traumatic visit," Rabin's daughter, Dalia, recalled years later. "She was very, very bitter." The family buried Poraz alongside his father in Tel Aviv.

Rabin also called on the Wachsman home, where journalists still lingered outside. Inside, Esther was preparing for her son's funeral. She had managed to get through the night only with the help of sedatives. Rabin arrived with several military officers, but Yehuda asked to speak to the prime minister alone. In the basement of the home, where the family had watched the abduction video four days earlier, Yehuda said he understood the decision not to negotiate with terrorists and didn't fault Rabin for ordering the raid. But he couldn't comprehend why Rabin didn't stall in order to give the unit more time to prepare. In the final hours, Hamas had seemed ready to extend the deadline. Rabin said he hadn't trusted the group to keep Wachsman alive and repeated a line from his press conference—that the decision and the failure were his own. When Rabin emerged from the basement, Esther noticed his eyes had welled up.

At meetings throughout Sunday, Rabin's security team reviewed the events of the preceding week. The one redeeming aspect of the affair had been Arafat. The Palestinian leader had combed Gaza to find Wachsman. He detained some two hundred Hamas men for questioning. When he reported to Rabin that the missing soldier was not in his territory, he was telling the truth. "Yasser Arafat earned many points from Yitzhak Rabin, deservedly. He ordered all his men to assist in the search [and] did everything we asked of him," Carmi Gillon would write later in a memoir.

Haber came to view the ordeal as a defining moment in the interaction between the two leaders. Each Hamas attack on Israel had prompted a debate among Rabin's security advisers: had Arafat been unable to stop it or simply unwilling? In the Wachsman case, when Rabin brought pressure to bear, Arafat responded. "Rabin even said, 'Hey, he told us the truth,'" Haber recalled two decades later. And yet, the most he could muster for now was a slow thaw. When Haber proposed that his boss phone Arafat and acknowledge his efforts, the Israeli leader recoiled. "He said, 'That's my red line. I'm not going to apologize.'"

The contours of the relationship were forming. Arafat seemed to revere Rabin's military bearing and fear his temper. At meetings he addressed him as "Your Excellency." Rabin was coming to terms with the fact that Arafat could not shut down Hamas violence—certainly not from areas that remained under Israel's control. If the Palestinian leader was making a genuine effort, the peace process could continue. To his own advisers, Rabin said repeatedly that Arafat needed to have his *Altalena* moment, to take on those rivals who threatened his sovereignty. But he also understood the complexity of domestic politics. Rabin had his own extremists to deal with—and he often chose to avoid confrontation.

In an interview with the reporters Nahum Barnea and Shimon Shiffer soon after Wachsman died, Rabin mounted a defense of his agreement with Arafat, something Israelis had been accustomed to reading. But he also defended Arafat himself. "Making a deal with Arafat was difficult, given the history of terrorism. But I came to the conclusion that it's Arafat or Hamas," he said. "I certainly don't regret coming to an agreement that included reciprocal recognition with the PLO. Arafat is a strategic partner of this government." Pressed on the ways the Oslo process had come up short, Rabin said: "Arafat is disappointed that he didn't get certain things from this agreement, just as I am."

Yossi Beilin, who accompanied Rabin on some of his subsequent meetings with Arafat, noticed the improvement. But he also began to think that the strategy he himself had devised in the Oslo talks—an incremental advance toward peace between the two sides—was misguided. The approach aimed to build confidence between Israelis and Palestinians, enough to allow each side to make difficult concessions in the final agreement. No doubt it had altered the landscape. Israeli and Palestinian troops now patrolled together in Gaza, an astonishing sight for anyone familiar with the history of enmity between the two sides. Academics were meeting across the region in what came to be known as track-two talks—freewheeling discussions on ways to solve the conflict for good. Dialogue groups had sprung up in all the big Palestinian cities, often led by former political prisoners. Youth groups, artists, businessmen, parents who had lost children in the conflict—all were looking for counterparts to engage with. Oslo had started as a process between leaders and quickly filtered down.

But the slow, staged approach of the political process had also allowed opponents to mobilize against it. Their campaign of violence had been so effective that, thirteen months after the signing in Washington, it was not clear whether the peace process was enhancing confidence or eroding it.

Under the terms of their deal, the two sides had until May 1999 to complete a final peace agreement. But Beilin now worried that another five years of shootings and bombings, closures and crackdowns would drain Oslo of public support on both sides. As the process moved into its second year, Beilin approached Arafat's deputy, Mahmoud Abbas, about launching another secret channel, this one in Stockholm. He envisioned replicating the Oslo talks but instead of negotiating another interim deal, hashing out all the complicated details of a final peace accord, including where the border would run between Israel and Palestine. When the official final-status negotiations got under way, the two sides could work from the paper drafted in Stockholm instead of starting from scratch. Beilin appointed the two academics who had negotiated the Oslo deal, Ron Pundak and Yair Hirschfeld, to lead the talks. He informed neither Peres nor Rabin about the channel.

In the weeks that followed the Wachsman ordeal, the pendulum kept swinging between bad news and good news, trauma and euphoria. On October 19, just five days after the raid in Bir Nabala, a Hamas suicide bomber blew himself up on a Tel Aviv bus, killing twenty-two people. It was the deadliest attack yet by the group and a shock to residents of Israel's busiest city—who seemed to feel largely removed from the rising brutality of the conflict. The bomber had struck on Dizengoff Street, a main artery of the city lined with cafés and boutiques.

Rabin once again pressed Arafat to tighten his grip on Gaza. But the bomber turned out to be a resident of Qalqilya, a West Bank city under Israel's control. Israeli authorities had detained him six times in the preceding years. After cutting short a trip to London, Rabin told reporters in Tel Aviv that Israel must finally come to terms with sepa-

rating itself from the Palestinians and the land—much of it anyway—
it conquered in 1967. "I am prepared to fight them [Hamas] to the
finish because they are the enemies of Israel and the enemies of peace.
But I must also consider, what next? What is the solution? Should it be
separation between the Palestinians and Israel, or a continued blurring
of the line—continuing to create the conditions that led to fanaticism
among the Palestinians [in the first place]." He admitted there was
little Israel's security agencies could do against a lone suicide bomber
bent on destruction.

Rabin also said Israel was hunting for a certain engineer who made
bombs for all of Hamas's attacks. In meetings with the security team,
Shabak identified him as Yahya Ayyash.

Just one week later, Israel and Jordan signed a formal peace accord
in a stretch of desert on the border between the two countries. Israeli
troops had been clearing land mines in the area for weeks, preparing it
for what would now be a transit point. Though Israel and Jordan had
not fought a war in twenty-seven years, the agreement carried huge
symbolic weight. For the first time since its founding, Israel now had
more allies than enemies on its perimeter. Some five thousand people
attended in one-hundred-degree heat, including President Clinton,
whose face turned bright red under the desert sun. When it was over,
Israel and Jordan threw switches connecting their electric grids in
Eilat and Aqaba, twin cities on the Red Sea. Even Rabin's sharpest
critics praised the deal; the Knesset ratified it by a vote of 105 to 3.

Rabin had now been in office for twenty-eight months. Questions
surrounded his agreement with the Palestinians. Arafat had yet to
assert himself with Hamas and Rabin had still made no public commitment to a Palestinian state. Whether the two men could muster a
final treaty was by no means certain. But the messy accord with Arafat
had led to a comprehensive agreement with Jordan. And Rabin still
hoped to lock up a deal with Syria, the one bordering state that posed
a genuine threat. The Israeli leader had set out to change the country's
corrosive status quo and made good on that promise, unquestionably.
Israel looked nothing like it had when his term began.

The Nobel Prize ceremony took place in mid-December. In Tel
Aviv, it was still warm enough for dedicated beachgoers to swim in

the Mediterranean. At Oslo's Fornebu Airport, just five hours away by plane, technicians were de-icing the runway. Days before the event, Arafat's wife announced she was several weeks pregnant. Suha Tawil had been Arafat's secretary, more than thirty years younger than he was, when they married secretly in 1991. Now, she described the timing of the pregnancy as a harbinger of good things for the Palestinians. "It's a double blessing for Abu Ammar—the Nobel Prize and a baby," she said, using Arafat's nom de guerre.

Rabin had been irritated about having to share the prize with Peres. To Shimon Sheves, he said he needed no help "carrying the envelope." But offstage and later at the reception, Sheves noticed something surprising: an easy, almost demonstrative rapport between Peres and Rabin. The antagonism from more than two decades of quarreling had not quite dissipated—but it had been receding for some time now. Peres had several cuts on his face, having tripped the night before during a walk to an Oslo synagogue. When Norwegian security men watched him tumble, one of them thought someone had taken a shot at the Israeli foreign minister.

From Oslo, Rabin made a stop in South Korea for a meeting with President Kim Young-sam and then headed back to Israel. On a Saturday following his return, the red phone rang in his apartment on Rav Ashi. Rabin braced himself for bad news but the voice on the other end of the line sounded decidedly calm. It was Peres calling to inquire whether somehow the Nobel Prize medals had been switched. The one he was holding had the letters Y.R. engraved on the back—clearly it belonged to Rabin. Did Rabin have Peres's medal? Or was there a three-way switch with Arafat?

When Rabin explained the mix-up to the family over lunch, Noa, his teenage granddaughter, let out a derisive giggle. Did Peres have nothing better to do on a Saturday than admire his Nobel medal? But Rabin silenced her with a hand gesture. Peres had worked hard for the achievement and it was his right to revel in it, he said. Noa felt her jaw slacken. How strange it was to hear her grandfather defending the man he had loathed for so many years, not just his political rival but the antagonist-in-chief for the entire Rabin family. She made a mental note to hold her tongue from now on when it came to Peres.

CHAPTER 6

Under-the-Window Tales

"There was a lot of intelligence noise. This was one more item."

—HEZI KALO

The Nobel ceremony gave Yigal Amir one more reason to brood. If he thought the international community would conclude from the suicide bombings that Oslo had been a mistake, it had done the opposite: honored the dealmakers with one of the world's most prestigious prizes. In his own mind, Amir was doing everything he could to educate people about the evils of the so-called peace process. Yet he'd racked up nothing but failures: the failure to draw millions to the streets; the failure to form a serious militia; and the failure to stop Rabin.

On the Bar-Ilan campus, the first weeks of 1995 frothed with political activity. Some students had joined a hunger strike outside Rabin's office in Jerusalem. Others took part in a campaign to heckle Rabin wherever he appeared around the country. On January 22, the prime minister was scheduled to speak at Yad Vashem to mark fifty years since the liberation of Auschwitz. Shmuel Rosenbloom, the law student who had taken up with Nava Holtzman after she severed ties with Amir, organized a bus from Bar-Ilan to the memorial in Jerusalem. Amir decided to go along.

The students intended to protest Rabin's continuing partnership with Arafat in the face of Hamas violence. But they were also seething about something else: the government's decision to exempt most visiting foreign officials from touring Yad Vashem. The visits had been an unvarying ritual for decades. But by the 1990s, many Israelis felt the emphasis on Jews as victims had come to seem trite and manipulative.

To the students, the decision marked one more way the government was trying to dim Israel's Jewish heritage. A petition they circulated on campus featured a cartoon of Deputy Foreign Minister Yossi Beilin, the architect of the new policy (and of the Oslo talks), dressed as a traffic cop, directing people to Palestinian landmarks instead of Israeli ones. "How can the foreign ministry showcase Israel without showcasing the moral underpinnings of its very existence?" the petition asked. "People who don't go *there* won't understand why we are *here*."

On the morning of the rally, Amir woke up early at the house in Herzliya and walked to the neighborhood synagogue as usual. But during the service he did something out of the ordinary: quietly and alone, he recited the *vidui*, a confessional prayer that Jews say when they are preparing to die. Without much fanfare, Amir had decided he would try to kill Rabin at Yad Vashem, even if it got him killed. The prayer had different versions, usually beginning with an acknowledgment that God alone had dominion over life and death: "May it be Your will that You heal me with total recovery, but, if I die, may my death be an atonement for all the errors, iniquities, and willful sins that I have erred, sinned and transgressed before You, and may You grant my share in the Garden of Eden, and grant me the merit to abide in the World to Come which is vouchsafed for the righteous."

At home, Amir slipped the Beretta into his pants, then left for campus. Along the highway, from Herzliya south to Bar-Ilan, the bright bloom of the almond trees stood out against the gray of winter.

By now, sixteen months after the start of the deal with the Palestinians, Shabak had a file on Amir. It wasn't long—just a few sentences on a single page. It included references to the student weekends he'd been organizing in the settlements and also something about his idea of recruiting people for attacks against Palestinians. The agency had compiled a list of several dozen extremists overheard talking about the need to kill Rabin. From time to time, a Shabak officer would summon one of them for a meeting, warn him that he was being watched, and perhaps revoke his gun license, if he had one. In internal documents, the agency referred to these potential assailants as *b'dukaim*—literally, people who warranted scrutiny. But Amir's name was absent from the list. On campus and at the settlement weekends, Amir had been saying openly for some months now that *din rodef* applied to Rabin and that the prime minister needed to die. Smaller groups of people had heard him talk explicitly about killing Rabin with his Beretta. But somehow, Shabak knew only about his incipient plan to form an anti-Arab militia.

The Shabak officer in charge of thwarting Jewish extremism was a wiry man in his mid-forties, Hezi Kalo, who had spent most of his two-decade career in the Arab Affairs Department, battling Palestinian terrorism. In the agency hierarchy, Arab Affairs stood above everything else. The big budgets went to fighting terrorism, and the prestige lay with recruiting and running Palestinian agents in the West Bank and Gaza. The Jewish Affairs Department, by contrast, was the place where careers often stalled. Investigating settlers or rabbis meant tangling with their powerful patrons in government—and suffering the consequences.

Kalo took a sabbatical in 1992 to polish his Arabic and study Arab literature. He intended to return to the Arab Affairs Department. But by the end of his year away, the Oslo deal had transformed Israel's security landscape and shifted priorities in the agency. A withdrawal from parts of the West Bank and Gaza would rouse Jewish radicals and Shabak now wanted its most experienced officers to work the Jewish side as well. Kalo began his term as head of the Jewish Affairs Department in September 1993, the month Rabin and Arafat signed their deal in Washington. "We understood we were facing a major escalation," he recalled.

In his new role, Kalo found himself trying to infiltrate the very communities he'd spent years protecting—settlements where extremists were now plotting against Palestinians. In December, just three months after the start of Oslo, masked gunmen pulled three Palestinians from a car near Tarkumiya and shot them to death. Shabak suspected settlers but never solved the crime. Two months later, Goldstein committed his massacre in Hebron. Kalo quickly realized that Jewish extremists had advantages over Palestinian militants when it came to planning and perpetrating attacks. Most had military training and easy access to weapons. As Israeli citizens, they could travel anywhere without arousing suspicion. Around the time of the Hebron killing spree, Kalo drafted an internal memo outlining some worst-case scenarios. One was an attack on Jerusalem's Dome of the Rock, an event that would undoubtedly ignite the entire Muslim world. The other was an assassination attempt against Israeli political figures—chiefly, Rabin and Peres.

The memo coincided with some disturbing trends in the national religious community, including the rabbis' call on soldiers to defy their commanders should they be ordered to dismantle settlements. But it received little attention in the agency. Right-wing extremists tended to point their guns at Arabs, not Jews. The last time a Jewish leader had been assassinated was in 1933, murdered on a Tel Aviv beach in a crime that remained unsolved six decades later.

Still, Kalo and a few others in his department believed the rising radicalism among settlers made it conceivable at least that someone might take a shot at Rabin. Support for the theory came from the informants Shabak ran in the settlements. Several of them reported to their handlers starting around the summer of '94 that Jewish radicals were discussing openly whether it was permissible under Jewish law to kill a political figure in order to stop the peace process. One of the officers serving under Kalo, Yitzhak Fantik, relayed the information directly to Rabin in a meeting in July. Fantik had begun to regard all the ideological settlers—or many of them, anyway—as potential subversives. "At the moment of crisis, when there's a clash between the laws of the state and the laws of the Torah, they'll side with the Torah and turn against democracy," he would say.

To cope with the rising Jewish vigilantism, Kalo ordered his officers to recruit more informants in the settlements, a particularly complicated endeavor in close-knit communities. Their information had become critical. In the fall of '94, one of them informed Shabak that two brothers in Kiryat Arba, Eitan and Yehoyada Kahalani, were planning to murder a Palestinian randomly. In a clever bit of undercover work, the agency managed to neuter the guns the Kahalani brothers intended to use by removing the firing pins. On the appointed day, Shabak men followed them to an isolated road in the West Bank and watched them point their weapons at a Palestinian on a bicycle and then pull the trigger. When the guns misfired, they swooped in and arrested the brothers.

Weeks later, Shabak picked up on what it thought was an emerging plot to murder Peres. The details came from another informant but they were vague and circumstantial, not nearly enough to substantiate an indictment. Instead, authorities jailed the suspect without trial for several months under a procedure known in Israel as administrative detention.

The information Shabak had on Amir had also come from an informant—the blue-eyed Bar-Ilan student Avishai Raviv. The agency had recruited him eight years earlier from the ranks of the Kach movement and kept him on the payroll while he rose to prominence as a far-right agitator. His handlers found him difficult to control—he'd accumulated arrests for incitement, rioting, and assault. But Raviv was a prolific source. Though only in his late twenties, he'd already delivered thousands of tips about the radical milieu in which he'd ensconced himself. The agency had given him the code name Champagne for his bubbly energy: Somehow, Raviv managed to show up at just about every right-wing event—at the university and around the country.

Now, on the bus to Yad Vashem, in the frigid February of 1995, the firebrands from Bar-Ilan bantered across the aisle.

Jerusalem winds along the slopes of several hills, a tattered mesh of Jewish and Arab, spiritual and secular. Thanks in part to a long-standing ordinance requiring all buildings to be faced with chiseled limestone, the new neighborhoods of the city have the look of something consciously old and solemn—the architectural equivalent of distressed furniture. Amir sat near Har-Shefi and Skornik but said little. He envisioned himself standing outside the memorial, waiting for Rabin to approach, then lunging at him and firing his Beretta. Throughout the ride, he reminded himself that he had tried other approaches and was now spiritually ready. After a long stretch of highway, the bus heaved toward Mount Herzl, where Yad Vashem shares the crest with Israel's national cemetery.

But before it reached the top, a news bulletin announced a double suicide bombing at the Beit Lid junction north of Tel Aviv. A Palestinian bomber blew himself up at a bus stop teeming with soldiers near the town of Netanya. Moments later, a second bomber set off his explosives, killing people who rushed in to help the wounded. The attacks would be claimed by Islamic Jihad—Hamas's smaller and more radical stepsister. But Israeli investigators would discover that the bombs used at Beit Lid were built by the same Hamas operator involved in earlier attacks, Yahya Ayyash.

Amir listened to the descriptions of the carnage on the radio and began making calculations. Rabin would surely cancel his appearance at Yad Vashem. He might well decide to tour the bombing site, something officials often did in the aftermath of a major attack. If Amir could embed himself in the crowd pressing in on the Israeli leader, he might be able to take a shot at Rabin. He contemplated getting off the bus and finding his way to Beit Lid. But then he reconsidered. The assassination needed to be perpetrated in cold blood. "It occurred to me that I didn't want it to be an emotional response to something," he would say later. "If I'm going to act, it's only from a cerebral place. I won't do it in the aftermath of an attack." Amir remained with the group.

On the way back to campus, the radio delivered constant updates from the bomb scene. Rabin had indeed rushed to Beit Lid and was met by crowds chanting, "Death to Arabs." Now, Amir let loose. Once again, he announced openly that *din rodef* applied to Rabin and that the prime minister must die. An argument ensued, with students shouting across the aisle, debating whether the Halakhic decree had any relevance at all and, if it did, whether it allowed for the killing of the prime minister. Rosenbloom, who organized the protest, would say later that he was seated too far from Amir to hear his remarks. By now he and Holtzman had been dating for several months and were planning to marry in May.

Raviv filed reports to Shabak about many of the events he attended with Amir. But he never mentioned his threats against Rabin. Like many of the people who surrounded Amir, he simply did not give them credence. Raviv was a complicated character. He took seriously his work with Shabak and felt devoted to his handlers. The secrecy and intrigue of his life as an informant appealed to him deeply, so much so that he dreaded the prospect of being cut loose one day. But the world of far-right politics, the ideological certainty, the ethnic chauvinism and the bullying, tapped into something central in his character. Compulsively, Raviv needed to be the most provocative figure in any setting, the biggest attention hound. In Amir, he saw something similar—a young man who liked to talk big, liked the attention, and liked women. Not a guy who would murder the prime minister. Raviv himself blustered about the need to kill Rabin. Why should he have taken Amir's bombast seriously?

Shabak had two kinds of informants. There were those who joined the agency on a career track, received training in undercover work, and then got planted in target groups. As homegrown agents, there was rarely a question of their motives or loyalty to the agency. But their training and infiltration could take years. And as newcomers to the target group, they were often looked on with suspicion. As a rule, the more radical the group, the harder it was to infiltrate a homegrown agent. Then there were the "purchased" informants, people recruited from within particular communities or political groups whose credibility as activists was already established. These insiders would often deliver much better information but they could be difficult to control.

Raviv was a purchased informant. He had been active in Kach already as a teenager, hanging posters for the group in the Tel Aviv suburb where he grew up and showing up at rowdy protests and rallies. In high school, Raviv met Meir Kahane, the rabble-rousing leader of Kach, whose racist tropes included vulgar references to Arabs defiling Jewish women. To friends at the time, Raviv seemed spellbound. Among the messages he picked up from Kahane, Raviv liked to talk about the traitorous *smolanim*—leftists who cared more about the Arabs than their fellow Jews. Already then, he craved media attention.

Sometime after the army released Raviv on a disability, Shabak made the approach. By then he'd racked up several arrests and perhaps the agency enticed him with an offer to expunge his record. Once on the Shabak payroll, Raviv began branching out, operating with several groups at once. Dani Dayan, who encountered him while working for the right-wing Tehiya Party in the late 1980s, recalled something pleasant about Raviv, not exactly charisma but a kind of boyish enthusiasm and a stutter that made him seem vulnerable. But he could also be thuggish and breathtakingly reckless. Raviv dated a teenage girl the Dayans had informally adopted, often visiting her at their home in the settlement Ma'ale Shomron. One day he took her to the Palestinian town of Qalqilya in the West Bank to throw stones at passing cars. "We got very angry at him," he said.

Dayan, who would eventually become the chairman of the YESHA Council, heard rumors that Raviv worked for Shabak but dismissed them. Other friends had their suspicions. Raviv was constantly initiating hate crimes—running amok in Palestinian produce markets, organizing a militia summer camp, assaulting a leftist parliament member. But while his accomplices ended up in court, he seemed to have a knack for dodging indictments.

That knack was actually the deft maneuvering of his handlers, who repeatedly extracted their agent from trouble. If a policeman arrested Raviv, he might get a call from a Shabak officer asking him cryptically to release the suspect without raising too many questions. If somehow an investigation ensued, the state attorney herself—the one official in the Justice Department who knew Raviv worked for Shabak—would quietly quash the indictment.

By late '94, Shabak had grown tired of its informant's excesses. Raviv had formed his own group, Eyal, that was drawing media attention. With the help of a deputy, Benzion Gopstein, Eyal would circulate regular beeper messages to journalists announcing its latest provocation. In undercover work, agencies prefer for their informants to be observers, not initiators. Otherwise, it can look like authorities have planted a provocateur to deliberately smear the group. As the hooliganism mounted, Raviv's handlers summoned him repeatedly for rebukes and suspended him at least once.

But Raviv was delivering so much information that the agency, coping with spiraling radicalism in the settlements, felt it could not afford to sever the relationship. He was also making personal sacrifices to improve his intelligence gathering. Raviv had married a religious woman and started wearing a skullcap—though in reality he remained secular. For nearly a year now, he was living in Kiryat Arba, on the same block where Baruch Goldstein had lived, and reporting on the settlers of Hebron—extremists who fit the agency's profile of the Jewish terrorist or assassin.

Amir, who had begun actively stalking Rabin, did not fit this profile. He lived in Herzliya instead of a settlement and had no record of violence against Palestinians. The agency had an informant watching him but wasn't getting the picture.

———————

IN THE WEEKS that followed the protest at Yad Vashem, Amir couldn't help himself: He bragged separately to Har-Shefi and Skornik about having gone there to kill Rabin. Later, he confided it to Adani. Though nothing had actually happened at Yad Vashem, the event marked a psychological leap for Amir and a shift in his own self-perception. Until then, his discussions with Hagai focused on ways to kill Rabin and flee. The escape plan held as much importance as the killing itself. Now, Amir had begun thinking of himself as a living dead man, a martyr like the Palestinian bombers. From a tactical point of view, the shift offered tremendous advantages. If there was no need to hatch a getaway, the options for killing Rabin multiplied.

The awareness colored Amir's winter. He continued organizing protests and student weekends—mostly at far-flung settlements. But his parents noticed their son had become more pensive and withdrawn. Geulah thought Amir was still brooding over the breakup with Holtzman months earlier, or struggling with some other relationship.

At the settlement retreats, Amir would sometimes deliver the sermon after prayers Friday night or Saturday morning. One weekend, he told the biblical story of Pinchas, a Jew who witnesses another Jew transgress by lying with a Midianite. In a fit of rage, Pinchas kills them both—Zimri, the Jew, and his non-Jewish mistress. But instead of punishing him for his zealotry, God rewards the killer by declaring that the lineage of the High Priest will come from his descendants. Amir offered the story as evidence that murder can sometimes be justified. "If God wants a person to commit an act, He lets him commit the act." Then, he made a connection between Zimri and Rabin. Both men had turned their backs on their own nation for personal pleasure or gain, he asserted. To at least some of the students, it sounded as if Amir was saying God would reward the person who killed Rabin.

At home, Amir was now scouring the papers for information on Rabin's upcoming appearances. Rabin's government had been pressing ahead with negotiations over a wider pullback in the West Bank, one that would allow Palestinians control over six of the seven cities and many of the towns and villages. In a summit meeting, the two sides set a target date of July 1 for the start of the redeployment. Oslo II, as it had come to be called, would still leave the Jewish settlements untouched. But for Rabin's critics, the fact that he intended to cede more West Bank land to Arafat even as Hamas persisted with its bombing campaign amounted to folly or, worse, treason. Now Amir had a deadline. He told himself he must track Rabin before July 1 and kill him.

At school, Amir continued coasting on the hard work of others, skipping classes and borrowing notes from friends before the exam period. During the semester break, he threw himself into a new book about Rabin, a contemptuous assault on the Israeli leader that bracketed Amir's religious critique of Rabin with a quasi-scholarly one. Written by the philosopher Uri Milstein, the book focused on Rabin's early career in the military, highlighting certain episodes and depicting him as a serial bumbler on the battlefield. "It turns out . . . that Rabin amassed a string of failures and oversights that could well have prevented the establishment of the state of Israel," he wrote hyperbolically on the back cover. Israeli academics ordinarily pay publishing houses to print their books—the market is too small for profits.

In Milstein's case, some two hundred of Rabin's opponents donated the money.

But the book sold reasonably well and it added a veneer of academic legitimacy to what was now a street campaign of blistering agitation against Rabin. The settler journal *Nekuda* excerpted the book and allowed Milstein space to launch a broader attack on the Israeli left. "Rabin's character exemplifies the left in its entirety, which exerted its hegemony . . . through brainwashing and fraud. This approach eroded the social fabric of Israel and destroyed the Israeli spirit," he wrote.

As the street protests grew more aggressive, Shabak became increasingly concerned for Rabin's safety. It was now standard to hear protesters chant, "Rabin is a murderer," over and over, in pulsating fury; to compare Rabin to Hitler or his government to the Judenrat, the Jewish administrative bodies that enforced Nazi rule during World War II. The ugly invective came not just from the political margins but from the top echelons of the Likud Party. Ariel Sharon, who had founded Likud and now served as one of its senior deputies in parliament, favored the World War II comparisons. "What's the difference between the Jewish leadership in the ghetto and this government?" he said in a typical remark, months after the Oslo signing. "There, they were forced to collaborate. Here they do it willingly." Netanyahu generally stuck to calling Rabin a liar and accusing him of enabling violence against the settlers. "They [Hamas] receive signals from both the government and the PLO to kill Jews in Judea and Samaria."

Others said much worse. Politicians regularly likened Rabin's administration to the collaborating Vichy government in France during the Second World War, to the Quisling government in Norway, and to the Nazi regime itself. Settler leaders portrayed Rabin's peace deals as acts of treason for which the prime minister and his cabinet would one day stand trial.

Certainly, this wasn't the first time Israeli politicians reached for inflammatory rhetoric or made heinous Nazi-era comparisons. Left-wing activists depicted Sharon as a murderer for his role in Israel's 1982 invasion of Lebanon and the Phalangist massacre of Palestinians at Sabra and Shatila. But the invective on the right was being matched by a rising tendency toward violence on the right. In Shabak's Jewish

Affairs Department, Kalo was now wondering how long it would take before some hothead interpreted the verbal assaults on Rabin as a green light for a physical assault.

In early March 1995, Rabin named Carmi Gillon to head Shabak, an appointment that symbolized more than anything the new priorities in the agency. Gillon had never served in the Arab Affairs Department. He started his career with the Dignitary Protection Unit—the equivalent of the American Secret Service—and made his reputation in the Jewish Affairs Department, having broken up the Jewish Underground in the 1980s. No one in Shabak knew more about right-wing extremism than Gillon. On his sabbatical in 1990, he wrote a master's thesis about the radicalization process under way on the right, which he said "pushes the extremists even further towards the margins, both ideologically and in terms of their willingness to take dangerous action."

Almost immediately, Gillon took steps to protect Rabin. But he met resistance from an unexpected source—Rabin himself. In March, Gillon decided to order an armored car. Astonishingly, Israeli prime ministers to date had been chauffeured in regular American-made vehicles, usually a Chevrolet Caprice. The agency appointed a team to pick the right model. The most secure cars in the world were made by Mercedes, but because of the sensitivities involved—still, fifty years after the Holocaust—ordering a German car for Rabin was out of the question. Instead, Shabak purchased an armored Cadillac, similar to the model the Secret Service used to ferry President Clinton around at the time.

Rabin hated it. Luxury cars were uncommon in Israel and Cadillacs, especially, with their wreath-and-crest hood ornaments, had the air of American excess. When it arrived at the port in Haifa, an Israeli television crew filmed it being wheeled into the parking lot. The report aired on Channel One highlighted the car's lavishness, prompting opposition figures to criticize Rabin for wasting government money. From that point on, the car became a source of friction between the prime minister and his security chief. Rabin complained that the silver Cadillac, with its thick, cloudy windows and its excessive weight, made him claustrophobic. Often he instructed his driver to bring the Caprice instead—over the objections of the agency. Yechezkel Sharabi, who served as Rabin's driver for three decades, said later that his boss felt uncomfortable traveling in an armored car when ordinary Israelis risked being blown up on buses.

Rabin and Gillon also clashed over the issue of a bulletproof vest, which the agency had been trying for more than a year to get Rabin to wear. Gillon made the case that the threats against the prime minister were now specific enough to warrant wearing one at all public appearances. He argued that modern vests were light and flexible, not the bulky things Rabin knew from his military days. And he explained why they were so effective. Most assassins shot from the hip—raising the gun to eye level made them too conspicuous. From that low-down position, even a skilled shooter would have a hard time hitting a person in the head. The back, in contrast, formed a broad target. A good bulletproof vest would cover it entirely.

Rabin responded with a typical wave of the hand. "Are you out of your mind? I'll never wear a bulletproof vest in my own country, no matter what it's made of." In early spring, Rabin and Gillon both attended Israel's annual memorial service for fallen soldiers at Mount Herzl in Jerusalem. Right-wing protesters waited for the prime minister, chanting, "Rabin is a traitor." Gillon gestured at the crowd and raised the issue once again, only to be rebuffed. "I could understand his position," Gillon would write in his memoir later. "He was this Palmach soldier who fought in Israel's wars for thirty years, who commanded the army in the victorious Six-Day War . . . and he's supposed to suffer this humiliation?"

Though the relationship between the two men would eventually improve, at this early stage it remained awkward. Rabin had deliberated for months between Gillon and Gideon Ezra for the position of Shabak chief. Ezra had come from the Arab Affairs Department—it had been his idea to check car rental companies that led Shabak to Wachsman's captors. In a way, the choice between them mirrored the broader questions facing Israel: Was it genuinely ending its rule over the Palestinians or merely repositioning its occupation? Did domestic threats now require as much attention as external ones? Ezra had been considered extremely effective at antiterrorism but the agency's

new roles included coordinating with former enemies in the West
Bank and Gaza. Rabin wasn't sure Ezra could make the transition.
Still, terrorism had not subsided. On the contrary, it had mutated into
something deadlier and more fanatical. So torn was Rabin that he
offered the job to a third candidate, navy chief Ami Ayalon. When
Ayalon turned it down, Gillon finally got the call. But he entered
the job with the dispiriting knowledge that he wasn't Rabin's only
candidate—or even his preferred one.

The entire debate, of course, was concealed from the public. Shabak's culture was so secretive, it kept the very identity of the man
who ran the agency hidden. The Israeli press referred to Gillon only
by the first initial of his first name—Kaf, in Hebrew. Still, somehow
the settlers knew his résumé and complained about his appointment.

The matter of body armor was on Amir's mind as well: he wondered whether Rabin would be wearing a vest when he finally caught
up to the prime minister. Though Amir now regarded his plan as a
suicide mission, he still feared failing—and dying for nothing. Over
the spring semester, he and his brother went to a shooting range at
an isolated beach several times to test bullets Hagai had modified to
make them armor-piercing. He'd learned the technique from a book
about guns and ammunition. In his shed behind the house in Herzliya, Hagai had drilled into the top of a bullet and pressed a small
steel pellet into the groove he'd created. The extra weight would give
the projectile more force. Over the course of several weeks, he made
some forty of these bullets and gave half to his brother.

As part of the experiment, the brothers shot both hollow points
and modified rounds at a thick aluminum plate Hagai had attached
to a large telephone book—the equivalent of the American Yellow
Pages. The plate stopped the hollow points. But with Hagai's rounds,
the steel pellet pierced the aluminum and tunneled well into the
phone book. After additional modifications, Hagai was satisfied that
his homemade ammunition would penetrate a vest. From that point
on, Amir kept several stacked in his magazine, alongside the regular
casings and the hollow points. With the July deadline drawing near,
he felt an almost constant restlessness, a compulsion to put himself
close to the prime minister.

Rabin joined Palmach, one of the pre-state Jewish armed groups, as a teenager. Photo circa 1943.

Israel Government Press Office

With his daughter, Dalia, in Britain, where he attended the Royal Staff College at Camberley, 1953.

Israel Government Press Office

Rabin assumed command of the Israeli military at age forty-two. Pictured here on September 1, 1964.

Israel Government Press Office

Rabin and Defense Minister Moshe Dayan at the Western Wall, June 7, 1967,
after Israeli troops captured Jerusalem's Old City from Jordan.

Ilan Bruner for the Israel Government Press Office

With his grandson in 1977,
during his first term as
prime minister. Rabin would
say later that he lacked the
political experience to serve
effectively.

*Sa'ar Ya'acov for the Israel
Government Press Office*

Rabin with George H. W. Bush in Kennebunkport, Maine, August 10, 1992. Bush's decision to withhold loan guarantees from Israel's previous government over settlement expansion helped Rabin get elected.
Sa'ar Ya'acov for the Israel Government Press Office

Rabin and Arafat at the Oslo Accord signing ceremony outside the White House, September 13, 1993. Their handshake prompted gasps and then cheers from spectators.
Avi Ohayon for the Israel Government Press Office

Returning from China, October 1993. The Oslo Accord a month earlier helped improve Israel's diplomatic position around the globe. Seated across from Rabin are his chief of staff, Eitan Haber (right) and Mossad director Shabtai Shavit. Cabinet Secretary Elyakim Rubinstein is standing in the aisle.

Sa'ar Ya'acov for the Israel Government Press Office

With Jordan's King Hussein, shortly after they signed the Israeli–Jordanian peace treaty, October 26, 1994. "No doubt about it, Rabin and Hussein fell in love," Haber would say.

Sa'ar Ya'acov for the Israel Government Press Office

Rabin and Arafat in Casablanca, Morocco, October 30, 1994. Their relationship
was fraught at the outset but evolved into something workable.

Sa'ar Ya'acov for the Israel Government Press Office

Arafat, Peres, and Rabin receiving the Nobel Peace Prize in Oslo, Norway,
December 10, 1994. To avoid slights, the chairman of the committee
announced the winners alphabetically.

Sa'ar Ya'acov for the Israel Government Press Office

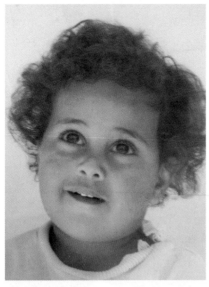

Amir as a toddler. His mother described him and his brother as the thinker and the tinkerer, Amir being the more studious and cerebral of the two.

Courtesy of the Amir family

Amir served in an infantry unit during the first Palestinian uprising in the West Bank. Pictured here with his squad.

Courtesy of the Amir family

Amir during a trip he took with his girlfriend, Nava Holtzman, to Egypt's Sinai Desert in 1994. Holtzman broke off the relationship soon after their return.

Courtesy of the Amir family

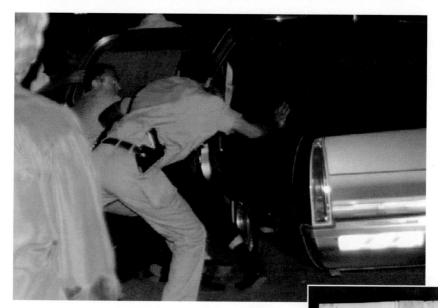

Moments after the shooting, November 4, 1995.
Police and security men lifting Rabin into the
back of the Cadillac.
Reuters

The song sheet Rabin tucked into his suit
jacket at the rally on November 4, 1995.
The title at the top: "A Song for Peace."
Sa'ar Ya'acov for the Israel Government Press Office

Rabin's family at the funeral, November 6, 1995. Left to right: son Yuval, wife
Leah, granddaughter Noa, daughter Dalia, and grandson Jonathan.
Tsvika Israeli for the Israel Government Press Office

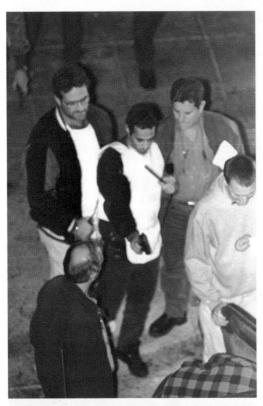

Amir reenacting the shooting for the police, days after the assassination. His interrogation-room bluster stunned investigators.

Nati Harnik for the Israel Government Press Office

At their trial, from left to right: Hagai Amir, Dror Adani, and Yigal Amir
(with a policeman seated between Adani and Amir).

Image Bank Israel/AFP

In April, Amir spotted an opportunity. At the end of the week-long Passover holiday, leaders of the Moroccan Jewish community would hold a banquet in Jerusalem to mark the end of the ban on eating *chametz*, or bread products—a Maghreb tradition known as Mimouna. Rabin would be there. In Israel's ethnically charged political climate, the Moroccans were a rising force, a group politicians regularly courted.

The event at the Nof Yerushalayim banquet hall fell on a Saturday night, April 22. Amir waited until after sunset, then drove to Jerusalem in Hagai's Volkswagen. He planned to talk his way in and sit as close to Rabin as possible. This would be his opportunity to reprise the wedding-hall encounter eighteen months earlier, when Amir could have killed Rabin but hesitated. But after a long wait at the entrance, organizers turned him away. The hall, perched on a hill overlooking the neighborhood of Bayit VeGan, could accommodate no more than twelve hundred people. Only ticket holders would get past the door.

Outside, Amir sized up his options. The banquet hall had two stories, its façade made almost entirely of glass. Rabin's Cadillac stood on the street abutting the entrance. Amir contemplated waiting near the car, hoping he could spot Rabin through the glass and charge at him when the prime minister emerged. But bodyguards congregated around the Cadillac and more security men sat with Rabin inside the hall. The protection procedures had clearly changed since the wedding. Amir recalled thinking at that early point, months after the Oslo signing, that he would regret not seizing the opportunity. And here he was, awash in regret. He spent one more minute considering whether he could force his way into the hall. But the lack of opportunity felt like a divine signal. "If God wants a person to commit an act, He lets him commit the act."

Amir slipped into the Volkswagen and drove back to Herzliya.

By the following month, Kalo at the Jewish Affairs Department had decided to sound another alarm over the possibility of a political murder. The prospect of a broader pullback in the West Bank had created more agitation in the settlements. YESHA Council rabbis were now drafting a new ruling calling on soldiers to refuse to evacuate army bases, an even more galling challenge to the sovereignty of the elected government than their effort to impede the dismantling of Tel Rumeida a year earlier. In early June, Kalo issued a "strategic warning" to agency officers and law-enforcement officials effectively saying that a Jewish assassin was out there, searching for an opportunity. To Kalo, the document reflected the increasingly dire picture his informants had been painting of radical settlers desperate to halt what they saw as a sacrilege against God. Intelligence analysts measured extremists in terms of their propensity for violence. Few were more dangerous than the religiously aggrieved.

But to others in the agency, it was one more intelligence assessment among many, one more document to read and file away. Analysts were paid to provide worst-case scenarios. Sometimes their reports pointed to real dangers and sometimes to what Israelis called *kisui tachat*, the ass-covering common to bureaucrats everywhere.

Kalo was certainly doing effective intelligence work—the kind he'd been trained to do against Palestinians. He had figured out that someone might try to kill Rabin and he had an informant, Avishai Raviv, watching the guy who was actually plotting murder. But the two ends weren't meeting. In part, it was Raviv's faulty estimation of Amir as nothing but a blowhard. But the agency itself had a too-narrow mental picture of the assassin based on its experience with Jewish terrorism. He would come from one of the hardcore settlements, as did Goldstein and members of the Jewish Underground. And his pedigree would be national religious, not ultra-Orthodox. The law student from Herzliya did not register as a threat.

In June 1995, a piece of information came in that should have helped the agency connect the dots.

Amir had continued bragging to people about his thwarted plot to kill Rabin at Yad Vashem, even five months after the event. One of them was Hila Frank, a twenty-three-year-old master's student in Bar-Ilan's history department. Frank had met Amir at one of the protests on campus and helped him organize the settlement weekends. She thought of him as a committed activist, smart and friendly, more radical than she was but certainly not a potential killer. Now, in the hallway of a building on campus, she stopped to talk to him about

Rabin. Alongside the things she'd heard him say before—that *din rodef* applied to the prime minister and he needed to be killed—he added the fact that he'd said *vidui* on the morning of the protest at Yad Vashem. The detail caught her attention. Religious Jews don't say the confessional prayer unless they really believe they're going to die.

Frank considered going to the police. If Amir was serious, the authorities needed to know. But if he said it just to impress her—he clearly liked flirting with women—she would land him in trouble over nothing. She shared the story with her boyfriend, Shlomi Halevy. A philosophy student at Hebrew University in Jerusalem, Halevy had served in an army intelligence unit and still did stints there as a reservist. He had also studied at Bar-Ilan before transferring to Jerusalem and knew Amir from the *kolel*. As she recounted the details, Halevy shot her a skeptical look. Lots of people on the religious right were wishing aloud that Rabin would die. "He didn't think it was a real threat," Frank would recall later.

Still, the two of them kept coming back to the *vidui*, a detail that seemed to give the story more credibility. Amir had a gun; everyone knew that. And there was an intensity to his anger at the government that set him apart. Could he be the kind of braggart who also followed through on his threats? Halevy proposed a compromise. He would convey some of the information to his commanding officer in the intelligence unit without naming Amir. On his own later, Halevy prepared his story. He would say that he overheard two young men talking in a public bathroom at the Tel Aviv central bus station, among the most teeming spots in the city. In their conversation, he would recount to his officer, one of the young men claimed to know a person who planned to kill Rabin and had already said the *vidui*. Halevy would claim no names were mentioned but that the young man described the would-be assassin as a short Yemeni guy with curly hair.

If Halevy had intended to test the efficiency of the separate intelligence agencies in Israel at sharing information, the bureaucracy scored well. After hearing the story, his officer wrote a report and sent it to Shabak, where it made its way to the Jewish Affairs Department. But officers in the department—the people more keenly attuned than anyone in the country to the possibility of a political assassination—found it unremarkable. The details were vague and there was no reason to believe the source had more to tell. "It didn't raise any red flags because this was a guy from inside the intelligence community. If he was a guy from Kiryat Arba, we would have interrogated him right away," Kalo would say later. "There was a lot of intelligence noise. This was one more item." Instead of summoning Halevy to Shabak for questioning, the agency asked the police to handle it.

At Jerusalem's police headquarters, Halevy stuck to his story, claiming he sat in one of the stalls while the two young men spoke to each other over the urinal. To the two investigators in the room, it should have seemed improbable. Witnesses who claimed to have overheard bits of information in random circumstances were often hiding something, so often that Israeli security officials had a name for their stories. They called them *yediot halon*, roughly translated as "under-the-window tales," as in: I was standing under a window when I heard someone above me say something incriminating. In real life, assassination plans are not overheard in public bathrooms. But instead of pressing further, the investigators made the mistake of assuming an intelligence officer would not withhold information. They took down Halevy's story and released him after a friendly exchange. Halevy told Frank later that he would have named Amir had police pressured him even slightly.

Shabak interrogators would surely have pressed harder—they were known to be thorough. But Kalo's department had waived the opportunity to have its own men sit with Halevy. Still, even with that misstep, it now had a pertinent bit of information. A short Yemeni guy with curly hair planned to kill the prime minister and had already said the *vidui*. Finding him might have been just a matter of circulating the tip among agency informants along with a question—does this description match anyone you know? The profile lacked the specificity required for tracing a suspect from a population of 5.5 million. But right-wing extremists numbered no more than a few thousand, and many of them operated under the gaze of Shabak informants. Avishai Raviv knew a short Yemeni guy with curly hair. By now, that guy had endeavored twice to kill the prime minister.

SOMEHOW, THE JEWISH Affairs Department saw no way to make use of the information. It did, however, relay the report to Dignitary Protection, the unit within Shabak responsible for guarding the prime minister and other VIPs. If Arab Affairs occupied the top rung on the agency ladder, the protection unit lingered at the bottom. Its senior officers had no role in intelligence gathering—the agency's core function—and met with the head of Shabak on average only once every two years. Guarding dignitaries at their offices and in their homes, as they made their way from one public event to another, involved complicated planning. But to outsiders it could seem like mere muscle work. It helped little that recruits often resembled nightclub bouncers, with gorged biceps and wraparound glasses. In Shabak's early years, the department had been known as the Escort Unit, a name some in the agency's other branches still invoked with a sneer.

Several people in the unit read the report, including Dror Mor, the officer in charge of Rabin's security detail. Though his job entailed more planning than actual guarding, Mor had served as a regular on Rabin's detail in the 1980s, picking him up from his home on Rav Ashi at five in the morning on many days and staying with him until midnight. With all those hours together—more than Rabin spent with his closest advisers or even family members on a given day— Mor came to know him intimately. How this man who had been a public figure for most of his life remained so painfully shy baffled him. Rabin seemed to relish the interaction with soldiers at dusty military bases while dreading the small talk at dinners and cocktail parties— and the attire as well. When Mor came to pick him up one evening in a jacket and tie for a formal event, Rabin groused softly. "If you're wearing one, I'm going to have to wear one," he said, and retreated to the bedroom to change.

Mor found the detail about the short Yemeni guy determined to kill Rabin noteworthy. For decades, the protection unit was certain of only one thing when it came to assassination scenarios: the shooter would be an Arab. But Mor and others knew that assumption no longer applied. After Oslo, the unit had introduced a new drill for coping with right-wing protests at events attended by Rabin. Known as *keren zavit* (translated roughly as "secluded corner"), the drill specifically factored the possibility of Jews perpetrating violence at or around Rabin. "We took it into consideration; we understood it could happen," Mor recalled later. Halevy's statement to police seemed to substantiate the threat. Mor conveyed the vague profile to the rest of the detail. At a meeting sometime later, he asked members of the Jewish Affairs Department whether they followed up on the report and what came of it.

But even as the perception of the threat against Rabin shifted, the unit did what bureaucracies tend to do: it remained fixed in its old approach. Dignitary Protection had a near perfect record, at least within the borders of Israel. It had never lost a VIP. Though much of the credit belonged to Shabak's intelligence gatherers, the bodyguards regarded themselves as the best in the world. All were graduates of military combat units and some had served in special operations forces. Shabak trained them to put a bullet in an assailant no longer than 1.8 seconds after the start of a potentially lethal event. Recruits who couldn't draw and fire fast enough did not graduate from the training course. "Dignitary Protection was a cocky unit. Good but cocky," recalled Shlomo Harnoy, one of its veterans.

The hubris bred a kind of institutional certainty that nothing bad could happen as long as the bodyguards showed up. It also fostered a culture of condescension toward outsiders, especially those who dared to offer suggestions or criticism. That, anyway, was the experience of a certain Shabak officer who served in one of the agency's other departments and happened to live in Rabin's neighborhood. The officer noticed that Rabin walked from his home to a country club in the area to play tennis every Saturday morning, often with Leah. Though it was a short walk and the prime minister had guards with him, he left the house at the same hour every week and took the same route to the club—basic mistakes in bodyguard tradecraft. "There were a lot of tall buildings around [where a shooter could set up] and the smell of assassination was in the air," he recalled. The officer took up the issue with the head of the Dignitary Protection Unit. The response he got amounted to a bureaucratic brush-back: Relax, everything's under control.

That arrogance extended to other parts of Shabak as well. When Mor raised the Halevy issue with the Jewish Affairs Department, he was similarly rebuffed.

Gillon, who had spent his entire career in Shabak, knew the agency's shortcomings. But he was still new to the job, serving a man who had shown only tenuous confidence in him and coping with the bloodiest waves of Palestinian violence on record—on top of the right's surging radicalism. In late June, Israeli and Palestinian negotiators engaging in marathon talks in the Egyptian resort town of Taba announced they would not meet their deadline for the Oslo II agreement. Gillon would have more time to prepare for the redeployment. But as the summer heat blistered across the country, members of the settler group Zo Artzeinu launched a new round of protests, blocking key intersections and creating huge traffic jams. Their rhetoric grew so nasty that Gillon decided to appeal directly to opposition leaders and members of the YESHA Council to help lower the temperature.

Most right-wing leaders welcomed the dialogue but the meetings produced nothing tangible. Gillon argued that hotheads on the right might misinterpret the references to Rabin as a traitor and a murderer as an explicit call for violence. He asked the leaders to exert their influence over the rank and file—or to simply refuse to speak at demonstrations where protesters engaged in incitement. The settlers, who suspected Gillon identified with Rabin politically, felt he was dwelling on the actions of a few insignificant rabble-rousers in order to tarnish the entire nationalist camp. They accused him of trying to stifle legitimate protests.

Gillon also made his pitch to a group of senior columnists, asking them to refrain from writing anything overtly inflammatory. The Shabak chief had rarely engaged with members of the media—most knew him only by the initial Kaf. Though meeting this man of secrets was clearly a dream for journalists, at least some resented his message as an attempt to mobilize the press on Shabak's behalf. Yoel Marcus of the left-leaning *Ha'aretz* newspaper wrote later that the interaction made him feel like he lived in a banana republic. "Israel is not a country of political assassinations, thank God," he wrote.

Gillon's initiatives were all meeting resistance: the Cadillac, the bulletproof vest, the appeals to settler leaders and journalists. Now he faced yet another challenge: Avishai Raviv's handlers felt they'd lost control of their agent. Raviv kept running amok, assaulting Palestinians and pushing the limits of what the agency thought it could justify. In the messy business of undercover work, informants sometimes broke laws. A reputation for delinquency helped an agent maintain his cover and attract the real criminals or extremists. But Shabak had been forced to intercede with the police or the Justice Department eleven times in the years it had been running Raviv in order to head off indictments. The agency had warned him repeatedly that he would lose his immunity. Yet he continued to demonstrate an almost obsessive hooliganism—and Shabak continued to protect him.

In late July, the agency summoned Raviv for what it termed a "peeling off" meeting: a daylong session in which the informant would come clean about his offenses and submit to a lie-detector test and a psychiatric evaluation. Raviv's handlers wanted a catalogue of every crime he'd committed, whether police knew about it or not. Over several hours, the informant spared no detail. He confessed to attacking Palestinians dozens of times, often in the Hebron area and often at random, using brass knuckles, slingshots, a crossbow, a flare gun, knives, and even a real gun he borrowed from a friend. He also admitted to teaching two minors how to make petrol bombs. It was a deeply troubling list. Innocent Palestinians were being victimized regularly by a man who drew his salary from Shabak. And by seeking publicity for his thuggery, Raviv contributed to the image of the settlers as violent extremists—a reputation already well established through the acts of Baruch Goldstein and others.

Still, Raviv had shown his value again and again and this was no time to forfeit intelligence assets. His handlers decided to deliver yet another rebuke. They ordered him to get prior permission for even the tiniest infraction. Raviv promised to comply, as he had on previous occasions. But he persisted with the provocations. Several weeks after the meeting, he staged a nighttime swearing-in ceremony for new members of his Eyal militia at the national cemetery in Jerusalem, complete with guns and balaclavas. With an Israeli television crew filming the event—it would air on Channel One's nightly newscast— each member pledged to fight the Rabin government to his dying breath. "Much blood will be spilled," Raviv promised from behind a ski mask. To the few people who knew that Raviv worked for Shabak, the paradox could not have been more stark. Gillon had been making the case to settlers and journalists—to anyone willing to listen—that inflammatory rhetoric would lead to violence. Yet here was his own informant engaging in precisely such rhetoric. Raviv's undercover work had created a complicated arithmetic: Even his handlers could no longer tell if the benefits canceled out the damage.

With so much going on, Gillon was now meeting Rabin almost every day. Over the summer, the two men reached an understanding about the Cadillac. Rabin would ride in the armored car whenever he attended events that appeared on his calendar—the kind a potential assassin might learn about from the media. For unscheduled events, he would have his driver bring the Caprice. Though Rabin occasionally strayed from the agreement, it seemed to set the relationship on a better footing. Rabin felt comfortable with security people, and Gillon warmed to his boss's forthrightness. He also identified with Rabin's social unease. At a gathering in the Caesarea home of President Ezer Weizman around midsummer, Gillon wandered through the house to get away from the crowd. He found Rabin alone in a back room, watching a soccer match on television. The two men remained there together until the game ended.

The delay in the negotiations gave the Amir brothers a respite as well. Three months had passed since Yigal's aborted mission at the banquet hall in Jerusalem. When he told his brother about it, Hagai became more determined than ever to forge a better plan, something other than a suicide operation. Killing Rabin with a handgun meant his brother would need to get within a few feet of the prime minister—and within easy range of his bodyguards. With an assault rifle, he could shoot him from a safe distance. Hagai had enough money to afford a rifle but by law, Israelis could only buy handguns; assault weapons were issued by the military.

Hagai called the liaison officer in his infantry unit and asked to sign out an M16 rifle. His official address remained at the settlement Shavei Shomron, where his uncle lived. Hagai argued that the hour-long drive between the settlement and his college at Ariel, also in the West Bank, took him through areas where Palestinians frequently stoned Israeli cars. He needed more than a handgun to feel safe.

His company commander turned down the request. The army had issued thousands of guns to settlers over the years and incorporated these armed civilians in community patrol units. By the 1990s, some military officials worried about blowback—the possibility that settlers might turn their guns against the army if it tried to evacuate them under a peace agreement. The Hebron massacre prompted a reassessment of the gun policy; Goldstein had used an army-issued weapon in the shooting. In a phone call, the liaison officer explained that only reservists with a rank of lieutenant or higher were now eligible to sign out rifles. Hagai was a sergeant.

With that idea nixed, the brothers talked almost obsessively about other ways to kill Rabin. Sometimes, Dror Adani joined the conversation. Amir had decided Adani would make a good match for his younger sister Vardit. He brought him to the house several times to get to know her. But Vardit showed little interest and, when they ran out of things to talk about, Adani would head upstairs to sit with Amir and Hagai. As the summer wore on, the brothers confided more in Adani than in anyone else. Ohad Skornik had proposed to a woman at the end of the school year—a fellow student he'd met on one of the settlement weekends—and lost interest in the militia plan.

The ideas they discussed together ranged from the impractical to the bizarre (just outside the room, two washing machines ran almost constantly, muffling their voices). Adani favored bombing Rabin's car but had no idea how to plant the explosives without getting caught. Amir talked about trying to get an interview with Rabin for a student journal and smuggling in a gun disguised as a microphone—or hiding a bomb in the tape recorder. Hagai's idea of injecting nitroglycerin into the pipes of the building on Rav Ashi prompted cackles. But even when the conversations strayed to the absurd, Adani, perhaps alone among Amir's friends, actually believed Amir intended to kill the prime minister. "He really wanted to kill Rabin," he would say later. And his outlook in those conversations seemed remarkably similar to Amir's. Adani believed fully that *din rodef* applied to Rabin. He agreed that a death sentence hung over the prime minister. Occasionally, he raised the concern that murdering Rabin would harm Jewish cohesion, itself a religious precept. But Amir insisted that preventing a withdrawal from the West Bank was more important. Without Rabin, the peace process would collapse in a heap.

At the close of summer, as Oslo's second anniversary approached, Amir tried one more time to come face-to-face with Rabin. The prime minister would be inaugurating an underpass designed to ease the rush-hour traffic at a junction north of Tel Aviv. In Taba, Israeli and Palestinian negotiators were close to finalizing the Oslo II agreement. Amir thought this might be his last chance to stop the handover of West Bank territory to the Palestinians. The Kfar Shmaryahu junction lay just ten minutes from his home; he knew the area well. An outdoor event would be easier to infiltrate, he thought. For the third time in nine months, he packed his gun and headed out to kill Rabin. But once again God seemed to offer no guidance, no help. Amir arrived at ten in the morning, noticed just a few people milling about, and decided to drive around for an hour. When he returned, Rabin had come and gone.

Amir had been pursuing Rabin for two years now while the prime minister moved closer to his objective: ending the corrosive military occupation in the West Bank and Gaza and forging peace agreements with all of Israel's neighbors. Rabin had taken huge strides while his stalker mostly blustered and schemed. But a fanaticism defined Amir's pursuit of Rabin—so much so that any honest interpretation of the Talmudic principle he fixated on would have pointed back at him.

Amir was the real *rodef.*

CHAPTER 7

Seam Zone

"You don't make peace by sitting in your living room.
Show up and make a difference."

—ADVERTISEMENT IN *Yedioth Ahronoth*

Rabin's negotiators clinched the Oslo II agreement with their
Palestinian counterparts on September 24, 1995. Amir, gloomy
and irritable, organized a student weekend in Hebron, where
the extremists would be gathering.

The agreement called for Israel to withdraw from all seven cities in
the West Bank, including Hebron—though hundreds of troops would
remain behind to protect the Jewish enclaves there. Israel would also
hand over hundreds of towns and villages in several stages. Oslo II
would not end the occupation. Large swaths of the West Bank and
Gaza, including the settlements and areas defined as "military zones,"
would remain in Israeli hands until the two sides negotiated a final
agreement. In the interim period, Israel would continue controlling
the borders, religious sites like the Cave of the Patriarchs, the water
aquifers, and other natural resources. But the deal would free most
Palestinians from many of the day-to-day encumbrances of Israeli
military rule. And it would signal to the settlers that their enterprise

had been a historic misstep, one the government was now bent on reversing. The settlement movement had grown accustomed to getting its way. It had amassed far more influence and power than its size merited. Rabin was now declaring that the tail would no longer wag the dog.

Rabin traveled to Washington toward the end of the month for another White House signing ceremony with Arafat. Though the agreement had far more breadth and detail than the original Oslo deal—it ran to 460 pages—the ceremony itself lacked the drama of the signing two years earlier. It took place in the White House East Room in the presence of a few hundred congressmen and diplomats. Journalists from around the world covered the event, but not a single American network transmitted it live. The exhilaration of 1993 had given way to temperance and even caution. But the two leaders now seemed more at ease with each other. Martin Indyk, who had left the White House to serve as the US ambassador in Tel Aviv, watched Arafat press his arm to Rabin's back at one point and marveled that Rabin let it linger there. "Today we are more sober," the Israeli leader said in his speech. "We are gladdened by the potential for reconciliation, but we are also wary of the dangers that lurk on every side."

At a reception hosted by Clinton at the Corcoran Gallery across from the White House that evening, Rabin spoke unambiguously about the Palestinian right to self-determination. His unscripted comment drew applause. When Arafat remarked warmly that Jews and Arabs had always been cousins but were now peace partners, Rabin responded with a tease. He explained that Jews were not famous for their athletic abilities but had a gift for speechmaking. Then he turned to Arafat and said playfully: "It seems to me, Mr. Chairman, that you might be a little Jewish." Indyk would write later: "At that moment many thought the Arab-Israeli peace process had reached a tipping point. It seemed only a matter of time before a Palestinian state would be established in most of the West Bank and Gaza."

In Israel, Rabin's opponents sensed the tipping point as well. Rowdy street protesters now clashed with policemen almost every day somewhere around the country. In the settlements, rabbis and YESHA Council leaders talked openly about sabotaging the deal, whether by seizing military bases the army would evacuate or urging soldiers yet again to disobey withdrawal orders. By signing the Oslo II agreement, Rabin had defied biblical injunctions and undermined the redemption process that messianists believed had been under way since 1967. That alone made it an abomination for religious rightists— even as they framed their opposition to the handover of more land as largely a security issue.

Amir headed to Hebron the day after the Washington signing, taking more than 500 students with him from Bar-Ilan. The large turnout should have pleased him—the school year hadn't even begun yet. The students, including Margalit Har-Shefi and Avishai Raviv, jammed the sidewalk at the entrance to the university, waiting to board the eight buses he and the other organizers had leased. But Amir bristled at the mingling and the banter. Where was the outrage? He'd been organizing protests since the first Oslo Accord, hoping they would help foment a rebellion. Instead, the events allowed these recreants to feel they were doing something significant while mainly shopping for spouses. He looked forward to interacting with the ideologues and the hotheads of Hebron.

They were all there. Though it would take months to implement Oslo II, activists had been heading to Hebron for days to try to block the agreement or at least vent their anger. By the time the buses from Bar-Ilan arrived, the scene outside the Cave of the Patriarchs resembled a Hasidic block party: music blaring from speakers, settler spokesmen leading tours of the area, men shouldering assault rifles, and women carrying babies. Along Shuhada Street, settlers had been waging a constant battle to displace Palestinian street merchants. Now Israelis who had only just set foot in Hebron scowled at the vendors. Amir instructed the students to set up their sleeping bags in the seminaries or prayer halls scattered around the enclaves—wherever they found room. He and Hagai, who came straight from a stint in reserve duty still clad in his military fatigues, climbed the roof of a building intending to sleep under the stars.

The weekend offered a little of everything. In a Saturday-morning sermon, Rabbi Eliezer Waldman excoriated Rabin for handing Jews over to the enemy. "We have total and absolute right to this place," he intoned from a podium. "The government is against us, collaborating with the Arabs." Later, Amir and other students joined settlers on a rampage through Arab areas of Hebron. The group smashed a windshield and broke the camera of a Palestinian photographer. At meals, Amir would stand up and announce upcoming events, sounding surly and impatient. At one point, he led a group to Baruch Goldstein's grave in Kiryat Arba.

On the way back to Bar-Ilan, Amir and the other organizers handed out forms asking people to check off what they could do to help the settlers of Hebron. The options included moving to one of the enclaves and, at a lesser level of commitment, joining settler patrols. Many of the papers ended up on the floor. For the two-hour ride, Amir sat with his friends at the front of one of the buses and said little. For all the spiritedness these weekends inspired, the rightists had been dealt a stinging defeat with the signing of Oslo II, he thought. If this was Israel's civil war, Rabin was winning.

Israelis marked Yom Kippur the following week, the holiest day of the year. Religious Jews fasted and prayed while secular Israelis, many of them anyway, spent the day on their bicycles. With a virtual ban on motorized travel, cyclists of all ages own the roads for twenty-four hours every year, swarming main arteries, riding even on highways. And yet, for all the reverence (and recreation), the political spasms continued. Rabin still had to win the endorsement of parliament for the Oslo II agreement, and the vote was sure to be close. As the debate got under way in Jerusalem on October 6, protests around the city grew steadily more sinister and frenzied, with the aggression directed mainly at Rabin.

In the afternoon, a group of extremists led by the former Kach activist Avigdor Eskin gathered outside Rabin's official residence to pronounce a kind of Kabalistic death curse against the prime minister. Known by its Aramaic name Pulsa diNura (blaze of fire), the curse involved a complicated series of procedures and carried certain risks for its invokers: it would rebound against them if the target of the malediction turned out to be innocent. But if guilty, he would die within thirty days. One of the participants would say later that the ritual in Jerusalem had been preceded by a more official ceremony in

Safed with some twenty rabbis and scholars, a sizeable gathering of extremists that Shabak somehow failed to detect. Eskin and the other participants recited the curse from photocopied pages: "Angels of destruction will hit him. He is damned where he goes. His soul will instantly leave his body . . . and he will not survive the month. Dark will be his path and God's angel will chase him. A disaster he has never experienced will beget him and all curses known in the Torah will apply to him."

Later in the evening, tens of thousands of people gathered at Zion Square for the largest anti-government protest in years. The square at one of Jerusalem's main intersections had long been a venue for right-wing demonstrations—and also tourist gatherings and the occasional terrorist attack. For some two hours, Benjamin Netanyahu and a phalanx of other right-wing leaders stood on the balcony of the Ron Hotel above the square and watched as protesters came unhinged, burning pictures of the prime minister, chanting "Death to Rabin" in a pulsating frenzy, then "Rabin the Nazi," and "In blood and fire, we'll drive out Rabin." One of the demonstrators had brought a stack of photocopied pages with distorted images of the prime minister, including one showing his head superimposed on the body of a dog and another of Rabin dressed in a Nazi uniform. Raviv, who drove from Kiryat Arba to attend the rally, spotted a youngster handing them out and saw an opportunity for more of the publicity he craved. He grabbed one of the Nazi images and delivered it to the hands of an Israeli television reporter, who promptly displayed it to viewers in a live broadcast.

On the balcony, Netanyahu seemed unfazed by the mayhem— even as protesters threw burning torches at the line of policemen. Any effort to call the crowd to order could well have turned the extremists against him, a risk Netanyahu evidently did not wish to take. Instead, he castigated Rabin for relying on the backing of Arab-Israeli parliament members to get his agreement through parliament. Lawmakers had yet to vote on Oslo II, but it was clear by now that Rabin would need the representatives of Israel's Arab minority to support it in order for the deal to pass. Though Arab-Israelis were full-fledged citizens and made up one-sixth of the population, Netanyahu and many other rightists were now arguing, unblushingly, that an endorsement that rested on the support of non-Jews would lack legitimacy. "The Jewish majority of the state of Israel has not approved the agreement," he said. "We will fight and we will bring down the government."

The protest ended around ten p.m., but instead of dispersing, thousands of demonstrators marched on the Knesset, where legislators would debate the accord into the night. All 120 parliament members had signed up to address the plenum before the vote; each was entitled to five minutes at the microphone. As the crowd outside swelled, hundreds of policemen rushed from other parts of the city to the parliament building and formed a human cordon. For the first time in Israel's history, it seemed the Knesset might be overrun.

Menachem Damti, who served as Rabin's alternate driver, happened to be making his way to the Knesset in the Cadillac. A block from the building, protesters swarmed the car, rocking it back and forth, climbing the hood and pounding on the roof. Fearing a lynching, Damti locked the doors and inched his way forward until policemen arrived and pulled people off the car. But in the melee, one of the protesters managed to rip the hood ornament from the Cadillac. A nineteen-year-old Kach activist, Itamar Ben-Gvir, held up the ornament during a television interview later and made what could only be interpreted as a death threat. "This is the ornament. People managed to remove the ornament from the car. And just as we got to the ornament, we can get to Rabin," he said.

One of Rabin's cabinet ministers, Binyamin Ben-Eliezer, got caught up in the mob as well. A retired general who had served in an elite commando unit and suffered war wounds, Ben-Eliezer told friends later that he felt more threatened in the car than in his toughest moments on the battlefield. When he reached the Knesset building, Ben-Eliezer tracked down Netanyahu in one of the corridors and launched at him. "You better restrain your people, otherwise it will end in murder. They tried to kill me just now. . . . If someone is murdered, the blood will be on your hands."

By the time lawmakers voted on the Oslo II Accord sometime after three in the morning, most of the protesters had gone home. Rabin managed to rally sixty-one votes to the opposition's fifty-nine—a narrow margin but a majority nonetheless. Yoel Bin-Nun, the settler rabbi who had been corresponding with Rabin for more than three years, now crafted his harshest letter yet to the prime minister. "Your success at passing the agreement . . . is formal and legal but cannot be binding on the entire nation of Israel, either morally or historically. It certainly cannot obligate Jewish history," he wrote. Still, he vowed to fight those members of the right-wing camp calling for an insurrection. "I will continue opposing any attempt to go against the law and against the democratic foundation, which remains the one thing that stands between us and a civil war."

From both sides of the political divide, the civil-war scenario now seemed at least plausible. Israel had reached a crossroads on a matter that would define its very character, with implications for territory, rights, and religion, and with two roughly equal camps pulling in opposite directions. What would Israel be and what would it do? Would it surrender land some regarded as a Jewish birthright or maintain a system of rule in the West Bank and Gaza that privileged Jews and disenfranchised Palestinians?

Amir, who had attended the rally at Zion Square and then made his way to the Knesset, somehow missed the ransacking of Rabin's car. When he spotted Har-Shefi on the street later, he told her he was mad at himself for having been elsewhere. But a certain line had been crossed in Jerusalem and Amir felt it. A few days later, he watched another right-wing outburst on television. At an annual gathering of American immigrants at the Wingate Institute north of Tel Aviv, a protester charged at Rabin, getting to within a few feet of him before being intercepted by a bodyguard. The assailant didn't exactly fit the profile of the right-wing hothead. He was later identified as Natan Ofir, a middle-aged rabbi employed by the Hebrew University. But the mayhem at Zion Square had set a new standard for protesters; Ofir kicked and spat at policemen who tried to arrest him. To Amir, the details were less important than the lesson the event offered: Had Ofir been armed, he could have killed Rabin.

The spiraling protests posed a dilemma for Rabin, who hoped to get reelected in a year's time. The demonstrations created the perception that Israelis overwhelmingly opposed his policies. But Rabin hated the idea of initiating a pro-government rally—it smacked of authoritarianism. Still, while his own polls gave him a small lead over Netanyahu, he worried that perceptions could shape political reality.

Haber shared his boss's reluctance. When two figures from outside the Labor Party—the former Tel Aviv mayor Shlomo Lahat and the French businessman Jean Friedman—approached the prime minister's office in early October with their own plans for a peace rally, his response was tepid. Haber felt that a small turnout, either due to bad weather or because people were more inclined to rally *against* policies than in favor—would create the impression that the public lacked confidence in Rabin. And if large numbers of people did show up, the government would be accused of using its influence with the labor unions to bolster attendance. It was a lose-lose.

Lahat, who had served alongside Rabin in the military decades earlier, came back with a new plan: a rally against violence—to address one of Haber's points—and in favor of peace. The theme would reference the right's rising hooliganism and its threat to Israeli democracy. It would also gesture at Hamas and its suicide attacks, recasting the regional conflict as a dispute between moderates and extremists, whether Palestinian or Israeli. As the idea circulated, Peres began pressing for the rally as well.

Sometime after the Wingate incident, Rabin relented. With the calendar out, Haber suggested November 4, a Saturday night following the prime minister's return from the United Nations General Assembly meeting in New York. Rabin would deliver the main address. The plan quickly gained momentum, with peace groups offering their help and popular musicians agreeing to perform. Lahat chose the Kings of Israel Square as the venue, a huge plaza adjacent to Tel Aviv's city hall building that could accommodate more than 100,000 people. The square had been the scene of the largest protest in Israel's history—against the Lebanon War in 1982. Friedman, a contributor to Israeli political campaigns over the years, paid for several large newspaper advertisements to promote the rally, including one in *Yedioth Ahronoth* that read: "You don't make peace by sitting in your living room. Show up and make a difference.

"Yes to peace, no to violence."

With the event now two weeks away, Rabin cycled between the parts of his job he liked most and least—the closed-door security meetings and the big public events. In Tel Aviv, he deliberated for several days whether to allow a Mossad hit team to kill Fathi Shaqaqi, the Islamic Jihad leader who had boasted to a British newspaper about his role in the double suicide attack in Netanya back in January. The assassination in Malta days later would come off cleanly. At the UN General Assembly, where Israelis often received icy receptions, Rabin drew more attention than just about any other political figure. Haber struggled to make time on the prime minister's schedule to accommodate all those world leaders who wanted their pictures taken with Rabin. Apparently, the memento had political value at home.

Amir spent the last days of October with the regulars from Bar-Ilan—though, as usual, not in class. He attended Skornik's wedding in Tel Aviv, a glitzy affair held at the same banquet hall where Amir had first seen Rabin in person two years earlier. Skornik would notice in a video of the reception later that Amir seemed to be brooding and off to the side much of the time. Amir also organized a birthday party for Nili Kolman at a makeshift settlement that Bar-Ilan students had been visiting regularly since the summer. Among scattered trailers and an improvised synagogue, the students talked about starting their own settlement when the Likud Party eventually returned to power and ended the construction freeze. Kolman had distanced herself from Amir months earlier to avoid leading him on. Now the two were friendly again.

The day before the rally, Amir pondered whether to try to kill the prime minister at Kings of Israel Square. The start of the dreaded pullback in the West Bank was now only weeks away. Already, Israel was handing over government compounds to Palestinians in Jenin and elsewhere. But police had announced road closures around the plaza ahead of the event, which meant security would be tight. After three failed attempts to get close to Rabin, Amir had begun to think God did not intend for him to do the job. In the early afternoon, he returned home from Bar-Ilan and spotted Hagai in the front yard. Impulsively, he suggested they drive to Shavei Shomron to spend the weekend with their uncle. Had Hagai agreed, the two brothers would have remained at the settlement until the end of the Sabbath and returned to Herzliya late Saturday, too late to get to the rally.

But Hagai felt drained from the long week at school. The sky had been gray since morning and the idea of driving back into the West Bank in what might be rainy weather seemed unappealing. Instead, Hagai tinkered in the shed and then lounged around the house. Amir spent the afternoon talking to people by phone, organizing another settlement weekend. To Kolman, one of the people he reached, Amir seemed irritable. They discussed the counter-rally that right-ists planned to stage at the plaza the next day, but Amir did not say whether he intended to go.

At Rabin's apartment, the family gathered for Friday night dinner at 8 p.m. sharp, as usual. Dalia had been hosting a group from abroad and could not attend, but Yuval, who had been living in North Carolina, was now back in Israel. He arrived with a new girlfriend, Tali Henkin, who seemed surprised to find so few bodyguards posted around the building. With extremists now openly threatening the prime minister, charging him at public events, and ransacking his car, she expected a small army at the entrance. "The security is a joke," she remarked in the narrow elevator. Yuval put a finger to his lips to indicate the issue should not be raised at the dinner table.

"We don't talk about things like that at home."

———————

AT AROUND NOON the next day, Police Chief Superintendent Motti Naftali began directing preparations at the plaza. A twenty-year veteran of the force who smoked a pipe during most hours of the workday, Naftali had helped write the operational plan for the event—the document that outlined how police would maintain security at the rally. Lahat had told him to expect up to 100,000 people, a huge crowd in a square the size of several football fields. If a Hamas suicide bomber managed to blow himself up at the rally, the casualty toll would be enormous. Naftali had seen the effects of suicide attacks. A year earlier, he had surveyed the scene of the Tel Aviv bus bombing.

Among the fragments and body parts, he spotted the severed head of the bomber. The security plan now included blocking roads to traffic around Kings of Israel Square and ringing the plaza with police barricades. Rally-goers would have to approach on foot and get searched by policemen on their way in.

Shabak took charge of security in the inner circle—the stage where the politicians and performers would gather and the open-air parking area just north of it. Though police bore overall responsibility for the event, officers from Shabak's Dignitary Protection Unit exercised a certain authority over police, at least as far as the security of Rabin and the rest of the dignitaries was concerned. With Shabak chief Carmi Gillon in Paris on a work visit for the weekend, the head of the Protection Department would be the agency's senior officer at the event.

The officers now walked the length of the plaza with Naftali and other police officials, pointing out rooftops where snipers should be posted and areas around the stage where they wanted walk-through metal detectors. The Shabak operational plan called for the stage and the parking lot to be "sterile zones," meaning only authorized personnel would be allowed entry, a group that included VIPs, accredited journalists, performers, and their roadies.

The parking lot demanded particular attention. The stage itself was on a raised platform, accessible by two separate staircases. Keeping crowds away was simply a matter of restricting admission at two points. But the parking lot, adjoining one of the staircases, was at street level, exposed from above and open at either end. In the language of dignitary protection, the parking lot was a "seam zone," a potentially dangerous corridor the dignitary would need to traverse in order to get from one relatively safe area to another—in this case, the car and the stage. Shabak cadets were taught that most assassination attempts occurred in seam zones, including the one against President Reagan in Washington in 1981. It was a lesson they learned on day one of their training. To secure the lot, Shabak had policemen stand at both ends—along a police barricade at one side and a rising and falling barrier gate at the other.

Around the plaza in what was now early afternoon, Tel Aviv came to life. A surge of Mediterranean sunshine had burned off the morning haze, drawing people to the sidewalk cafés that dotted the city. At one of the cafés across from Kings of Israel Square, Dror Mor, the Shabak officer who oversaw Rabin's security detail, sat with a friend and sipped a cup of milky coffee, *kafeh hafuch*. Mor had no role in the security plan that day, but his subordinates would be working the event, including the two young bodyguards, Shai Glaser and Yoram Rubin. Though Glaser was just twenty-five and Rubin thirty, both had already protected Rabin at hundreds of events.

At one point the conversation turned to politics. Mor's friend, a well-known sports analyst, probed whether the prime minister was taking seriously the threat posed to him by right-wing extremists. "Rabin is going to be assassinated," the sports analyst said suddenly. "You guys need to be aware of it and if you want, I'll explain it to him." Mor had spent much of his time in the preceding months assessing the potential for right-wing violence, but his friend's vehemence surprised him.

At Rav Ashi, some fifteen minutes north of the square, Rabin worked in the den of his apartment through the afternoon. Earlier in the day he had denied the army's request to target a certain Lebanese militant whose location intelligence analysts had suddenly pinpointed. The potential retribution seemed to outweigh the benefits of the strike. Now he tried on the phone to defuse a crisis with Peres, who had been threatening to challenge Rabin in the upcoming Labor Party primaries if he didn't get more say in future political appointments. The two men had come to accept their partnership in the preceding years as a kind of providence but the occasional argument still stirred up old resentments.

Throughout the day, Rabin worried whether people would show up at the rally. The night before, Lahat reassured him the square would be full. If not, he joked, the two of them would have the plaza to themselves. "You bring Leah, I'll bring [my wife] Ziva. The performers will be there. . . . We can dance alone at the square." Sure enough, by 7 p.m., the official start time, Israel Radio reported that thousands of people had arrived and thousands more were streaming toward the plaza. Lahat had asked Rabin to get there at 8:15 p.m.

for his address. At 7:45 p.m., Yoram Rubin, who commanded the five-member close-protection team that night, knocked on Rabin's door to say the Cadillac was waiting downstairs.

In the car, Rubin sat up front, alongside Rabin's alternate driver, Menachem Damti. The prime minister and his wife sat in the back, where dark curtains covered the windows. Three other bodyguards rode in the Caprice, which trailed the Cadillac. In his earpiece, Rubin could hear the communications between various Shabak officers. At one point, he turned toward Rabin to report what was being said: Intelligence gatherers had picked up something about a Palestinian suicide bomber intending to strike at the rally. Perhaps this was Islamic Jihad trying to avenge the assassination of its leader in Malta the week before. Within minutes, Danny Yatom phoned the car to deliver the same news. Then he called Shabak to ask that security around the prime minister be enhanced. Leah felt a wave of dread wash over her, but Rabin seemed unfazed. Intelligence warnings were often false alarms.

By 8:15 p.m., the crowd had swelled to more than 100,000. Lahat met Rabin at the car and walked him to the edge of the platform to take in the view: A stunning mass of people, bobbing and swaying to the music blaring from the stage. Rabin's supporters had filled every inch of the plaza and its surrounding streets. On a side road, police had cordoned off an area for the counter-rally. Only a few dozen rightists showed up, including Avishai Raviv.

Amir was on his way. In Herzliya, he'd kept to himself throughout most of the day. After telling Hagai in the morning that he'd decided to try to kill Rabin at the rally, he made no further mention of it. He ate lunch with the family, then sat in the living room and read from one of the religious texts stacked tightly on the shelf. At synagogue in the evening, Amir quietly asked God to let him accomplish the thing he'd been endeavoring to do for two years now and he repeated the *vidui*—the prayer Jews say before death. Though Hagai didn't know it, Amir had paid a quick trip to the *mikva* the day before, the ritual bath where observant Jews purify themselves. It was one more way he prepared himself for death.

When the Sabbath ended after nightfall, Amir took his Beretta and several boxes of ammunition and closed himself off in the room next to the one he shared with Hagai. He had read about the Kahalani brothers a year earlier—how Shabak had secretly neutered their gun before they set out to kill a Palestinian. To make sure no one had replaced his rounds with blanks, Amir emptied his magazine and reloaded it with new ammunition. He started with three of his brother's modified shells, then alternated between regular rounds and hollow points. Then he pressed the magazine back into the handle and fit the gun in his pants.

Amir slipped out of the house at 7:45 p.m. without saying goodbye, and made his way to the bus stop. If Shabak had somehow been on to him, he thought, better to avoid traveling by car, which agents could tail. He took the 247 line and got off two blocks from the plaza. To blend in, Amir took off his black skullcap and stuffed it into his pocket. In dark jeans and a T-shirt, he looked like every other demonstrator.

Amir had no real plan. But as he drew closer to the stage, he spotted the prime minister's two cars parked in the lot, the Cadillac and the Caprice. The lot teemed with people, including policemen and security guards but also roadies and drivers, and just bystanders hoping to catch a glimpse of some famous person. The police barricade blocked the entrance only partially and the men who guarded it seemed to come and go. Amir was about to make his way in when he spotted a fellow law student from Bar-Ilan, the careful note-taker Amit Hampel, and quickly retreated. Hampel would wonder what he was doing at a peace rally and why he was not wearing his skullcap, Amir thought. He might become suspicious.

Instead, Amir pressed into the crowd. Onstage, the performers and politicians alternated at the microphone, grating on him equally. In the square, he bristled at these Hellenizers, the peaceniks. To Amir, this was the other Israel, the one with no regard for biblical warrant, no reverence for Jewish heritage. He walked the length of the plaza and then turned back toward the parking lot, approaching it this time from the west. At the electric gate, he had no trouble getting past policemen. Once inside, Amir walked to within fifteen feet of the Cadillac, leaned on one of the equipment vans, and waited. From there, he had a clear view to the staircase where Rabin would likely descend from the stage.

Now Amir gave himself over to God. If a policeman approached, he told himself, he would walk away. But if no one questioned his presence there, it would be a divine signal. *If God wants a person to commit an act, He lets him commit the act.*

For forty minutes, Amir lingered, either leaning against the van or sitting on a planter at the base of the stairs. The policemen around him seemed to mistake him for a roadie or a driver. To allay possible suspicions, he chatted casually with one of the cops about the musician Aviv Geffen, a rocker in white face makeup. "What a weirdo," Amir remarked when Geffen came down from the stage. Twice, he noticed another policeman coming toward him but veering away at the last moment. The Shabak officer charged with maintaining a sterile environment in the parking lot stood less than two car lengths from Amir, leaning on the Caprice. He'd been privy to the intelligence about a "short Yemeni guy with curly hair" wanting to kill the prime minister. And yet he paid no attention to Amir. At a moment when the threat to Israel's leader loomed larger than ever, Shabak's seam zone—the very place where assassination attempts were known to occur—was unsecured.

Onstage, Rabin huddled with the other men in suits and waited for his turn to speak, trailed constantly by the bodyguards Rubin and Glaser. Leah looked out at the crowd and noticed a few dozen young people standing waist-deep in a fountain at the front of the plaza, shouting, "Rabin, King of Israel." It was a pleasant alternative to the chants she'd been accustomed to hearing outside her window. While she scanned the square, the wife of an Israeli journalist approached and asked her if Rabin was wearing a bulletproof vest. Though Leah had certainly been aware of the growing threat to her husband, the question seemed somehow out of place to her.

Rabin's turn came after Peres finished his speech and as the two men intersected at the podium, they lingered for a moment facing the plaza. In an unscripted and uncharacteristic display, Rabin threw an arm around Peres's waist and Peres reciprocated, prompting cheers from the crowd. The speech had been written to include references to the growing danger posed by right-wing extremists. Though Rabin lacked the theatrical impulse required to be a rousing orator, he now found his rhythm. "Violence is undermining the foundation of Israeli democracy," he said into the microphone, a staccato echo bouncing off the low-slung apartment buildings around the square. "I was a military man for twenty-seven years. I fought as long as there was no chance for peace. I believe there is a chance now, a great chance, and we must take advantage of it."

The rally would soon draw to a close. For a finale, one of the performers lined up the politicians for a rendition of "A Song for Peace," a late-1960s anthem that echoed the American antiwar folk songs of the era. "*Sing a song for peace, don't whisper a prayer. Better to sing a song for peace, shout it out loud.*" A microphone passed down the line picked up Rabin's discordant baritone; the prime minister, it was now evident to 100,000 rally-goers, could not carry a tune. When it was over, he folded the page with the lyrics printed on it and placed it into the breast pocket of his jacket. The national anthem followed and by 9:30 p.m., the crowd began to disperse. From a phone on the stage, Chief Superintendent Naftali called his wife to say he'd be home soon. "Everything went smoothly, *Gott sei dank* [thank God]," he said, using the German he'd learned during a posting in Europe.

Rubin led Rabin toward the staircase but the prime minister kept getting stopped for another handshake, another photo. Partway down, Rabin realized he'd forgotten to thank Lahat for organizing the rally. He walked back to the stage and gave him an embrace. Now the prime minister headed once again toward the exit, with Glaser on his left, Rubin on his right, and two other Shabak men trailing. On the staircase, Rubin saw the crowd in the parking lot and a horde of people to his right, pressing up against the police barricade. He had been trained to look at hands and faces—what people were holding and what their expressions indicated. If danger lurked, it would come from the right, he thought, where bystanders were reaching over the barricade to shake Rabin's hand. The parking area to his left, where Amir still waited, was supposed to be secure. Toward the bottom of the staircase, Rabin turned his head and asked about his wife.

"Where is Leah?" She had fallen behind but was there at the top of the stairs.

By this point, Rabin had entered Yigal Amir's field of vision. From behind the planter, Amir watched Yoram Rubin place his left arm on the prime minister's back to direct him toward the Cadillac. He waited one more moment until Rabin drew close to the car, then circled the bodyguards who trailed the prime minister and found a gap. Amir pulled the Beretta from his pants and lunged at Rabin in one fluid motion, firing three shots from a distance of about two feet. The first round sliced into Rabin's upper back, causing him to fall forward. Amir had hit his target. The second shot struck Yoram Rubin's left elbow, the one he'd draped over Rabin. It bore through the bodyguard's arm and exited his shoulder. As Rabin tumbled to the ground, the third bullet entered his lower back, left of the spine.

The next few moments unspooled like a series of snapshots: The Beretta falling from Amir's hands and bouncing off the pavement; policemen piling on top of him. The Dignitary Protection Unit had a rule that if someone managed to fire a shot at one of its VIPs, the second bullet must come from the gun of a bodyguard, directed at the assassin. Yet Amir had squeezed off three rounds and no one fired back. The head of the unit, who had followed Rabin down the stairs, watched the event with a sense of confusion that quickly gave way to horror. Behind him, or perhaps off to the side, someone else called out: "It's not real, it's not real."

On the pavement, Rubin now crouched over Rabin and tried to lift him into the Cadillac. "Listen to me and no one else," he said. But his arm ached badly and the prime minister's body felt limp and heavy. Glaser, who had been a step ahead of Rabin when the shots rang out, spun around and dropped to the ground. Together the two bodyguards hoisted Rabin into the backseat of the car and Rubin dove in behind him. "Get going, now!" Rubin shouted to Damti. As the Cadillac sped away, the rear door still open, Glaser glimpsed an image that would stain his consciousness for years: Rabin, the man he was charged with protecting, lying on the backseat of the car, with Rubin sprawled out on top of him.

From the plaza, Ichilov Hospital was only minutes away. But the hysteria of the shooting and the crowds that still lined the streets disoriented Damti. At the first stoplight, he turned north instead of south and then lost his bearing. In the back, Rabin was bleeding heavily but still conscious. He managed to tell Rubin he thought he'd been hurt but not too badly. Then he fell into a coma. With his left arm barely functioning, Rubin leaned down and blew short quick breaths into Rabin's mouth.

Damti punched the gas pedal, running red lights and swerving to avoid pedestrians. But he was unsure about his direction. In his rearview mirror, he saw Rubin crouching over Rabin. "What's his condition? How's Rabin?" he asked several times. After turning east on a main artery, Damti spotted a policeman and pressed the brakes hard. He reached across the front seat, opened the passenger door and yelled for the policeman to get in. "Guide me to Ichilov," he said. The policeman, Pinchas Terem, took control of the megaphone, calling cars out of the way. Two minutes later, at 9:52 p.m., the Cadillac pulled into the driveway of the hospital. Some ten minutes had elapsed since the shooting.

In the emergency room, Rabin was not breathing and had no pulse. The doctor on call, Nir Cohen, noted the bullet wounds in Rabin's back and then turned him over to examine his chest. Only then, when he bent down to listen to his lungs with a stethoscope, did Cohen realize this elderly man in his elegant suit was the prime minister. Other doctors gathered around his bed while a nurse phoned the surgery department: send people now, she said. Forty-one-year-old Mordechai Gutman, the most senior surgeon in the building, came running. The emergency-room doctors had pulled off Rabin's jacket and shirt by now and inserted an IV. Gutman, sensing that air had seeped into Rabin's right chest cavity, plunged a tube into his rib cage to drain it. A gust of air and blood burst from the cylinder. Suddenly, a pulse appeared; the prime minister was alive.

Gutman wanted Rabin in the surgery room immediately, where he could cut him open and treat the internal wounds. He and several other doctors wheeled the gurney into a long, fluorescent corridor and began running. Gutman expected the waiting area they passed through to be teeming with people—Rabin's wife and children, his staff members and security team. It was strangely empty.

Leah at that moment was at Shabak headquarters across town, unsure of her husband's condition. She'd witnessed the shooting from the staircase but by the time she reached the parking lot, Rabin was gone. Glaser, who had just watched the Cadillac speed off, took Leah by the arm and pushed her into the Caprice, to get her away from the danger zone. "What happened?" she kept asking. Glaser had felt Rabin's limp body on the ground, but he had also heard the confusing words "It's not real" spoken immediately after the shooting. Now his earpiece had gone quiet. Until he was told something definitive, he decided, it was better to reassure Leah. As the car raced north toward the imposing red building that served the agency, he echoed the words from the parking lot. "Don't worry, it's not real."

Leah and Rabin had planned to attend a party in Zahala, north of Tel Aviv, after the rally in honor of the diplomat Avi Pazner, who'd been named Israel's ambassador to France. For a moment, she thought Glaser might be taking her there. But the driver was tearing through the city, running red lights and cutting curbs. It made no sense. When they arrived at the Shabak office, the details began to emerge. Leah overheard one officer telling another that two people had been wounded in the parking lot, one lightly and the other seriously. Both were now at Ichilov. From a phone in one of the rooms, she called her daughter, Dalia. "Your father has been shot," Leah said. Dalia heard the words but struggled to grasp their meaning. How could it have happened? And what was her mother doing at the Shabak building? "Why aren't you at the hospital?"

Leah hung up and demanded to be taken to Ichilov.

By the time she got there, Israel Television had interrupted its scheduled program, the movie *Crocodile Dundee II*, to report that the prime minister had been shot and that his condition was unknown. The news brought hundreds of people to the street outside Ichilov, along with journalists and their broadcast vans. Inside, several of Rabin's cabinet ministers and staff members had already arrived. The American ambassador, Martin Indyk, was on his way. Haber had been

at the party in Zahala at the moment of the shooting, along with Ichilov director Gabriel Barbash. At 9:59 p.m., Barbash's beeper went off
with an urgent message to call the hospital. The two men rushed out
together.

Barbash met Leah at the entrance and walked her to a private room
near the surgery theater. For the first time, she learned that her husband had been struck by two bullets, that his situation was dire, and
that the shooter was not a Palestinian but a Jew. It was too much to
absorb. She felt herself disconnecting from the events around her. Leah
thought about the protesters who had gathered outside the building
on Rav Ashi every Friday afternoon, the vile things they chanted.
Slowly, the room filled with people, including Dalia and her family,
Sheves, Yatom, Haber, and Peres.

In operating room number 9, other senior doctors had joined Gutman by now, having rushed from their homes, among them Joseph
Klausner, the head of Ichilov's surgery complex. With the anesthesi-
ologists and nurses, as many as forty hospital staff circled the patient.
The rounds that struck the prime minister—the first and third to
emerge from Amir's gun—were hollow points. They'd caused massive internal bleeding and remained lodged in his body. It occurred
to one of the doctors that a protective vest would likely have stopped
these particular bullets, with their scooped-out tips. Gutman had
removed Rabin's spleen and cracked open his chest. More than twenty
units of blood had been pumped into the prime minister intrave-
nously. When a dose of adrenaline was injected into his heart, Rabin's
vital signs seemed to stabilize. Barbash left the room to report to Leah
that the doctors now had some hope.

In the hallway, Haber immediately swung into action. He spotted
a high-ranking Defense Ministry official and told him to begin setting up a makeshift office at the hospital, with phones and fax lines.
The prime minister would need to run the affairs of the country from
Ichilov while he recuperated.

But Rabin quickly lapsed again. To keep him alive, Gutman
reached into his chest cavity and pumped his heart manually, repeat-
ing the motion again and again, until he lost track of time. Around
the room, the grim realization was setting in that the prime minister

could not be saved. Gutman sensed the futility as well but he couldn't bring himself to pull away from Rabin's heart. At 11:02 p.m., eighty minutes after the shooting, Klausner touched him on the back and said it was time to stop.

Rabin was dead.

———————

THE OPERATING ROOM fell silent. Then some of the surgeons, trauma specialists who had seen terrible ordeals, began to weep. Gutman stepped away from the table and let other doctors stitch up the body. He found a corner outside the room to smoke a cigarette. Someone brought him coffee.

Barbash took several doctors with him to break the news to Leah and the rest of the family. The hallway outside the private room now swarmed with people—members of Rabin's cabinet, military officers, and security officials. For a moment, the crowd huddled around Leah. Then Barbash led a small group including Leah; Sheves; Peres; Yuval; Dalia; her husband, Avi Pelossof; and her two children, Noa and Yonatan, to a reception room where Rabin's body had been wheeled. A white sheet covered everything but his head. To Noa, who was now eighteen and a private in the army, her grandfather seemed to be smiling slightly. His face had retained its color but he was cold to the touch. After taking turns standing at Rabin's bedside, the group filed out.

By this point, masses of people had gathered outside the hospital, including rally-goers who'd made their way to Ichilov straight from the plaza. From media reports, Israelis had learned that the shooter was a twenty-five-year-old Jewish extremist from Herzliya who studied law at Bar-Ilan. But they still knew little about Rabin's precise condition. Haber was about to stun the nation. At 11:15 p.m., he walked out of the hospital alone, looking pale and deeply shaken. He stood in front of television cameras and asked for quiet. Beyond the ring of journalists, the crowd pressed forward to hear him. "The government of Israel announces with shock, with great sorrow and grief, the death of Prime Minister and Defense Minister Yitzhak Rabin, who was murdered by an assassin this evening," he said. At the word "death," some people erupted in shouts of "No, no!" Others gasped loudly.

Haber continued: "The government will convene in an hour to mourn in Tel Aviv. May his memory be blessed."

The announcement plunged Israel into a haze, a gloomy twilight zone where everything seemed surreal. At a movie house not far from Ichilov, an usher went from theater to theater to convey the news. Audiences filed out in a daze. On Channel One, television's most distinguished anchor, Haim Yavin, could not bring himself to say the words "Rabin is dead." Instead, he announced that the prime minister was "no longer among the living." *Yedioth Ahronoth*, the country's largest-selling newspaper, had already laid out its front section for the next day. Its editors now threw out the material and began working on a new edition for what would be a different country in the morning. The columnist Nahum Barnea, who had covered the peace rally earlier in the evening, sat down and wrote: "Ever since Israel was established people believed, rightly so, in the stability of the regime. Only in Arab countries are leaders assassinated. Only in Arab countries, people who strive for peace pay with their lives. . . . We were mistaken. We are not immune."

In Washington, Clinton's aides patched the president through to Leah in the hospital. Clinton's national security adviser, Anthony Lake, had been the one to inform the president ninety minutes earlier that an attempt had been made on Rabin's life. The long wait for word on his condition felt excruciating. To steady his nerves, Clinton walked out to the putting green on the South Lawn of the White House—the same grassy field where the Oslo Accord had been signed two years earlier—and swung at golf balls aimlessly. Eventually, he spotted Lake walking toward him from the Oval Office. "From the look on his face, I knew that my friend was gone," Clinton would say later.

On the phone, he tried to comfort Leah. "This idiot took my Yitzhak away," she told him. After hanging up, Clinton ordered the flag over the White House lowered to half staff, summoned reporters, and delivered an anguished tribute to Rabin, straying into Hebrew at one point and adding to the sense of delirium in Israel. "Yitzhak

Rabin was my partner and my friend. I admired him and I loved him very much," he said at the podium of the Rose Garden. "Because words cannot express my true feelings, let me just say, *Shalom, haver.* Goodbye, friend."

Eitan Haber had been careful not to assign blame with his statement outside the hospital. But to many Israelis, the murder felt like an assault by one political camp against the other, another step toward civil war. Amir clearly stood on the margins of the right-wing camp. But its mainstream leaders had goaded the extremists with their ugly rhetoric and its rabbis had furnished the religious justification for violence. Even now, as the horror of the country's first political assassination set in, some Israelis celebrated.

Within seconds of the shooting, policemen had cuffed Amir on the ground, then lifted him to his feet and ran with him to the outer wall of a small shopping mall that bordered the parking lot. At least fifteen men pressed up against him, clutching his arms and patting him down but Amir heard the voice of just one policeman asking questions in rapid succession: Were the bullets real? Was the prime minister the intended target? Amir had regarded his lunge at Rabin as an act of suicide, yet somehow he was alive. He responded loudly enough to be heard over the chaos: Yes, he intended to shoot Rabin and yes, the bullets were real. Inspector Yuval Gershon pushed him into a police had car, a late-model Subaru, and got in behind him.

Already on the ride to the station, Amir delivered a full confession. He was a law student at Bar-Ilan, he owned the Beretta that police had picked up in the parking lot, he had gone to the square intending to shoot the prime minister, and he was reasonably sure his bullets had struck Rabin. For the policemen in the car—Gershon and three others—the incident itself had been a bewildering experience. Amir's swagger, his nonchalance, added another layer of astonishment. One of the men asked Amir if he'd been aware that his actions could cause Rabin's death, information that in court would help establish intent. Amir, who had completed two full years of law school, including at least two courses in criminal law, understood the question. Not only was I aware, he said. That was my objective.

The bluster continued pouring out at the precinct, along with a giddiness that made Amir seem weirdly detached from the enormity of his crime. Before he was even booked, he asked First Sergeant Yohanan Ronen to reach into the pocket of his jeans, pull out his skullcap, and put it on his head. The policeman obliged. While pressing his fingers to an inkpad, Amir noticed that his wrist was bare. "My watch fell off in the parking lot," he remarked to the lab technician. "Can you check if someone found it?" To the technician, it must have seemed like the suspect had mistaken him for a summer-camp counselor. "We'll let you know," he said.

Throughout the booking, Amir kept replaying the shooting in his mind. Though it remained unclear to him whether Rabin had survived, Amir was now certain that God had wanted him to act, that he'd managed to fathom God's will, in the words of that settler rabbi. The proof was in the outcome. Only divine intervention could account for the fact that he eluded police for forty minutes, outmaneuvered Rabin's vaunted protection force, and fired at the prime minister without getting shot himself. In one of the waiting rooms, he told a policeman his act would cause people to rise up. "I don't want people to think I'm crazy. Otherwise, I won't achieve my goal." To Ronen, he explained that *din rodef* amounted to a death sentence for Rabin—an explication that only people familiar with the internal discourse in the Orthodox community over the preceding year would have understood. When the policeman pointed out that even the most hardline political parties would condemn the assassination attempt, Amir seemed untroubled. "I didn't do it in order to go down in history," he said. Then he added: "But you guys will be famous."

In the interrogation room, Amir faced Motti Naftali, the chief superintendent who had helped draft the security plan for the rally. Word had reached the precinct by now that Rabin had died on the operating table. With his pipe wedged in the corner of his mouth, Naftali told Amir he would be charged with the murder of Prime Minister Yitzhak Rabin. Amir's response nearly unhinged the police officer. Amir threw up his cuffed hands and declared, "I did it." Then he asked Naftali if he could bring a drink—a "schnapps," he said—to toast the news.

While the interrogation continued, several policemen and Shabak investigators made their way to Borochov 56 in Herzliya, to search the house and pick up Hagai. Forensic technicians had already discovered the modified bullets at the bottom of Amir's magazine. When Naftali asked about them, Amir said they were the handiwork of his brother and bragged about Hagai's technical skills. Now he was a suspect as well.

In Herzliya, Hagai waited for a knock on the door. He'd been watching a television movie earlier in the evening when a newscaster interrupted the program to report that shots were fired in Rabin's vicinity at Kings of Israel Square. Though the initial details were scant, Hagai knew immediately that it was his brother. He turned to his father and told him to brace himself—Amir had tried to kill Rabin at the peace rally. Shlomo erupted: What did you and your brother do? How could you do this to me? Then Hagai set about hiding his ammunition and explosives.

Elsewhere in the neighborhood, Geulah watched the same news bulletin at the home of a friend and had a similar stirring about Amir. She dialed the home number and asked one of her younger sons to check if he was there. Geulah had noticed the Beetle in the driveway when she left, but her son reported back that Amir was not in the house. At that moment, with the phone still pressed to her ear, she heard the news anchor read out a description of the suspect—a short, dark-skinned resident of Herzliya. Geulah felt a crushing pressure in her chest. A few minutes later, Israel's two networks broadcast the first footage of Amir—surrounded by policemen against the wall of the shopping mall.

By the time she got home, friends from the neighborhood were making their way in and the phone was ringing constantly. One of the callers was Margalit Har-Shefi, who had seen the bulletin at her parents' home in the settlement Beit El. When Hagai came to the phone, Har-Shefi probed for information. "You don't think . . ." she started. But Hagai worried that Shabak might already be tapping the line or even surrounding the house. He cut her short and said, "We'll cry later." Har-Shefi asked him to give Amir her regards.

An hour passed and somehow the police had still failed to show up. Hagai considered dismantling some of his homemade armaments, including the grenades and the timers. The parts alone would be less incriminating. But he worried that investigators would walk in as soon as he got to work. Instead, he grabbed what he could from the bedroom and the shed and stashed it in a small chicken coop he'd built over the summer in the backyard—on the left side, near the incubator. The deadlier munitions, the TNT sticks and C-4 explosives, remained hidden in the attic and inside one of the walls.

Back in the house, he spotted a relative who lived in the neighborhood and had come over to console the family. Hagai still had a few things left to hide, a supermarket bag with fuses, explosives, and the handcrafted silencer. He pulled the relative, Uriel Ben-Yaakov, to the back patio and asked if he'd be willing to stash the munitions in his home. In the dimly lit yard, Hagai opened the bag and showed him the contents. When Ben-Yaakov refused, Hagai pointed to the hiding place in the coop and asked him to remove the materials after he was arrested.

The policemen and Shabak agents, delayed apparently by the chaos, finally pulled up around midnight. On the street, journalists were knocking on doors to interview people about their neighbor, the assassin. Inside, the friends still lingered; Shlomo sat alone in a bedroom reading Lamentations. The officers took Hagai to a bathroom, told him to undress, and searched him. Then they combed the shed and the bedroom he shared with Amir, confiscating whatever items seemed relevant. In several boxes, they carted off the ammunition Hagai left lying around and tools from his shed but also a phone book, four photo albums, a camera with film in it, and a worn copy of *The Day of the Jackal*. Near Amir's bed, they found a book titled *Baruch the Man*, a paean to Baruch Goldstein with tributes written mostly by settlers and rabbis. Amir had not only devoured the 533-page book, he'd recommended it to Har-Shefi and others.

The officers walked Hagai out and cuffed him in the car. Borochov, the sleepy suburban street, swarmed with people. At one in the morning, the day was not over yet.

In Tel Aviv, Peres had gathered Rabin's cabinet ministers to formalize the transition of power. Alongside his responsibilities as foreign minister, Peres held the title of deputy prime minister, which meant he would be leading the government through the transition period. Dressed in the same suit and tie he'd worn onstage a few hours earlier, his face pale and heavy, Peres looked wretched. He struggled to deliver a brief eulogy for Rabin and kept his gaze down through much of the meeting. Peres had preceded Rabin in the parking lot by a few minutes. In updates he received from the interrogation room, he learned that Amir had considered shooting at him but decided to wait for the prime minister. Had the two men come down together, Amir told Naftali, he would have killed them both. The trifecta—losing Rabin, having the country's leadership thrust suddenly upon him, and realizing he'd barely escaped death himself—had induced in Peres a kind of post-traumatic stress.

Rabin had now been dead for three hours. His body remained in a room at Ichilov Hospital, waiting for the autopsy. Doctors had left the clothes he'd been wearing in a neat pile, a pack of Parliaments still stuffed in his jacket pocket. At two in the morning, the government's chief pathologist, Yehuda Hiss, walked in with an assistant and began to probe what precisely killed Rabin. Speaking into a tape recorder, Hiss described what he saw: "The body of a man who looks to be about seventy, nutritional condition looks normal, measuring 172 centimeters from his left heel to the top of his head, naked and covered in sheets." He noted the obvious and the obscure: The long lines of stitches crisscrossing Rabin's chest and abdomen where surgeons had cut him open and the yellow stains between his index and middle fingers from a lifelong smoking habit. In back, Hiss traced the pathway of the bullets into Rabin's body. One hollow point entered his lower back, ruptured his spleen, then traveled up and to the right, where it punctured his left lung. The other pierced his back below the clavicle, smashed through the rib cage, and entered the right lung.

The massive bleeding alone and the collapse of his lungs had made Rabin's chances of surviving the shooting extremely low, Hiss concluded. But it wasn't until doctors wheeled the body to a lab room for a brain scan that the full picture came into view. In the computerized image, they noticed an embolism in one of Rabin's cerebral arteries, a large pocket of air that entered his bloodstream in the lungs and made its way to his brain, restricting the flow of blood and oxygen. The blockage, it was now clear, had hindered the resuscitation effort and, with every passing moment, eroded the prime minister's mental capacity.

In effect, Rabin's brain died well before his body did.

CHAPTER 8

Killing a King

"I used the talents that God gave me and came up with all kinds of things—whether ideas or actual things—and for that I'm not ashamed."

—HAGAI AMIR

A vaporous chill hung over the city through the rest of the night. Leah sat with family members and close friends in the living room at Ravi Ashi until four in the morning, then took a sedative and fell asleep. Dalia and Noa climbed into bed alongside her. Peres worked until dawn, consulting with advisers and talking to President Clinton by phone. He retreated to his apartment around the corner from Rav Ashi for a short nap and then returned to work. At the spot where Amir had murdered Rabin, hundreds of Israelis kept a vigil, some holding candles and lounging on sleeping bags. When the sun came up, a *Yedioth Ahronoth* truck dropped a bundle of newspapers near the site with the headline: RABIN MURDERED; ISRAEL ACHES AND WEEPS.

The morning brought a raft of questions for the new Israel: Would the peace process survive Rabin's death? Could Peres step into the shoes of a man whose military background had underpinned his role as a peacemaker? And could the country ever bridge the chasm between its pragmatists and messianists—between the people who viewed Israel as a secular nation-state and those who saw it as the realization of biblical prophecy? In the American embassy building overlooking the Mediterranean, Martin Indyk typed a cable to Washington that referenced some of these issues. "The . . . assassination of Prime Minister Yitzhak Rabin has no precedent in Israel's forty-seven year history," he wrote, addressing his memorandum to the secretary of state and the White House and designating it "classified." While the loss of Rabin marked a devastating blow to the peace camp, Indyk reported that rightists stood to suffer a broad backlash. "Opposition leader Binyamin Netanyahu told us last night that Likud and the right will be directly blamed for the violence leading to the assassination of Rabin. He called the death of Rabin a 'disaster for the Jewish people, a disaster for Israel and a disaster for the right which will be decimated if elections are called soon.'"

A second cable, written by the American consul general in Jerusalem, Edward Abington, summed up the Palestinian reaction. Abington wrote that Arafat seemed severely shaken and distraught, according to his advisers. The Palestinian leader had ordered his security forces to prevent Hamas and Islamic Jihad from celebrating Rabin's death in the areas under his control. Many ordinary Palestinians felt relief that the perpetrator was a Jew and not an Arab, Abington added.

To the two diplomats, the uncertainties seemed overwhelming. But Israel had more immediate matters to address—starting with how to stage Rabin's funeral. More than a quarter century had passed since a prime minister died in office. The government had no protocol for the ceremonial observance and, with the assassination, no precedent to follow. According to tradition, Jews bury their loved ones as soon as possible, usually within twenty-four hours of death. But by Sunday morning, more than one hundred foreign dignitaries and heads of state had expressed interest in attending the funeral. Washington alone had sent Israel a list with thirty-eight names, including those of two ex-presidents, three former secretaries of state, and nineteen senators and congressmen—in addition to President Clinton and members of his administration. All wanted to pay Rabin their respects.

To accommodate the requests, Israel pushed the funeral to Monday and announced that Rabin would lie in state at the plaza of the Knesset in Jerusalem until then. Safeguarding the events would fall on Shabak at an excruciatingly difficult moment for the agency. Shabak had just committed the worst security lapse in Israel's history, allowing a lone gunman to kill the prime minister in what should have been a secured area. Its Dignitary Protection Unit, whose members would be tasked with guarding the foreign statesmen, was in turmoil. Several of the agency's senior officials were already talking to lawyers about what would surely be a state probe into the circumstances of the murder. And its chief, Carmi Gillon, was only now getting up to speed, having returned earlier in the morning to Israel from Paris.

Gillon had been on his way to the airport in Paris the night before when his chief of staff called with the news that the prime minister had been shot. At the El Al terminal in Charles De Gaulle Airport, he joined other Israelis around a television set just as the French network reported that Rabin had died of his wounds. Gillon spent the next five hours contemplating all the ways the murder could have been prevented. "The flight back to Israel was the longest I'd experienced in my life," he would write in a memoir. "The plane was dark, most people around me slept, and I sat there alone with myself, resting my head against the window and gazing at some meaningless point in the distance. I couldn't shut my eyes." When the plane landed in Israel at five thirty in the morning, Gillon headed straight to the assassination site to try to understand exactly what had happened.

At his office later, Gillon consulted with the agency's top officers and then made several decisions. A team of three retired Shabak officers would investigate how the failure had occurred. Former agency officers would be brought back to help Shabak through the transition period. With the funeral to look after, the ongoing threat of Palestinian attacks, and the possibility of another assassination attempt—a copycat event could not be ruled out—Gillon felt a constant anxiety. He had quit smoking four months earlier. Now he couldn't go for more than a few minutes without lighting a cigarette.

Throughout the day, thousands of people streamed to Jerusalem to pass by Rabin's coffin and greet the grieving family. Leah had woken up that morning with a feeling that something horrible had happened the night before. For a moment, she struggled to recall what it was. Through the window of the car on the way to Jerusalem, she saw hand-painted signs hanging from bridges and stretched out along highway barricades with the Hebrew words that Clinton had spoken in his Rose Garden tribute to Rabin the night before, SHALOM HAVER. But it was only when she glimpsed the coffin outside the parliament building that the "inconceivable reality" set in, as she would write later. By midnight, more than a million Israelis had filed past the casket to honor Rabin. Dalia woke up at three in the morning and turned on the television to see the plaza still teeming with people. She roused her mother so that Leah could view the spectacle herself.

The funeral at noon the next day marked the largest gathering of international leaders the Middle East had ever known, with more than two thousand foreign guests. Nearly eighty countries had sent senior representatives, including Egypt, Jordan, Oman, Mauritania, Morocco, Qatar, and Tunisia. The headwear told the story: Jews in skullcaps but also men in kaffiyehs, turbans, military berets, and baseball caps. For a country that had suffered isolation in the region throughout its history, the display underscored just how far Israel had come in the preceding three years. Airport authorities canceled all regularly scheduled flights for several hours in order to free the runways for the government planes. Only Arafat among world leaders was conspicuous by his absence. Israel decided it would be too difficult to protect him from potential assassins.

Clinton and the rest of the American delegation had arrived on *Air Force One* early in the morning. On the flight over, Israel's ambassador to Washington, Itamar Rabinovich, delivered a briefing to a select group on the situation in Israel. The notables, including former presidents Bush and Carter, wanted to know what to expect of Peres— could he assume Rabin's security mantle and reassure Israelis about the risks involved in further peacemaking? Rabinovich explained that Peres had been a security figure throughout his career—the father of the Israeli nuclear program and a former defense minister. But the question would come to seem prescient in subsequent months. Rabinovich took in the luxury of the plane—all eighty seats were first-class recliners. George Shultz, the former secretary of state, leaned over and explained to the Israeli official that it was President Reagan who had ordered the upgrade. Only Reagan could spend lavishly on comforts for the president and get away with it, he said. Several rows behind them, House Speaker Newt Gingrich complained loudly about having been seated so far in the back.

A bevy of leaders eulogized Rabin, including King Hussein, who addressed him as a "brother, a colleague and a friend—a man." Clinton recalled helping Rabin straighten his bowtie at an event in Washington two weeks earlier, a prop the prime minister borrowed from a US Secret Service agent. "Look at the leaders from all over the Middle East and around the world who have journeyed here today for Yitzhak Rabin and for peace," Clinton said. "Though we no longer hear his deep and booming voice, it is he who has brought us together again here, in word and deed, for peace." Haber held up a blood-stained sheet of paper that doctors had retrieved from the inside breast pocket of Rabin's suit jacket with the lyrics to "A Song for Peace." "I want to read from this page but it's difficult," said Haber. "Your blood covers the printed words." But it was Rabin's granddaughter, Noa, whose tribute prompted a teary outpouring: "Others greater than I have already eulogized you, but none of them ever had the pleasure that I had to feel the caress of your warm, soft hands, to merit your warm embrace that was reserved only for us, to see your half smile that always told me so much," she said.

At two o'clock, a siren wailed throughout Israel, precisely the way it does on Holocaust Memorial Day every year. Traffic stopped and people across the country stood at attention for two minutes. At Mount Herzl, Yuval Rabin recited the Kaddish—the traditional Jewish mourners' prayer—as pallbearers lowered Rabin's casket into the grave. Haber, who had studied at Orthodox schools as a child and was well versed in Jewish liturgy, noticed that Yuval mispronounced many of the words in the prayer, a complicated Aramaic text. Rabin had been the paradigm of secular Israel, he thought, and had raised his children that way as well.

The outpouring of grief across the country and the picture of millions standing at attention to honor Rabin created an image of solidarity in Israel. But the extremists had not gone away, and most were unrepentant. In Kiryat Arba, several people rejoiced at the assassination and continued celebrating through the week. "I am very happy that the dictator Rabin is dead," one resident, Aryeh Bar-Yosef, told a news crew. Bar-Yosef had been seen blowing a shofar—a biblical ram's horn—on the night of the murder and singing "Happy Holidays." Another settler explained that Jewish law required people to "enjoy the fact that Yitzhak Rabin, the head of the traitors, got what he deserved." When a journalist asked the head of the Kiryat Arba local council about the remarks, he received a lesson in civil rights. "In a democratic state, I'm allowed to demonstrate. I'm allowed to scream and express my opinions. . . . They want to shut our mouths but they won't succeed."

Some non-settlers delighted as well. In a few places around the country, graffiti appeared praising Amir. On a wall in Jerusalem, someone scrawled the words PERES IS NEXT.

Benjamin Netanyahu, his popularity plunging, tried to draw a line between the extremists and the rank and file of his own party. "These people are not in Likud and won't be in Likud and I have a message for you and the message is: I don't want your votes, I don't want to be elected by you," he said in a television interview. But he rejected the idea that the vicious campaign against Rabin—the signs calling him a traitor and a murderer, the rabbinical pronouncements, the references to Nazis and their sympathizers—had somehow contributed to the assassination. The YESHA Council complained in the days following the murder that settlers were being blamed collectively when in fact the gunman had never been part of the settler community. Israel Harel, who headed the council at the time, took it further. He said many religious Jews now felt vulnerable walking around in their skullcaps and compared the environment to the climate in Nazi Germany on the eve of World War II. "You couldn't board a bus if you had a skullcap on your head. . . . It was terrible, really terrible," he recalled.

The truth was not nearly so dramatic; no one was rounding up rightists. But in a broad sense, the murder had created a binary landscape—

right and left, religious and secular. A skullcap identified a person with the camp that included the murderer, even if he found the assassination abhorrent. Yedidia Stern, who served as the dean of the law school at Bar-Ilan and was horrified to learn on Saturday night that the shooter was one of his students, felt the antagonism almost instantly. Raised in an Orthodox home, Stern had cultivated a kind of moderate observance that eschewed political or religious extremism. Yet on the stairs outside his home the next morning, a secular neighbor scolded him: "What did you people do to us?" he said.

Harel, who headed the YESHA Council, had known Rabin from the occasional meetings settlers held with the prime minister over the years. After the funeral, he conveyed a message to Leah through a friend that he wished to make a condolence visit to Rav Ashi during the shiva—the seven-day mourning period. But Leah, who felt a constant churning of anger and grief, could not stomach the idea. Settler leaders and right-wing politicians had orchestrated the incitement against her husband. She regarded them as Amir's accomplices.

The shiva gave Leah a way to pass the time without wallowing alone in her husband's death. She greeted visitors starting early in morning, recounted the moments of the murder, and reminisced about Rabin. Outside, large groups of Israeli youngsters kept vigils going through the week—on Rav Ashi and at the site of the shooting. Candles burned constantly.

On Thursday night, an unexpected guest arrived. Yasser Arafat had arranged through an Israeli intermediary to be flown in a military helicopter from Gaza to Tel Aviv and driven to Rav Ashi. It was Arafat's first visit to Israel, a secret mission accompanied by his two deputies, Mahmoud Abbas and Ahmed Korei. He entered the apartment in his customary fatigues but without the kaffiyeh, a look that made his facial features more striking than usual. Arafat kissed Leah and the other family members, then sat for ninety minutes drinking tea in the living room where Rabin had lounged only days earlier. The Palestinian leader described how an aide had told him about the shooting and how he'd phoned his Israeli contacts every few minutes, pleading for updates. For all the tensions he'd experienced with Rabin in the preceding two years, the murder had left Arafat in despair. He wondered whether the peace process could continue without him.

The following morning, Harel read in the newspaper about Arafat's visit with Leah and bristled. She had agreed to host this arch-terrorist in her home but not me? he thought to himself.

By now, the three retired Shabak officers had concluded their internal investigation. Peres had already announced that the president of the Supreme Court, Meir Shamgar, would lead a state commission of inquiry into the circumstances surrounding the murder. But his probe would take months to complete. In the meantime, the agency would adjust its security procedures based on the conclusions of the retired officers.

Not surprisingly, the three men found serious flaws in both the planning and implementation of Rabin's protection on the night of the murder. Among other things, the Cadillac should not have been parked at the base of the stairs. It revealed to Amir where the prime minister would end up after the rally. But the failure to keep people out of the parking lot amounted to the unit's biggest lapse. Many in the agency would end up pointing a finger at one man in particular, the bodyguard who stood alongside Rabin's car during the forty minutes that Amir lingered in the lot. Though the distance between the two was measured at just four meters, the agent never approached Amir to verify whether he posed a threat. "Forty by four" became the shorthand locution in the agency for the bodyguard's catastrophic negligence (Shabak has never identified him publicly). He would end up leaving Shabak a few months after the assassination. Regarding Glaser and Rubin—the latter of whom spent several days in the hospital recovering from the wounds to his arm—the panel had no complaints.

The retired Shabak men recommended suspending four senior officers in the agency and overhauling the Dignitary Protection Unit. From now on, dozens of bodyguards would ring the prime minister wherever he went and keep the public well away. Israeli leaders would no longer have the routine interactions with people that Rabin had—attending parties and weddings, playing tennis in a country club teeming with people, and occasionally driving himself to events.

The almost small-town intimacy that had existed between Israelis and their politicians was over.

The panel left other issues for the Shamgar Commission to investigate, including whether the intelligence side of the agency—the Jewish Affairs Department—should have known in advance about Amir's intentions. For the time being, responsibility for the security lapse rested squarely on the protection department. The failures on the intelligence side would emerge soon enough, seeping from the rooms where Amir and Hagai were being interrogated.

———————

THE AMIR BROTHERS opened up easily. Yigal Amir spent the first night recounting the preceding two years since the Oslo deal, how he spotted Rabin at a wedding and realized it would be possible to kill him, then tried three times to hunt him down. He stretched his arms up and behind his head from time to time, whistled to himself during pauses in the conversation, and responded sarcastically to questions he didn't like (police videotaped many of the interrogations). When an investigator—several of them switched off during the night—asked him if he uttered anything while firing at Rabin, Amir sneered: *"Allahu Akbar?"* To the question, "Did you work on your shooting recently to improve your aim?" he replied: "At that distance, you don't have to be a genius to hit the target."

Amir explained *din rodef* and *din moser* several times. When the investigator Yoram Ben-Haroush asked him if he had something to add about the murder, Amir gave a short sermon that seemed rehearsed. "I don't regret it and I would do it again right now, for God, for the nation, and for the country. I'm just sorry that the family is suffering." Yours or Rabin's? Ben-Haroush wanted to know. "Both," Amir replied. At one point the investigator announced they would be heading to the crime scene soon to reenact the shooting, something police often did with suspects following a confession. Amir pleaded for a hairbrush and shampoo. The man who had murdered Rabin in cold blood a few hours earlier now wanted to look good, in case the media was on hand. "Let me near a faucet so I can wash my hair," he said. But with so many people still lingering at the plaza, police put off the reenactment.

Hagai, by contrast, conveyed a twitchy nervousness during his first interrogations. He drank several glasses of water and coffee and asked to go to the bathroom three times in the span of a few hours. His initial instinct was to let his little brother take the blame alone for the murder. The first time an investigator asked him whether he'd ever heard Amir say Rabin needed to be killed, Hagai insisted he had not. The murder, he said, was unacceptable to him. But by morning, after investigators staged an encounter between the two brothers, Hagai changed his story. We planned the assassination together, he now told them.

The questioning continued intermittently throughout the day and night, with police and Shabak interrogators taking turns in the room. In the traditional division of labor, police tended to prod the suspects for confessional statements that would cement the indictment. Shabak focused on exposing the broader picture, including who else took part in the plot and what threats still loomed. The Amir brothers would satisfy both masters, describing the militia plan and the various schemes for killing Rabin and naming accessories—those who participated in the planning and those who merely knew about it.

By midweek, the two brothers had met with the lawyers who would represent them, sat through remand hearings in Tel Aviv, and huddled briefly with their parents. They received phylacteries to pray with and religious texts to help pass the time. The ongoing interrogations, initially a source of anxiety for Hagai, would soon offer a reprieve from the loneliness and monotony. Hagai told investigators about the munitions hidden in the chicken coop and about asking Ben-Yaakov to remove them. Once he'd confessed to his role in the murder, there was no reason to withhold the details. Police paid another visit to the house on Borochov Street and found the stash precisely where Hagai had left it. Ben-Yaakov had never touched the munitions.

Back in his cell, Hagai wrote his first letter home, an apologia aimed at shoring up his parents and assuring them that his brother (Gali, as they called him) had been guided by God. Amir had "managed to kill the king," Hagai wrote, placing the assassination in the tradition of Jewish rebellion against apostasy. "According to Judaism, killing a king is profoundly significant," he would add later with devastating prescience. "It affects the entire nation and alters its destiny."

Dear Mom, Dad and the rest of the family,

Gali and I are very sorry for the damage and suffering we've caused you in these difficult days. I hope that after you read this letter, you'll feel a bit better and you'll have a more optimistic way of grasping the situation.

I saw a picture of Dad and Mom coming out of my hearing, Mom wearing her glasses and Dad with his eyes closed. It caused me much pain. I'm accustomed to seeing Dad with happy, tranquil eyes, but it all disappeared. Dad, I expect you of all people to be strong inside. After all, you know that things happen for a reason in our world and especially in this age of anticipation for the messiah.

I thought a lot about what Gali did and to this moment I can't believe he did it. Gali was ready to sacrifice his life in order to kill Rabin. This shift was not clear to me until after the fact and I'm still amazed. . . . I used the talents that God gave me and came up with all kinds of things—whether ideas or actual things—and for that I'm not ashamed. I was careful of course not to leave them [armaments and explosives] someplace where they might endanger people's lives, or in a form that might be dangerous. That was one of my basic approaches to the work. The fact is that nothing happened to anyone, with God's help. I'm glad I didn't share the information with you because that would have made you accessories.

In any event, I expect you, Dad, to understand that the fact that Gali survived is a huge miracle for our family. I had discussed with him how unlikely that would be. For that alone—we're thankful.

The very fact that Gali managed to kill the king suggests that the incident has long term implications for the life of our people in Israel. And as far as I know, what it means for the people of Israel is, at the end of the day, positive. For this reason, the fact that Gali managed to do what he did without getting hurt [proves] it was divinely guided. And because this tragedy happened to our family—to people who are all honest, sim-

ple, doers of good deeds, there's no reason for you to suffer so much. This again suggests that the consequences will be only good for the people of Israel.

For this reason, Father, in the same manner that you accepted the good things in life, with joy and with gratitude to God, you must also accept the things that at first look bad and believe that they are ultimately for the better. Because it's quite possible that this is the way God wants to save [the people of Israel] and Gali from what might have happened in the future. You will one day thank him for this.

You must understand that Gali and I will most likely be in prison for a long time (then again, maybe not) and I expect you to be strong and to project strength outwardly because that will help us be strong as well. The path ahead is still long and full of struggles and I'm only at the start. But I have faith in God that it will all turn out well, and that you'll one day get to have grandchildren from me and from Gali.

Dad, I have no doubt you will one day serve in the Jewish Temple as a poet . . . so go back to work and trust in God that it's all from him. By the way, you know that Gali himself did not intend to go to the protest because on Friday when I came back from classes, he suggested that we go to Shavei Shomron and I said no.

Mom, I'm very proud of you for your strong stance and I hope that you'll continue this way. Don't be afraid to tell the press (scums) what you really think of them. Don't apologize to anyone because you're not to blame, and they'll only use it as a weapon against you. . . .

With love from Hagai. Be strong and courageous.

Hagai's appeal for support and understanding brought mixed results. For all of Amir's ranting about Rabin at home, the murder had stunned his parents. Their son boiled at the government's peace deals with the Palestinians, that much they knew. But neither contemplated the possibility that he would assassinate the prime minister—how could they? Israelis did not murder their politicians; there was no precedent for it. Geulah spent the first phone conversations with Amir screaming into the receiver—*What got into you?* Eventually, she would come to defend him (and later, to embrace conspiracy theories and deny he'd actually committed the assassination). But in her first television interview days after the shooting, Geulah renounced her son. "He's not mine anymore. He left the borders of this house. . . . I can't be a partner to this. He betrayed us in a way that's difficult to describe . . . I don't wish on any Jewish mother—even an Arab mother or a non-Jewish mother— the suffering that I'm enduring." The interview prompted Hagai to write a second letter, this one harsh and insistent: "I'm unwilling to accept any kind of criticism from you and I demand that you support him and stop saying he's a stranger to you. . . . I don't want you to argue with him about the incident every time he calls. It doesn't change anything anyway. Just give him the love that a family can give at these difficult moments when he needs it most."

Over the course of the week, police brought in Amir's friends from Bar-Ilan, starting with Ohad Skornik and Margalit Har-Shefi. A spreadsheet pulled from Amir's computer identified the students who had attended the settlement weekends. Phone logs showed which of them he'd spoken to in the days leading up to the murder. Based on Amir's testimony—he talked so much that by the third day he needed a throat lozenge—police put Har-Shefi and Skornik in the first circle of possible co-conspirators. Amir had told each about his attempts to kill Rabin and talked to both about joining his militia. But their interrogations would unfold in dramatically different ways.

Skornik had anticipated his arrest. Already on Sunday morning, he consulted with one of the country's most well-connected lawyers, Jacob Weinroth. The advice he got would keep him out of prison: Say little, be polite, and write down every question and answer in the interrogation. His unhurried longhand made the questioning tedious and frustrating for investigators. In at least a dozen interrogation sessions during the weeks that followed the murder, he studiously refrained from incriminating himself, making it difficult for police to substantiate an indictment against him.

Har-Shefi did the opposite. She spoke at length, defended Amir, insulted her interrogators, and insisted that Rabin had indeed betrayed his people.

Har-Shefi's first interrogation began just as the siren for Rabin sounded across the country. She refused to stand up—there was no reason to honor his memory, she said. The defiance would set the tone for the weeks to come. Outside, most Israelis were reeling from the details of the murder and enraged by Amir's triumphalism—he had smiled throughout his remand hearing. But Har-Shefi, who had turned twenty several months earlier, seemed unable to process the social environment, even if just to help her own cause. "We spoke about the murder of the prime minister and she failed to express sorrow or condemnation," one of the investigators noted. "She stated that Rabin is a traitor, no doubt about that, and that he caused the murder of Jews. She . . . prayed and hoped that he would suffer a heart attack or get arrested and tried for treason. She admits and is proud of the fact that at protests she shouted 'Rabin is a traitor.'"

In her defense, Har-Shefi said she never believed that Amir would actually kill Rabin. Like many others who heard his bluster, she simply underestimated him. But the potentially mitigating value of the explanation seemed to be eclipsed by her plainly evident loyalty to Amir, the sheer number of times she heard him talk about wanting to kill Rabin and having already tried, and her grating surliness in the interrogation room. When investigators told her after eight hours of questioning that she would be formally arrested for failing to prevent the murder, she scowled. "So what?"

If Har-Shefi had left room for doubt about the sway Amir held over her, it came through clearly in notes he passed to her through the interrogators. Allowing the suspects to write notes and letters formed part of the investigative strategy. The texts would then be entered into the file as evidence.

In one of the notes, Amir wrote: "You should continue with the Sabbath gatherings when your questioning ends and make sure to get the list of activists. Nothing is over. I feel terrific and I'm doing everything I thought to do. My parents need shoring up. Have people go over there and talk to them about me. They don't exactly understand what happened here. They live in [a bubble] and have no idea what's happening in the country so the shock for them is total.

"Tell the whole truth, you have nothing to lose. On the contrary, if you don't say everything, you're liable to get hurt. Don't try to look like a hero when it's not necessary. . . . You're on the outside in order to continue the activities so don't mess things up. I miss everyone and especially Nili and Hila. Give them my warm regards.

"You're my voice on the outside. Only you know precisely why I did this and only you can get the message out, so don't mess up. No one is beating me in the interrogations and all the information they have about you is from me. I was only trying to lessen the damage. . . . You have nothing to fear, you didn't do a thing. . . . See you in the next life."

At the end Amir added: "Make sure that friends help my family by visiting them and talking about me. My family doesn't know me like you guys know me."

Only Dror Adani among Amir's friends spoke as much and as candidly in the interrogations as Har-Shefi. In his very first sit-down with police he confessed that he, too, believed Rabin needed to die. "By definition, yes. Someone had to stop Rabin. According to the *Shulchan Aruch* [the Code of Jewish Law], a person who hands over the cities of Israel to a foreign ruler is a *moser* and in principle a death sentence applies to him so that he doesn't cause the death of others." Adani tried to explain certain theological nuances that distinguished him from the killer. And like Har-Shefi, he claimed to have harbored doubts about whether Amir would go through with it. But Amir and Hagai had already described to investigators by now how Adani sat with them in the bedroom on Borochov Street and suggested ways to kill Rabin—making him an accessory to the murder. Adani did not deny it.

Other friends helped round out the picture but were not viewed as suspects. Nili Kolman described Amir's role in planning the settlement weekends and his admiration for Baruch Goldstein. Rachel Adani told police about the assassin's interest in astrology and Rabin's zodiac sign. When investigators summoned Hila Frank for questioning, they expected to learn more about Amir's behavior on campus. Frank, whose boyfriend, Shlomi Halevy, had fabricated the story about a conversation overheard in the public bathroom at Tel Aviv's central bus station, had a more dramatic tale to tell.

Frank had slipped into near catatonia when she saw Amir's mug on television the night of the assassination. The very real possibility that she could have prevented the attack filled her with dread. She spoke to Halevy by phone and then paid a visit to the home of a lawyer who was also a family friend. Once in the interrogation room, she recounted her conversation with Amir in a campus hallway several months earlier, how he told her he'd recited the confessional prayer, *vidui*, before setting out to kill Rabin at Yad Vashem. She explained to investigators how Halevy ended up telling police that "a short Yemeni guy with curly hair" might be plotting to kill Rabin while withholding Amir's name.

In the already battered agency, the testimony landed hard. Shabak had chosen at the time not to summon Halevy for questioning by its own interrogators. Now, it turned out, his strange bathroom tip contained the key to preventing the assassination. Even after the murder, no one connected the intelligence Halevy had delivered with the suspect himself—the short Yemeni gunman with curly hair. When the details of the story surfaced in the Israeli press a few days later, the stench of failure that had clung to Shabak's protection unit now infected the intelligence side as well.

In his office in Tel Aviv, Carmi Gillon struggled to cope. In the few hours' time he had to sleep at night, he found himself thinking over and over again about the moment of the shooting. Peres had rejected Gillon's offer to resign, but the decision had not been a vote of confidence—more like a desperate measure to keep Shabak functioning. Soon, the agency would suffer yet another embarrassment.

Among the friends Hagai and Amir discussed with interrogators, Avishai Raviv's name came up several times. To Shabak, it was no surprise; Raviv had mentioned Amir in his reports. But the brothers both included Raviv on their short list of people who'd heard Amir talk specifically about plotting to kill Rabin. That detail distressed Raviv's handlers. Why did their agent withhold the information?

Three days after the murder, they summoned Raviv for a meeting. To the media, it looked like the agent was one more extremist being hauled in for questioning. Over several hours, Raviv came clean to his handlers, once again unloading information he'd kept from them. Yes, Raviv had heard Amir talk about *din rodef* applying to Rabin, sometimes in group settings and sometimes in conversations alone. And yes, he'd heard him say that Rabin needed to be killed. On one occasion, Raviv said, Amir went further, actually specifying that he intended to murder the prime minister.

The confession bewildered the Shabak officers. At the very least, the agent had failed spectacularly. He'd heard someone scheming to assassinate the prime minister and reported nothing. But was it more than just negligence? A debate would ensue over Raviv's future with the agency, specifically whether to fire him and put him on trial for failing to prevent the murder. For Raviv, it was a frightening prospect; he could not imagine a life outside Shabak. He explained to his handlers that many people in the milieu where he'd embedded himself talked about *din rodef* and the need to kill Rabin. He simply did not take Amir seriously. Still, it was his job to report on potential threats—not to assess their veracity.

While Raviv's fate hung in the balance, an Israeli journalist learned about his relationship with the agency. On November 17, nearly two weeks after the murder, Channel One's Amnon Abramovich reported that Raviv was a Shabak mole operating under the code name Champagne. The journalist inserted the detail at the end of an in-studio report focused mainly on the exchanges Amir and other suspects had with their interrogators. Among other things, Abramovich described how Margalit Har-Shefi refused to stand during the siren for Rabin. But it was the detail about Raviv that caused an uproar. Within days, the agency would be forced to confirm the report.

Once again Shabak found itself on the defensive. In opinion polls, huge numbers of Israelis now regarded the entire agency as incompetent—its bodyguards, its intelligence gatherers, and its informers. Settlers and other rightists blamed Shabak for running an agent provocateur in their midst with the aim of smearing the entire right-wing camp. Though most of the incitement against Rabin had been generated by activists and politicians with no connection to Shabak, the Champagne ordeal allowed them to slyly shift the blame to the agency.

The Raviv debacle would also nurture conspiracy theories about the assassination—that, in hindsight, would be its lasting legacy.

Given the relationship between Amir and Raviv, the conspiracists would claim, Shabak must have known what was coming and allowed it to happen. Over time, the theories would morph and mutate. They would migrate from the far right to the Israeli mainstream. Though no evidence would surface to support these theories, they would prove to be exceedingly resilient.

———————

SHABAK'S TROUBLES WORRIED Peres. He needed a functioning security agency if he was to proceed with the hand-over of West Bank territory to the Palestinians—which he intended to do. With the trauma of the assassination still lingering, he also needed to feel personally secure. The protection unit now had dozens of men guarding the prime minister. They took extraordinary precautions whenever he moved around, halting traffic, putting up curtains to hide his passage through seam zones, and keeping even journalists far away. But instead of inspiring confidence, the measures radiated overcompensation and self-doubt.

Peres had spent the first days after Rabin's death considering whether to call a quick election or serve out the year that remained on Rabin's term. To most of the political figures surrounding him there seemed to be one clear answer. Rabin's murder had prompted an outpouring of sympathy for Peres and contempt for Netanyahu. Though the Likud leader had nearly matched Rabin in popularity polls before the assassination, a new survey showed him losing to Peres by a huge margin, more than 30 percentage points in a head-to-head contest. Winning an election would give Peres four full years to complete a final accord with the Palestinians and negotiate a peace deal with Syria. The region would be transformed.

Yossi Beilin advocated strongly for elections. The architect of the Oslo Accords had been in New York on the night of the murder. He flew back to Israel on a commercial flight, seated next to Ehud Barak, who had left the military to serve as Rabin's interior minister. In Jerusalem on Sunday, Beilin spent nearly an hour with Peres.

His old mentor looked haggard and unfocused. For the first time, Beilin informed Peres about the yearlong backchannel negotiation he'd been conducting with Arafat's deputy, Mahmoud Abbas. The two men had completed the draft of a full-blown peace accord days before the murder. Though it was nonbinding, the so-called Beilin–Abu Mazen agreement—Abu Mazen being Abbas's nom de guerre—would give the official negotiators a huge head start once the talks on a final accord got under way.

Beilin had been planning to show the draft to Rabin at a meeting already scheduled for November 8. Now he was suggesting that Peres win a mandate of his own in a snap election and then wrap up the Palestinian track quickly. The longer he waited, the more time opponents on both sides would have to undermine the process with violence, he said.

But Peres wavered. The murder had created a mesh of complicated emotions for Peres, not just trauma and survivor's guilt but also a tinge of envy that his lifelong rival had been immortalized by the assassination—leaving him alone with the fallout. "Rabin became a saint that night," the columnist Nahum Barnea would say later. "So Peres was envious." Peres's string of electoral defeats over the years had left him craving public approval. But a victory now would really be Rabin's victory. Peres wanted to earn it himself.

Beilin and others sensed the old rivalry reasserting itself, even in Rabin's absence. In his own philosophical way, Peres would admit it himself, years later. "I thought it was unfair to take advantage of this occasion that was created after the murder of Rabin. I thought it wouldn't be . . . correct historically." But in the moment, he framed it as a practical issue. The government had a year to press ahead with the peace agenda, including the West Bank pullback, Peres told Beilin. He was leaning toward serving out the term.

The rivalry between Peres and Rabin would be a factor in other ways as well. Since Rabin had also served as defense minister, that position now needed to be filled. Barak, who had been a popular army chief and the most decorated soldier in Israel's history, was the obvious choice. But Peres preferred to keep the job for himself, just as Rabin had done. Uzi Baram, who served as the tourism minister, quarreled openly with Peres over the issue. He argued that Barak would bring some of Rabin's badly needed security mettle to the table. And he would provide Peres some distance from the electorally damaging suicide attacks, in case they persisted. But Peres stood his ground. Why didn't you urge Rabin to surrender the position? he growled. At a moment in Israel's history when the challenges seemed particularly complicated, Peres would not allow himself to assume a lighter load than Rabin's. He kept the portfolio and made Barak his foreign minister.

Those first days had an endless quality to them, stretching from four or five in the morning until after midnight. Rabin's aides had turned over classified documents for Peres to read and briefed him on issues Rabin had kept from his cabinet ministers. Among other things, Peres learned that Rabin had given Washington a tentative pledge to evacuate the entire Golan Heights in exchange for a satisfactory peace agreement with Syria. The willingness to withdraw violated a promise Rabin made during the 1992 election. Israel had captured the Golan in 1967, along with the West Bank and Gaza; successive governments had described it as vital for Israel's security. Peres seemed surprised.

Rabin had told the Americans to keep the pledge tucked away until Syrian president Hafez al-Assad agreed to Israel's terms on security and other issues. Among Clinton's peace team members, it became known as "the pocket." Itamar Rabinovich, the Israeli ambassador to Washington and lead negotiator with the Syrians, would make sure to correct anyone who referred to it as a commitment. It was a "hypothetical, conditional willingness to withdraw in return for a satisfactory package of peace and security," as he put it. Though Rabinovich had been negotiating with Syrian representatives for more than two years, Assad had failed to offer what Rabin regarded as an acceptable package.

After Rabin's funeral, Peres and Clinton met at the King David Hotel in Jerusalem to discuss the Syrian track. The hotel had housed the offices of the British Mandate when it was blown up by Jewish militants in 1946. The reconstruction made it Jerusalem's most elegant and stately hotel, with its Art Deco lobby and spectacular view to the walls of the Old City. Members of the American peace team, including Martin Indyk and Dennis Ross, had long regarded the Syrian track as more important than the process with the Palestinians. Now Clinton wanted to know if Peres would honor Rabin's pledge regarding the Golan Heights. The new prime minister tarried for a moment, then agreed to embrace his predecessor's formula: for the right deal, he would cede the Golan in its entirety.

By the end of the week, Peres had taken the option of a quick election off the table. He would serve as prime minister for a year, establish his own record of success, and then compete against Netanyahu. It was his first big decision as prime minister and it would turn out to be a fateful one. Now he faced a second dilemma. Peres would need a significant achievement to point to in his election campaign. A year was enough time to work toward a full peace accord with either Syria or the Palestinians but not both.

Peres had invited Beilin to Jerusalem on Saturday night, November 11, to hear more about the agreement with Abbas and review the maps the two men had drawn up. He hosted Beilin in the living room of a small apartment that the government made available to him as foreign minister—Peres had yet to move into the prime minister's residence.

With the help of their teams, Beilin and Abbas had produced a thirteen-page agreement that settled all the difficult issues facing the two sides. Considering how intractable the conflict had been, it was a remarkably straightforward document. The Palestinians would get a state of their own on about 95 percent of the West Bank and Gaza. Israel would incorporate some large Jewish settlements into its borders—about 5 percent of the West Bank—but would dismantle all the rest. To compensate Palestinians for the annexation, Israel would cede roughly the same amount of land from its own territory. The two sides would redraw the borders of Jerusalem to include several large Jewish settlements and then share the city, with Arab neighborhoods run by Palestinians and Jewish neighborhoods by Israel.

Regarding what Palestinians referred to almost sacredly as the "right of return," Abbas agreed that the repatriation to Israel of refugees displaced in 1948 was impractical. Instead, these refugees and their progeny would settle for "compensation and rehabilitation for moral and material loss."

The parameters far exceeded the positions Rabin had articulated publicly. In his last address in parliament weeks earlier, the prime minister referred to a Palestinian entity that fell short of a state. But Rabin had repeatedly shown himself willing to be far more flexible than his public positions indicated—that much was clear from his readiness to cede the Golan Heights. And his closest aides, including Haber and Sheves, believed that withholding support for full Palestinian sovereignty until the final status talks was part of his negotiating strategy. Ron Pundak, who had helped lead the back channel in Stockholm, felt sure Rabin would recognize the benefits for Israel. "Based on everything we knew, we were confident he would say yes."

Peres was more dovish than Rabin. But making dramatic concessions to the Palestinians in the aftermath of the assassination now struck him as divisive, not exactly what he aimed for in an election year. When Beilin unrolled a map that corresponded to the plan, Peres pointed to the Jordan Valley, a territory that the Labor Party had traditionally sought to retain for Israel's security. Israelis are not ready for it to come under Palestinian control, Peres said. The plan would have to wait until after the elections.

That left him with Syria. Peres hoped he could entice Assad to negotiate with him directly, as Egyptian President Anwar Sadat had done with Israeli Prime Minister Menachem Begin at Camp David seventeen years earlier. If the two sides could agree on the outline of an accord, the election would become a referendum on a peace deal with Syria. "Peres was very seasoned at timetables," Rabinovich would recall. "For an election in November, he wanted a major achievement by May." Preferring the Syrian track, then, would be the second big decision of his premiership. In less than a week, Peres had laid down two wagers, one on himself and one on Assad. Both were risky bets.

The seven-day mourning period lasted through Saturday evening. Though it drizzled over the weekend, many thousands of Israelis made their way to Rabin's gravesite on Jerusalem's Mount Herzl, where patches of freshly packed dirt had turned to mud. That night, one of the darkest weeks in Israel's history ended with a downpour.

On Sunday evening, Leah left Rav Ashi to speak to a huge crowd that had congregated once again at the plaza in Tel Aviv, this time to commemorate Rabin. From the stage, the gathering looked even larger than it had the week before. More than 200,000 people stood in silence, listening to songs and speeches and, at the request of organizers, withholding applause. "Never have so many people stood in one place so quietly. Not in Israel," Nahum Barnea would write. The public outpouring over the preceding week had persuaded Leah that the murderer failed. Instead of wrecking Rabin's peace process, he had given it momentum. Now she addressed her husband: "I want to believe that this terrible tragedy which has befallen me, us, all of us, this monstrous price that you and we have paid, was not a vain sacrifice. For we have all risen from the nightmare to a different world."

The event ended on a hopeful note: Tel Aviv mayor Roni Milo announced the plaza would now be called Rabin Square. But it would take more time to determine whether Amir had failed or succeeded. And the nightmare would not go away so quickly.

Four nights after the gathering, investigators brought Amir to the plaza for a reenactment of the murder. The suspect, his ankles bound together in a long chain, vaulted from a white police van just after two in the morning, followed by guards and a police camera crew. For twenty-five minutes Amir directed the action, positioning the stand-ins and retracing his own steps from the night of the murder. On the roof of the adjacent shopping mall, Shabak officers watched in dismay, including the bodyguard Yoram Rubin, his arm still in a sling. Police had barred them from bringing their sidearms, fearing one of them might be tempted to take a shot at Amir. Beyond police barricades, a small crowd gathered.

When Amir drew a toy pistol and made the sound of gunfire, gasps of horror rose from the crowd. Yoav Gazit, an investigator in the case and the stand-in for Rabin, lunged forward as if hit with real bullets. Though they'd never met on campus, Gazit and Amir had been fellow students at Bar-Ilan.

"OK, so after you took us through the event, do you have some-thing to add?" another investigator asked Amir, holding a microphone to his mouth to record the exchange.

"No regrets," Amir said.

"Excuse me?" the investigator asked, leaning in.

"It needed to be done and that's it."

CHAPTER 9

The Man Who Voted Twice

"Our last chance is this election and if the Labor Party wins again, this is the end of Judaism and you are also responsible."

—YIGAL AMIR

Political assassinations don't necessarily change a country's direction. In democratic societies, an extremist who kills in order to prevent certain policies from going forward can end up accelerating them—in part by infusing them with a sense of historic inevitability.

In Israel, Rabin's murder seemed to rouse the peace camp and weaken its opponents. People who had been largely silent in their support for Oslo now made themselves heard, displacing the rowdy hardliners at the plazas and town squares. Settlers and other rightists toned down their rhetoric, some from a recognition that lines had been crossed, others simply because the climate had changed. The novelist Amos Oz captured the feeling of peace's inevitability in a short essay he penned a week after the murder. "The peace process between Israel and the Palestinians, Israel and the rest of the Arab world will continue; there will be a comprehensive peace agreement,"

Oz wrote. "There is simply no alternative to a historic compromise between Jews and Arabs."

In reality, the murder did not make peace inevitable, and neither did it settle the great debate in Israel. Large segments of the country still viewed the ceding of land as dangerous or sacrilegious. Extremists on both the Israeli and Palestinian sides remained determined to sabotage any reconciliation. Israel's direction now depended on how adroitly Peres would maneuver in the two hundred days ahead—the coda to the Rabin story.

He was off to a shaky start.

Peres had learned that the Israeli negotiation with Syria foundered mainly over the security arrangements. Rabin demanded limits on Syrian troop deployments along the border and the posting of early warning stations following a retreat from the Golan, a mountainous region that towered over much of northern Israel. To President Assad, these seemed like infringements on Syrian sovereignty. Rabin also wanted a staged withdrawal, stretched out over several years. Assad expected to get the Golan within months of a peace treaty.

Peres had ideas for breaking the logjam. In late November, he discussed them with Uri Savir, the former Oslo negotiator who would now run the talks with Syria. Peres would be willing to bend on security if Assad agreed to make the Golan the hub for a thriving commercial relationship between the two countries. The more Syria benefited economically from its relationship with Israel, he told Savir, the less incentive it would have to violate the deal and rekindle old hostilities. In effect, industrial zones and high-tech ventures would trump military measures as the real guarantors of Israeli security.

Peres also raised the idea of a summit meeting between the two leaders. Assad had ceded almost no authority to the negotiators he dispatched to meetings with Israelis over the years, making the talks slow and frustrating. Peres felt sure he could move quickly to the essence of the dispute in direct talks—as he had with Arafat whenever a disagreement arose among lower-level negotiators. Assad's reluctance to meet face-to-face reminded Peres of an old joke he shared with Savir: A young man who was too shy to confess his love to a woman directly, put it in writing, sending her a letter every day. After a year, the woman married the mailman.

In December, Peres conveyed a series of questions to Assad through US Secretary of State Warren Christopher regarding the way forward in talks. They included references to Peres's schedule—one year to complete the first draft of a peace agreement. Assad did not rule it out but didn't explicitly embrace the timetable either. His willingness to entertain the idea encouraged Peres, who set about formulating positions for a new round of talks. But Rabinovich, one of Israel's most astute Assad watchers, sensed a rebuff. "Assad generally preferred to make an agreement with Israel in the beginning of a prime minister's term," allowing time for an Israeli withdrawal before an election brought someone new to power. "I don't think he ever intended to complete a deal with Peres," he would recall.

By late in the month, Assad's reticence would become evident to Savir as well. The Syrian leader dispatched a delegation for several days of talks with Israel at the Wye River Conference Center on Maryland's Eastern Shore, a rustic lodge with grassy knolls and rows of cherry trees. It was the most intensive interaction Assad had allowed between his representatives and their Israeli counterparts to date—a significant upgrade in the process. But on the Israeli proposals Peres thought of as deadlock-busting—the economic development that would substitute for security guarantees—the Syrians conveyed an ambivalence that seemed to flow directly from Assad. "They were interested in an accommodation with Israel but feared being overwhelmed by the economic strength of their Westernized, democratic neighbor," Savir would write in a memoir, years later. "The solution they were seeking was aid without influence and peace without engagement."

By the end of the round, the teams had failed to make significant headway.

At home, Peres struggled as well. In the days after the murder, the outrage Amir had inspired across the political spectrum prompted coalition and opposition figures to rally around the new prime minister. But the more time passed, the less the assassination factored as a political consideration. When Peres presented his new government to parliament on November 22, eighteen days after the assassination, a large majority of lawmakers endorsed it. But his decision to press ahead with the hand-over of West Bank cities to the Palestinians restored the political realm to its fractious self, minus the ugly invective (at least at first).

The hand-over also ate at the margin Peres held over Netanyahu in opinion polls. He still led by a lot—20 points, according to some surveys. But the trend line looked troubling. Netanyahu, who had rated his own chances of defeating Peres at zero in the days after the murder, seemed to be regaining his footing. In a conversation with Labor's Uzi Baram in December, he offered a new assessment: If Palestinian terrorism picked up in the winter, Netanyahu said, Peres's popularity could plunge dramatically. To Baram, the remark seemed breathtakingly calculating. The assassination had changed so much about Israel's political culture, he thought—and yet it had changed nothing at all.

Amir's regular remand hearings kept the horror of the murder firmly in the public consciousness. His courtroom polemics and his relentless triumphalism drew scorn. But the publicity also galvanized extremists who were quietly finding ways to venerate the murderer—just as they had venerated Baruch Goldstein. Letters of support now flowed to Amir's home from Israel and abroad, bundles of them. When Amir's younger sister, Vardit, got married in December, supporters mobilized to make sure no one interfered. "Thankfully, God heard our prayers and sent hordes of Haredis to keep out the few Hellenizers who came to cause trouble," Hagai would write in a diary he kept in prison. "And some anonymous person made sure to supply security people and a car for the bride."

The support buoyed Hagai, who worried that his siblings would bear the stigma of the assassination. It also suggested to him that certain religious figures were ready to quietly embrace the Amir family. When his sister sought benedictions from rabbis before and after her wedding—privately, in their offices—some conveyed their blessings to Amir and Hagai as well. "Many of the rabbis in the Haredi world supported us," Hagai would say years later. "If they would have attacked us, it would have been a problem."

Determining whether rabbis—those or others—had given Amir a religious authorization to kill Rabin remained a priority in the police investigation. Amir denied it. He didn't need rabbis to interpret Jewish law for him, he told his interrogators. He knew it well enough himself.

But Hagai admitted several times that his brother *had* consulted with rabbis and received at least an implicit confirmation that *din rodef* applied to Rabin and that targeting him was thus permissible. On November 6, one investigator who questioned Hagai wrote in his notes: "The subject repeats that he heard from his brother about having received corroboration from a rabbi regarding the fact that *din rodef* and *din moser* apply to him [Rabin]." Another investigator wrote the following day that Hagai described Amir as having driven to a Jewish seminary in Samaria to ask a rabbi there for permission to assassinate Rabin. "After Yigal received the permission," the interrogator noted, "he came home and told the subject [Hagai] about it and together the subject and Yigal decided to carry out the murder."

Hagai provided no names; he claimed that his brother withheld them. But investigators had already put their hands on the letter the three settler rabbis had written earlier in the year suggesting Rabin was an accomplice to murder through the tenets of *din rodef* and *din moser*. And Yoel Bin-Nun, the moderate settler who had maintained a correspondence with Rabin, implicated at least one other rabbi. The assassination had caused a crisis of faith for Bin-Nun. He announced days after the murder that he would expose the agitators if they did not come forward on their own. "The problem is these Torah authorities, without whom, no kid would have dared do such a thing," he said at a public meeting of settlers and other rightists. "If they don't resign their rabbinic posts by the end of the seven-day mourning period, I will fight them, even to the death."

Police questioned rabbis throughout the fall and winter, including Dov Lior and Eliezer Melamed, two of the letter's three authors. Both claimed that the references to *din rodef* and *din moser* were theoretical inquiries—a scholarly attempt to verify whether the edicts applied to current events. All the rabbis questioned denied having made specific rulings regarding Rabin. Chief Superintendent Ofer Gamliel, who helped lead the murder investigation and spent many hours with Amir, felt sure the rabbis were lying. But with no hard evidence, police eventually closed the file against them. "The letter was examined but the contents could not substantiate criminal charges," the attorney general wrote about the three rabbis. Regarding suspicions against other religious figures, he was clear: "Rumors alone cannot form the basis for criminal charges."

Gamliel would come to see the inquiry into the rabbis as a failure. "I have no doubt in retrospect that certain people encouraged him [Amir], either directly or indirectly," he said years later. But the tendency of the religious community to close ranks around its leaders and punish the rare whistle-blower hampered the probe. Amir, who had no trouble incriminating his friends at Bar-Ilan and elsewhere, would not implicate rabbis. Bin-Nun, who did, would suffer death threats and eventually be driven from the settlement where he had lived for years.

For Gamliel, who had worked on some of Israel's biggest cases in the preceding two decades, the murder investigation presented few other challenges. Amir had provided enough information to support indictments against himself, Hagai, Adani, and Har-Shefi, on counts ranging from murder and conspiracy to the much lesser charge of failing to prevent a crime. A military court would convict one other suspect, the active-duty soldier Arik Schwartz, for stealing explosives from his base and giving them to the Amirs.

But Gamliel did puzzle extensively over one issue: Who cried out, "It's not real" at the murder scene? At least a dozen people in the parking lot and beyond heard the words or variations on them, including "it's fake" and "blanks, blanks." Reports about it, coupled with the disclosure that Avishai Raviv had worked for Shabak, were already fueling conspiracy theories about the murder. If Amir had fired blanks, clearly someone else killed Rabin.

The conspiracy theories surged when Amir cited a rumor during one of his remand hearings about a Shabak bodyguard who died mysteriously after the assassination. The story turned out to be incorrect. The theories continued to circulate even after a video shot by an amateur photographer surfaced showing Amir lunging at Rabin and firing his gun, and the prime minister falling forward. The photographer, Roni Kempler, submitted the video to the Shamgar Commission probing the murder and sold the rights to Israeli media some weeks later.

As part of their inquest, investigators drew up a table with the names of all twenty-five policemen on the scene and asked each one to report what words he heard and who said them. None could point to a specific person. Gamliel considered the possibility that it was Amir himself, uttering the phrase as he squeezed off his rounds. He and his brother would certainly have been crafty enough to calculate the effect of it—how it might sow confusion and deter Rabin's bodyguards from firing back. It seemed like the kind of detail Hagai might have read in a thriller or a manual for the amateur assassin.

But Amir denied it repeatedly. Gamliel, who shared Amir's ethnic background, felt he had some insight into the suspect's character. He found him easy to read. Whenever Amir seemed to be withholding something, Gamliel would deliberately underestimate him—you aren't smart enough to have thought of that. The slight would launch Amir into bragging mode and draw out the information Gamliel was seeking. To the investigator, Amir's denials seemed genuine. If he had survived the shooting because of his own clever tactic, Gamliel felt sure he would have boasted about it.

At some point, Gamliel began focusing on members of the Dignitary Protection Unit. Shabak's culture of secrecy made interrogating agency officers a delicate affair. To put them at ease, Gamliel summoned the bodyguards in the evenings, when the precinct emptied out, and questioned them alone. Often, he would leave their names off the interrogation log and include only their positions or other identifying details. Eventually, one of them provided an account that would clear up the mystery, at least partially.

The Shabak man told Gamliel he'd heard the shots fired from Amir's gun and lost his focus. The words "it's not real"—in Hebrew, "*ze lo ameetee*"—flew from his mouth almost involuntarily, as an expression of his own disbelief: This could not be happening. Around him, people trained to respond to a shooting instantly had failed to fire back at Amir. His own inaction and the possibility that others had hesitated because of the words he uttered filled him with shame. He asked that his name not be disclosed.

The story failed to explain how some people had heard variations of the words the Shabak man shouted. But Gamliel had a theory. He surmised that others at the murder scene echoed the cry—not precisely as they heard it but in the manner they construed it. In what he thought of as a real-life version of the game Telephone, "it's not real," became "it's fake," which in turn became "blanks, blanks." A cry of incredulity had morphed into a hint at something sinister—through serial reinterpretations. Gamliel took down the account and agreed to keep the Shabak man's identity a secret.

Toward the end of the year, Israel completed its withdrawal from each of the cities in the West Bank except Hebron and from many of the towns and villages. Oslo II, the agreement that cost Rabin his life, was quietly taking shape. Peres remained focused on the talks with Syria but in the final days of 1995, another issue vied for his attention: Yahya Ayyash, Hamas's master bomb maker, was finally in Israel's sights.

After hiding in the West Bank for years, the Hamas bomb maker responsible for the deaths of more than fifty Israelis had quietly crossed into Gaza, where his wife and child lived. Among the people he took into his confidence there was a certain Palestinian businessman who also happened to be an informer for Shabak. Through the informer, the agency learned that Ayyash was hiding in a safe house in Beit Lahiya, on the northern edge of Gaza. On Peres's order, Carmi Gillon now informed the prime minister, Israel could eliminate the most formidable terrorist it had ever faced.

To Gillon, the decision seemed easy. Ayyash had headed Israel's most-wanted list since 1992. He excelled not only at engineering but also at persuading young men to become suicide bombers, a skill that troubled Shabak almost as much as his technical aptitude. Killing him would end a sustained manhunt that had taxed the agency's resources.

Gillon hoped it would do something else as well: redeem Shabak, and perhaps himself, from the failure of the Rabin assassination two months earlier. "The morale was low. In addition to the grief and the feeling of failure, the entire Shabak was talked about in the media as incompetent," he admitted.

For Peres, the arithmetic seemed more complicated. Hamas had not carried out a suicide attack in more than four months, the longest stretch since the Goldstein massacre. Whether killing Ayyash would reinforce the trend or trigger a new wave of bombings and undermine Peres's political standing was anyone's guess. In effect, Israel would be gambling on the idea that Ayyash alone possessed the skills to engineer large deadly attacks. If he had trained others, a reasonable assumption, they would certainly want to avenge his death.

Like Gillon, Peres seemed to have had motivations beyond the immediate battle with Hamas, including a drive to match Rabin's security record. And he needed a standout achievement now that hope in the Syria talks was fading. In late December, he authorized the strike.

On the first Friday of the New Year, Ayyash answered a call on a cell phone he had received from the Palestinian businessman, expecting to hear his father. Shabak technicians had embedded a small explosive in the phone with a minimal blast radius. When a surveillance team identified Ayyash's voice on the line, soldiers on a plane overhead triggered the explosive, blowing out the side of the man's head.

It would take several hours for Shabak to corroborate that Ayyash had died. When the confirmation came, Gillon felt enormous rélief. "After the killing of Yehiya Ayyash, people . . . stopped talking about the agency as worthless," he would write in his memoir. "I personally felt that I had now made good on my promise to Peres that I would put the agency back on track and restore its sense of confidence." Gillon tendered his resignation two days after the cell-phone strike.

He would not be around to face the consequences.

BY THE END of January 1996, Peres grew tired of Assad's dithering. At his office in Jerusalem, he wrote the Syrian president a note, taking a tougher line this time. The only way forward was through a series of meetings between the two leaders, Peres wrote. If Assad was serious about peace with Israel, now was the time to move. Secretary of State Warren Christopher carried the letter to Damascus on February 5 and brought back a reply the following day: Assad realized that a meeting would be necessary eventually but he was unwilling to set a date.

To Peres, the response meant one thing: With virtually no prospect of clinching a deal in the coming months, his November election gambit had failed. The prime minister still had a double-digit advantage over Netanyahu in polls, but his aides wondered how long he could sustain the lead as the anguish over Rabin's assassination faded. Peres pondered the question himself; perhaps he'd committed a mistake back in November when he decided to serve out Rabin's term. A week after Christopher's shuttle mission to Damascus, Peres convened a press conference to announce a new decision: he would bring up the date of the elections to May.

The announcement effectively launched the race between Peres and Netanyahu. It would be a referendum on the peace deals with the Palestinians and a contest over the status of the West Bank and Gaza: would they continue to be military-ruled enclaves where settlers strove to bring about Jewish redemption—or would Israel cede them to the Palestinians? A change in the election law meant that for the first time, Israelis would elect their prime minister in a direct ballot and cast a second vote for the party they preferred. The new system was devised to minimize the agonizing horse trading that went on after elections, when left and right vied for the support of the ultra-Orthodox parties to form a majority coalition. It seemed to favor Peres. With his commanding lead and his incumbent status, the election was his to lose.

The winter of 1996 was colder than usual; the campaign ramped up slowly. Peres and Netanyahu both rented office space for their headquarters and hired American political consultants. Both scheduled political events around the country. Among Israelis, the feeling that this election carried particular weight seemed palpable. It even permeated the Tel Aviv courtroom where Amir's trial had been under way for more than a month now. Edmond Levy, who led the trial's three-judge panel, struggled to prevent the defendant from turning every hearing into a political spectacle.

Amir seemed adept at creating chaos in his new environment. In the first weeks of the trial, two of his lawyers resigned, leaving his defense in the hands of a Texas-born immigrant who appeared to know little about Israeli law and almost no Hebrew at all. Amir took over from the lawyer at one point, questioning the witnesses himself. In prison, he somehow wheedled extra phone privileges from a guard, using the minutes to call Margalit Har-Shefi and Nili Kolman. Both women hung up on hearing his voice. When Har-Shefi's father complained to police about the call, prison officials punished Amir and the guard.

Hagai passed the time in his cell adding entries to his diary, a yellow notepad he hid from the guards. In pages and pages of tight little handwriting, he recounted dreams, complained about the guards, and fantasized about a natural disaster striking Israel—a huge earthquake—so that he and his brother could flee prison. Hagai even expressed a modicum of regret for his actions, though not from any sense of sorrow at Rabin's death. "Sometimes I think, did we really need all this? Why did we get involved?" he wrote on February 10. "We could have lived our lives like everyone else, without a care. I know it's a defeatist attitude but I can't stop thinking about it in these difficult, depressing moments."

In another entry, Hagai admonished himself for having cooperated with his interrogators. "It turns out from the testimony that I talked too much and that I have only myself to blame for my situation. Not only that but I harmed other people, like Dror and Margalit," he wrote. "I hate myself so much for it, for my stupid gullibility. . . . The experience shattered a myth I had about myself that I'm good at withstanding pressure. No one exerted any real pressure on me, and yet I kept talking, out of sheer stupidity and gullibility. I feel bad for the suffering it's causing my family. I have no words. I deserve everything."

Hagai ordered books from the prison library and kept a record of the ones he got through. It included some classics like Fyodor Dostoyevsky's *Crime and Punishment* and William Golding's *Lord of the Flies*, but also the self-help bestseller *I'm OK—You're OK* by Thomas A. Harris and a book on meditation. Years later, he would add the Harry Potter series to the list.

In mid-February, the traditional Muslim forty-day mourning period for Yahya Ayyash came to an end. Shabak had assumed that if Hamas had the capacity to avenge his death, it would do so immediately following the interlude, as it had in the aftermath of the Goldstein massacre two years earlier. So as the days passed and the group remained passive, Peres felt a wave of relief. Though his campaign was off to a strong start, he had squandered large leads in three previous elections. Winning in polls but losing elections had come to be known as the Peres curse. Carmi Gillon, now in his final days as head of Shabak, shared the sense of relief. On February 22, he briefed his successor, the former navy chief Ami Ayalon, took part in a hand-over ceremony in Tel Aviv, and cleared out his office.

A day later, Ayalon convened the agency's top officers and announced that, starting Sunday, he would be reviewing all of Shabak's old policies and directives. The Rabin assassination had brought about a general collapse of the agency, he said. It needed to be rebuilt. Ayalon spent the weekend at his home in the Carmel Mountains near Haifa and told his driver to pick him up at six on Sunday morning for an early start. But the agency review would be overtaken by something else altogether.

On his way in to work, just before seven a.m., a radio news announcer broadcast the first details of what seemed like a suicide attack on a bus in Jerusalem. From the backseat of his agency car, Ayalon asked the driver to turn up the volume. Bus number 18, which ferries residents from the southern neighborhoods of the city to the busiest part of downtown and then on to the central bus station, blew up toward the end of its route. The damage to the bus and the buildings surrounding it looked to be extensive, according to a reporter on the scene. Ayalon could hear the wailing of ambulances through the radio. The casualty toll would likely be high.

Nahum Barnea, the *Yedioth Ahronoth* columnist, heard the radio report as well. At his home in Jerusalem, he put on a striped dress shirt and a black leather jacket and rushed to the scene. Barnea's son, Yonatan, a twenty-year-old soldier in an intelligence unit, rode the 18 line to his base on Sunday mornings. Barnea wondered whether Yonatan had been on the bus—whether he would be reporting on his own son's death.

At the scene, Barnea opened his notebook and wrote the date at the top of an empty page: February 25. Around him, body parts lay strewn on the street, alongside glass and twisted metal. The blast had reduced the bus to a burned-out shell. But before he launched into his reporting routine, Barnea received a message from his editor in Tel Aviv, Eitan Amit, instructing him to leave the area and report to the newspaper's Jerusalem office at once. Amit had learned that Yonatan Barnea had indeed been on the bus and had died in the blast— along with twenty-five other passengers. He worried that his reporter would learn of his son's death in the most horrific of ways: by seeing his body, or perhaps fragments of it, on the street.

When Barnea reached the bureau, Amit spoke to him by phone from Tel Aviv. "I'm sorry to have to convey the worst possible news. . . . Your son is among the dead," he told him. Barnea had covered or written about nearly every one of the suicide attacks in the preceding two years. He had coined the term "victims of peace" to convey the irony of a peace process that had caused a surge rather than an ebb in violence. Now he held the phone to his ear and tried to understand the words. When a cabinet member paid a condolence call later in the day, Barnea confided that Yonatan had been a Peres supporter. "You lost a vote," he said. Then he added: "You probably lost a lot of votes today."

Within days, Shabak pieced together a chronicle of the attack. Soon after the strike on Ayyash, a Hamas operative had slipped out of Gaza and crossed to the West Bank to plot the group's revenge. He assigned the Jerusalem bombing to a cell in Al Fawar, near Hebron. Members of the cell, the agency learned, were now hiding out in Ramallah, one of the cities that had come under Palestinian control months earlier. A second suicide bomber they had sent to Ashkelon blew himself up at a junction an hour after the Jerusalem attack but managed to kill just one person other than himself.

Ayalon now faced a dilemma. Arresting the cell would require Israeli forces to enter a Palestinian-run city, which the Oslo II agreement expressly forbade. But waiting until the Hamas men returned to Al Fawar, a town still under Israeli security control, would mean putting off interrogations that might produce time-sensitive information. What if the cell had already set a third attack in motion? After consulting Shabak's top officers, he chose to wait.

It would prove to be the wrong decision. On Sunday morning, exactly a week after the Jerusalem bombing, the cell struck again—on the same bus line. This time, the assailant killed fewer people, nineteen, perhaps because some regular passengers had decided to avoid public transportation altogether. But the psychological impact of the third suicide attack in a week was devastating. Israelis who had withstood wars and sieges now talked about staying away from buses and public events. The government had sealed off the West Bank and Gaza, and yet Hamas continued its campaign. Its attacks seemed unpreventable.

Peres, who had been at his apartment in Tel Aviv when the second bus exploded, set out to see the horror for himself. Years later, he would recall it as a traumatic experience. As he entered Jerusalem, some ninety minutes after the bombing, a heavy rain began to fall. "There were thousands of people around. The bodies of the dead were still there and the blood covered the whole square. . . . As I came in, they all started to shout, 'Murderer, look what he did to us.' What could I say to them?" Peres left without addressing the crowd.

But Hamas was not done yet.

The day after the second Jerusalem attack, a suicide bomber tried to enter Dizengoff Center, Tel Aviv's largest mall. When a policeman turned him away, the assailant walked into an adjacent intersection and detonated the forty-four-pound nail bomb he had strapped to himself, killing thirteen people. The afternoon crowd outside the mall included many children in costumes—Israelis would be celebrating Purim that evening. Five teenagers were among the dead.

For the first time, Ayalon comprehended the encumbrance he'd taken on in agreeing to lead Shabak. Fifty-nine Israelis had died in his first ten days on the job. He now recommended to Peres that the army impose a cordon around the West Bank's main cities. Palestinians would not only be barred from entering Israel, they would also be unable to travel from one part of the West Bank to another. Outside the Defense Ministry, where Ayalon briefed cabinet members, a few hundred protesters burned torches and shouted angry slogans—mostly directed at Arabs but also at Peres.

That evening, Barnea's editor called to ask if he would write a column for the next day's paper. The mourning period at his home had ended just a day earlier and the idea of resuming his work routine so soon seemed jolting. But Barnea could not bring himself to say no. He pondered whether to write something personal, to tie in the country's sudden turn with his own tragedy. But Barnea had the instincts of an analyst, not a memoirist. Instead, he wrote that Peres stood to lose the election if he could not stem the violence. "The man who was the central figure in Oslo sees the process withering with every strike by a Hamas bomber." The polls seemed to bear it out. In just a week, Netanyahu had closed most of the gap between himself and the prime minister.

In the days that followed, Peres spoke to Arafat several times by phone, demanding that he crack down on Hamas. The Palestinian leader rounded up several hundred members of the group and confiscated some weapons. In a conversation with reporters, his remarks suddenly sounded like those of Israeli officials. "We have to . . . destroy their infrastructure and to uproot terrorism," Arafat said. To Peres, it seemed that Arafat had finally understood how destructive Hamas could be to the process.

But the emotional tide in Israel had already shifted—from grief over Rabin's assassination to anger at Palestinian violence. For months, the country's most ubiquitous bumper sticker had been SHALOM HAVER, the line from Clinton's remarks after Rabin's death meaning "Goodbye, friend." Now someone coined a variation in plural that summed up the new sentiment: SHALOM HAVERIM, "Goodbye, friends"—a reference to the scores who had died in the Hamas attacks.

Clinton followed the transformation in Israel with a sense of foreboding. In early March 1996, he organized a "summit of peacemakers" that would focus on ways to combat terrorism in Israel and the region. In reality, it was an effort by the American president to stem Peres's political free fall. The event at Egypt's resort town of Sharm el-Sheikh had all the trappings of the Oslo-era ceremonies, including lofty speeches and camera-friendly interactions between Arab and Israeli leaders. In his address, Peres framed the Hamas attacks as the last thrust of a waning nihilism in the Middle East. "Our region is going through a period of transition. The dark days are at an end. The shadows of its past are lengthening."

But Israelis had grown tired of peace conferences. And it wasn't at all clear whether the extremists, Arabs or Israelis, were declining or ascending.

─────────

TOWARD THE END of March, the election campaign intensified. Pictures of the two candidates, the seventy-two-year-old Peres and the forty-six-year-old Netanyahu, suddenly appeared on billboards and banners across the country, most framed in the blue and white of Israel's flag. In the West Bank and Gaza the combination of Israel's cordons and Arafat's clampdown seemed to be working. With Hamas neutralized, the prime minister maintained a small but consistent lead over Netanyahu in opinion polls, usually of 5 or 6 points.

Peres had hired two outside advisers, the Israeli advertising man Moshe Teumim and the American Democratic Party consultant Douglas Schoen. Two senior members of Labor, Ehud Barak and Haim Ramon, led the campaign's strategy team. But for all the experience and talent in the room, the operation suffered from a constant drone of chaos and indecision.

Schoen had first worked in Israel during the 1981 campaign, representing Peres's adversary, Menachem Begin. His impression of Peres from that earlier time stuck with him. Peres seemed smart and visionary, but he lacked Begin's scrappy resourcefulness, a vital ingredient for winning elections. He also suffered from image problems. Though Peres had been a founding father who had worked with David Ben-Gurion, many Israelis viewed him less as a statesman and more as a politician, a shifty and manipulative one. Peres had led Begin in opinion surveys throughout the '81 campaign. When voting ended, Israeli Television announced Peres the victor on the basis of exit polls. But by morning, Begin had surged ahead, winning by a small margin.

Schoen had actually been hired by Rabin back in November, a full year before he would stand for reelection. The American consultant prepared his first poll for Rabin on Friday, November 3, and intended to issue it after the weekend. The assassination sent him back to the United States. When he returned to Israel in February to work for Peres, the candidate struck him as wildly overconfident. "He simply couldn't fathom the idea that he might lose—particularly to someone as radical and polarizing as Benjamin Netanyahu," Schoen would recall. Schoen suggested targeting specific groups with discrete campaigns, starting with women and Russian immigrants. But Peres brushed him off: "Doug, we don't really do that here."

Oddly, Peres seemed uninterested in going after Netanyahu directly. In part it was his notion that even criticism would somehow legitimize Netanyahu as a candidate. Peres had a real track record, a vision for the country's future, and a huge lead in opinion polls. He outmatched his opponent so dramatically, it was better to ignore him, he thought.

The two men also had a history that appeared to soften Peres's attitude toward Netanyahu. Peres had served as defense minister when Israel staged the Entebbe rescue in 1976, the operation that took the life of Netanyahu's older brother, Yonatan. He seemed to retain latent guilt over it; in effect, he had sent Yonatan, the commander of Sayeret Matkal and the pride of the Netanyahu family, to his death. While Peres could summon real malice for other adversaries, he seemed mostly indifferent toward Benjamin Netanyahu.

After the bombings Schoen pushed Peres to begin using Rabin's assassination to his advantage. The issue prompted raucous debates among members of the campaign staff: how to invoke the murder without sounding manipulative. It also revealed to Schoen the can-

228 <   KILLING A KING

didate's obsessions and how they were sabotaging his own race: his rivalry with Rabin and his determination to win the election on the merits of his own achievements. Somehow, the strategists ended up leaving Rabin out of the campaign much of the time and spurning Leah, who had offered to make appearances around the country. "In retrospect, I feel I should have perhaps insisted, but I was so reluctant to push myself and so sure they were going to succeed anyway," she would write in her memoir.

The campaign also suffered from internal strife. Peres suspected that Barak would eventually challenge him for leadership of the party. Barak, in turn, saw Ramon as his adversary in Labor's future succession battle. As long as Peres enjoyed a substantial lead over Netanyahu, the rivalries remained submerged. But his sudden decline infused the campaign with an air of hostility and dysfunction.

Netanyahu, by contrast, managed to squelch Likud's infighting and utilize every advantage he could possibly muster against Peres—starting with the suicide attacks. His American consultant, the Republican Party strategist Arthur Finkelstein, had a record of keeping his candidates on message. With his Israeli client, the message sought to exploit the increasing vulnerability Israelis were feeling. Netanyahu, the terrorism expert and former commando, would restore Israel's security, while Peres would divide Jerusalem. Peres had balked at using footage of Netanyahu at rowdy right-wing protests and drawing a connection to the Rabin assassination. Instead, burned-out buses—the ones attacked by Hamas suicide bombers—became the defining image of the campaign.

Yigal Amir's trial did keep Rabin in the public consciousness for part of the race. The hearings continued through the winter, and though judges barred journalists from broadcasting the proceedings, Israelis followed them closely. When the panel delivered its verdict and sentence on March 27, 1996, several hundred people showed up, packing the small Tel Aviv courtroom and fanning out into the hallway. Eitan Haber, who had left his government job soon after the assassination, sat near the front.

Amir had spent the preceding months arguing that he had not actually intended to kill Rabin but only paralyze him. As evidence, he cited the fact that he had aimed for Rabin's back and not his head. Now, in his final remarks, he called the proceeding a "show trial" and complained that he had been denied his right to explain his motives fully. "This is not a regular murder trial, but a trial about the existential problem of the State of Israel, the contradiction between a Jewish state and a democratic state," he said. "This subject was not dealt with at all."

Israeli law allows for capital punishment only in rare circumstances, including genocide and treason. In this case, the judges sentenced Amir to life in prison for the murder plus six additional years for wounding Yoram Rubin, the bodyguard. Haber, who had vowed after the assassination to stalk the Amir family for the rest of his life, felt no real sense of satisfaction. "I very much hope that before this scum of the earth rots away in jail, he will get to see that the murder has achieved precisely the opposite of what he had intended," he told reporters outside the courtroom. "For Yitzhak Rabin, peace will avenge his blood."

In his prison cell, Hagai wondered whether his brother would ever be freed. Israel's president routinely commuted life terms to twenty- or thirty-year sentences, but he doubted Amir would get a reduction. Hagai comforted himself with the thought that the messiah would appear soon—or that Israel would be struck by some devastating force. "I'll be surprised if the country continues existing for more than a decade," he wrote in his diary.

The day after judges announced the verdict, the Shamgar Commission issued its findings. By now the media had examined the lapses at the murder scene so thoroughly—through interviews with witnesses and an analysis of the Kempler video—that the panel had little new to say. Not surprisingly, it faulted Shabak for the failures that allowed the assassination to happen and singled out officers from the protection unit. Carmi Gillon bore overall responsibility as head of the agency, it concluded.

In a secret annex (parts of which the government would eventually declassify), the report criticized Shabak's handling of Avishai Raviv, but once again said nothing particularly illuminating in its conclusions. "Every reasonable person understands that gathering information is vital and that the people involved in the endeavor are not necessarily righteous and honest. But the agency needs to guard against provocateurs who would take advantage of the backing they get and initiate illegal activities," the report said. "The conclusion is that the agency must wield effective control over the agent and prevent misconduct."

Oddly, the panel said it had failed to determine who shouted "It's not real" at the murder scene. Though one of the Shabak bodyguards had confessed to Chief Superintendent Gamliel that the words came from his mouth, his witness statement was somehow left out of the murder file reviewed by the Shamgar commission. The fact that Gamliel had solved the mystery would remain unknown until 2009, when he disclosed the testimony to an Israeli television news program. Even then, fourteen years after the assassination, he refused to name the Shabak man.

Other legal proceedings related to the assassination would continue for years to come, including a separate conspiracy trial for Amir, Hagai, and Adani, as well as several appeals. Judges would sentence Hagai to a total of sixteen years in prison and Adani to seven years. But Amir's murder trial had been the main event and once it ended, interest dropped off. Margalit Har-Shefi's legal ordeal would wind on till 2001. She would eventually serve six months of a twenty-four-month sentence, express "sincere regret" over the murder, and have the rest of her jail time commuted.

In April, seven weeks before the election, Peres faced one more complication, this one on Israel's northern border. A partial truce the United States had mediated between Israel and the Islamic Hezbollah group in Lebanon three years earlier seemed to be disintegrating. The group had fired Katyusha rockets at Israel several times in the span of a few days, forcing thousands of Israelis to take cover in bomb shelters. For Netanyahu, it was yet another opportunity to call into question Peres's handling of the country's security. Israeli analysts attributed the escalation to Syria, which wielded a certain amount of influence over Hezbollah. The way Itamar Rabinovich saw it, Assad wanted to remind Peres that Syria could still inflict pain on Israel through its Lebanese proxy.

On April 11, Peres ordered a broad assault against the group, with air strikes across Lebanon. The prime minister hoped with the operation to reprise the earlier understandings Israel maintained with the group—essentially that neither side would target civilians. He also thought he might recoup some of the public confidence he'd lost with the Hamas suicide attacks. But as Operation Grapes of Wrath wound on, the images of Lebanese families streaming north by the thousands made Israel's Arab population decidedly uncomfortable. With Israelis now electing their prime minister directly, the nearly 1 million Arab-Israelis would play a decisive role on Election Day. Peres expected to get at least 80 percent of their votes.

A week into the offensive, tragedy struck. An Israeli Special Forces unit combing southern Lebanon for rocket launchers came under heavy fire from a Hezbollah team. The unit's company commander, a twenty-four-year-old officer named Naftali Bennett, used his field radio to order an artillery strike. But instead of hitting the Hezbollah men, the 155mm shells he summoned struck a UN position near the village of Qana, where some eight hundred civilians had taken refuge. The bombardment went on for seventeen minutes, killed more than a hundred people, and dealt Peres yet another setback. To most Israelis, it seemed like a tragic mishap, the kind of botched targeting that sometimes occurs in wars. But many Arab-Israelis thought of it as something worse—if not a deliberate massacre, at least an example of Israel's disregard for the lives of civilians on the other side of the border. When the operation ended after sixteen days, prominent Arab-Israelis called on members of their community—fully 18 percent of the population—to sit out the election.

For the first time since the start of the campaign, Peres felt a deep despair. He still led in opinion polls but every decision he made seemed to somehow work against him. Peres also suffered from fatigue. "These were sleepless nights, all the time telephone calls during the night," he would recount years later. "I think of myself as a strong man physically but there are limits."

Peres had been accustomed to hard-fought elections, but the stakes in this one felt particularly high, perhaps higher than at any time in Israel's history. If Netanyahu won, the Likud leader would do his utmost to roll back the agreements with the Palestinians and tighten

Israel's hold over the West Bank and Gaza. Rightists viewed it as even more decisive. Peres would use his mandate to cede more God-given land and end the redemptive dream of Greater Israel.

Yigal Amir had done his part to tip the balance in the right's favor by killing the one man who had both a vision for peace with the Palestinians and the public confidence required to keep it going, even in the face of terrorist attacks. Now, with characteristic pomposity, he thought of another contribution he could make: persuade religious Jews abroad to move to Israel in the weeks before the vote so that they could invoke their right to immediate citizenship, cast their ballots, and help defeat Peres. As the date of the election drew near, Amir crafted a letter in English to family friends in the United States. "Dear Rachel's Children in the Diaspora," he wrote.

> *Yigal Amir writing you from the prison in a desperate attempt to save the "holy land" from the sons of Israel. The holy land belongs not only to its inhabitants but to every Jewish soul around the world in our days and all generations which past and [which are] going to come. Therefore, this government has no right to give up our claim on the holy land, which has been promised to us by God itself three thousand five hundred years ago. . . .*
>
> *The Jews in Israel have lost their spirit, they have lost their belief, the love to the land. The Arabs inherited these values. That's why they succeeded to get the land. Now the Arabs kiss the earth when they return and it seems as if they are the sons of Israel who came back. The Jews are not sacrificing for their beliefs, only the Arabs.*
>
> *We still have hope. The majority of the Jews in Israel, the moral people, still have the faith. Our problem is that this minority . . . who prefer the culture of emptiness, they control all the powerful posts in the state and mainly the media. The majority has had no way to express protest in the past three years. The government . . . turned it into materialistic and the media washed its brain until we came to the situation that people abroad know better than us what is really happening in Israel. . . . People are afraid to talk against the peace process. I get a lot of letters with no name and people write me that they are afraid to talk and support me. It's not a democracy any more.*

Our last chance is this election and if the Labor party wins again, this is the end of Judaism and you are also responsible. The only hope is for you to come here and vote and repair the damage that has already been done. We are in the Great Days but the people are tired. Please save us from ourselves.

He signed it simply, Yigal Amir.

The last weeks of the election brought new promises from the candidates, both of whom now targeted swing voters. Peres vowed to submit any peace agreement with Israel's neighbors to a referendum before signing it. Netanyahu acknowledged that Israel could not renege on the parts of Oslo already implemented; he would not try to reoccupy Gaza or send troops back to the West Bank cities now under Palestinian control.

On May 27, two days before the vote, Peres and Netanyahu met at a television studio in Tel Aviv for the taping of a thirty-minute debate moderated by the journalist Dan Margalit. The two men had agreed to the event earlier in the campaign and as the date drew near, some members of Peres's staff felt he should back out. Netanyahu, twenty-six years younger than his opponent, simply looked better on camera. He had spent years in Washington and New York mastering the art of the television interview, delivering minute-long responses that sounded both eloquent and unassailable, albeit in English. At least one member of Peres's campaign conjured the American presidential debate of 1960—the first one ever televised—which propelled the younger, better-looking John F. Kennedy to an election victory over Richard Nixon. But Peres ruled out the suggestion that he should cancel his appearance.

Though Peres could be inspiringly eloquent himself on good days, he had spent the last months filling two extremely demanding positions (serving as both prime minister and defense minister), coping with suicide attacks and a war in Lebanon, and watching his double-digit lead in opinion polls shrink to almost nothing. From his opening remarks through the last minutes of the debate, when each candidate posed a question to the other, he seemed irritable and defensive. He referred to Rabin only once, some two-thirds into the debate. Somehow, the event that had consumed Israelis just two hundred days earlier, that had triggered the chain of events that led to the election—the Rabin assassination—never came up.

Netanyahu, by contrast, gave a polished and disciplined performance. He began nearly every response with the words, "I'll answer that, but first . . ." and then delivered a short but effective retort to whatever point Peres just made. He attacked Peres relentlessly over the suicide bombings and the security anxieties they had created for Israelis. In less than fifteen minutes of actual airtime, Netanyahu invoked the word "fear" more than a dozen times.

When the taping was over, Netanyahu stepped into an elevator and spotted Uzi Baram, the tourism minister he'd had the exchange with in December about his election chances. So, who won the debate? Netanyahu wanted to know. Baram conceded that Peres had not done well. "You did, but you're still going to lose the election," he said. In the edit room, Margalit, the moderator, watched the tape several times and drew the same conclusion: Peres had lost badly. Israel's Channel Two television aired the debate that evening. An opinion poll conducted after the broadcast showed Peres's lead dropping to three points. With the margin of error at 3 percent, the candidates were in a dead heat.

On Election Day, Peres woke up early and voted in his neighborhood polling station before heading to the Defense Ministry. Though Tel Aviv's oppressive humidity had made a pre-summer appearance earlier in the week, a slight chill hung in the air. Leah Rabin stopped by the same polling station later in the morning. It occurred to her that she had never voted without her husband at her side—at least as far back as she could recall. Netanyahu cast his ballot in Jerusalem before setting out to visit activists in several cities around the country. In Kiryat Malachi he sat with a prominent rabbi of the Hasidic Chabad movement, which had organized a last-minute billboard campaign with the slogan "Bibi Is Good for the Jews." In a country where non-Jews made up nearly one-fifth of the population, it was an almost gleefully divisive campaign.

Israel's election law allowed convicts to vote at polling stations in prison. Around midmorning, five guards escorted Amir from his cell to a booth at the Ohalei Kedar penitentiary, where he was presently serving his sentence in solitary confinement. The guards waited while he stuffed a square of paper with Netanyahu's name on it into an envelope and then slipped it into a cardboard box. Thomas L. Friedman, the *New York Times* columnist, would refer to Amir later as the Israeli who voted twice—first with a bullet and then with a ballot.

During the course of the day more than 3 million Israelis would vote in the election, for an official turnout of above 79 percent. Analysts would put the actual participation level at close to 90 percent, a calculation that involved discounting Israelis not present in the country on the day of the vote. Few Western countries had higher turnouts.

Israel Television broadcast the results of its commissioned exit poll a little after ten o'clock at night. Based on interviews with voters as they departed balloting stations around the county, the Channel One exit poll held a kind of hallowed status in Israel. With the exception of the 1981 debacle, it had been predicting elections accurately for more than two decades. Now, the channel's most renowned anchor, Haim Yavin, announced that Peres held a small lead over Netanyahu—50.7 percent to 49.3 percent. But he urged caution. Until the real tallies from polling stations around the country came in through the night, the race would be too close to call.

At the Cinerama auditorium in Tel Aviv, Labor Party activists chanted and cheered. Peres remained out of sight for the time being, chastened by the experience of 1981. But his campaign managers told reporters that the exit poll seemed to support other polling conducted over the preceding week. If anything, the real numbers would look better for Peres, they said. The optimism percolated at Leah's apartment on Rav Ashi as well, where she watched the broadcast with some twenty friends and family members.

But by one in the morning, Peres seemed to be losing his advantage, a trend that would continue throughout the night. Netanyahu, who had also kept himself secluded, appeared suddenly at the main Likud gathering in Tel Aviv to buoy his supporters. "The race is very, very close. Do not lose hope," he said. In the morning, with all but the absentee ballots counted, Netanyahu was ahead by half a percentage point.

He had won the election.

To the Israeli peace camp, it was the second devastating blow in six months. At Rabin's murder site, someone left a sign saying: "Rabin was killed on November 4. Peace was killed on May 29." Among the Oslo originators, Yossi Beilin felt particularly crushed. His draft agreement with Mahmoud Abbas, which might have resolved the conflict with the Palestinians for good, was now a dead letter. Beilin showed up at Peres's office the next day expecting to find his mentor wallowing in misery. Instead, Peres seemed less tired than he had in months and relieved that the election was finally over. His electoral defeats over the years had made him remarkably resilient. Peres was talking to his wife on the phone, asking what was for lunch. Chicken, Beilin could hear her saying. Peres told her he would be home soon.

In Herzliya, the Amirs rejoiced. Geulah and her husband had voted for Netanyahu, along with Amir himself. Hagai refrained from casting a ballot; he felt it would be wasted. But in his diary, he marveled at the results. "It's nice to see Peres, the evil one, fall," he wrote. "Gali saved the country."

Epilogue

The eleven-hour flight from Tel Aviv to New York, over Europe and across the Atlantic, can pass like an easy night's sleep or it can feel interminable. In the countless trips I made back and forth over the years, I had forged a strategy: book the red-eye and swallow an Ambien while the plane is still on the ground. The jostling of bags, the swapping of boarding passes between Hasidic men horrified to find they'd been seated next to women—the general chaos of the Israeli condition starts to dim even before the cabin doors close. But in the late summer of 2013, I was too agitated to sleep. I had been nervous about the security check at Ben-Gurion Airport, where vigilant young screeners specialize in detecting anxiety. If one of them decided to search my luggage, how would I explain the bloody clothes wrapped carefully in large sheets of white butcher paper and stuffed in my carry-on?

I had been living in Israel since 2010, filing dispatches to *Newsweek*, the steadily withering publication that had been my professional home for more than a decade. Sometime during the posting, I decided I would write a book about the assassination of Yitzhak Rabin. The murder of the Israeli leader by a fellow Jew in 1995 had profoundly shifted the course of events in Israel. It had also left a deep impression on me. I had covered Israel during the Rabin years, reported from the peace rally where he was assassinated, and then attended every session of the murder trial. Now almost two decades later, I wanted to reconstruct the twin narratives of Rabin's endeavor to forge peace with Israel's neighbors and Yigal Amir's fanatical effort to stop him. But in one of my first interviews with Dalia Rabin, the sixty-three-year-old daughter of the slain leader, I got sidetracked. "Do you know about the hole in the front of the shirt?" she asked me at her Tel Aviv office.

I did not.

At our next meeting, Dalia produced a cardboard box and in it the clothing Rabin was wearing the night of the assassination: a white Marks & Spencer dress shirt, encrusted entirely in blood; a sleeveless undershirt, similarly stained; a dark, tailored suit jacket and pants made of heavy wool; a pair of white cotton underwear; black socks; and leather shoes. She laid out the dress shirt on the table, holding the edges with the tips of her fingers. It had been torn in several places, presumably on the operating table. First she showed me the back side, where two bullets had struck Rabin. Amir had approached the Israeli leader from behind and fired three rounds from a 9mm Beretta. The first and third bullets entered his back—one high and to the right of his spine, the other low and to the left—and lodged in his body. The second bullet missed its target and passed through the arm of Rabin's bodyguard Yoram Rubin.

Dalia then turned the shirt over to show me a third hole in the front, on what would have been Rabin's lower left side. It was perfectly round and a little smaller than a dime, about the size of the perforations in the back. She showed me a similar hole in the front of the undershirt. Then she laid the undershirt inside the shirt, the way the garments would have hung on her father's five-foot-six-and-a-half-inch frame. The holes seemed to line up. In hospital records and other documents I'd reviewed relating to the assassination, there was no mention of Rabin being shot from the front, no evidence of an exit wound or other anterior injuries. Yet something had punctured the face of the garments, quite possibly while Rabin was wearing them (otherwise how to explain that the defects lined up?). The holes, Dalia said, had come to her attention ten years after the murder and had never been properly investigated. They were a mystery.

Murder cases, no matter how thoroughly investigated, almost always leave in their wake a trail of unanswered questions or just bits of evidence that don't add up. With political assassinations—and no one knows this better than us Americans—those loose ends tend to become the source material for theories about cover-ups and conspiracies. The main questions surrounding Rabin's murder were broad and sweeping: how did Amir elude Israel's esteemed intelligence and security agencies and how could the Israeli leader have been so exposed? But there were little ones as well, including discrepancies over the precise distance between the shooter and his target, and the time it took Rabin's driver to get him to the hospital. Most vexing was the testimony of nearly a dozen witnesses who heard someone at the scene shouting that the shots fired were "not real" or "blanks."

That odd detail in particular fueled conspiracy theories almost from the outset, mainly from the right side of the map—the political camp to which Amir belonged. In opinion polls over the years, at least one-quarter of Israelis have said they doubt the official version of the assassination. Among religious and right-wing Israelis, the number rises above 50 percent.

Dalia, of course, was no conspiracist. A lawyer by training and a former parliament member and deputy defense minister, she had spent much of her time since the killing nurturing the legacy of her late father. But she had her own questions about the night of the murder. In one of our conversations, she said she felt the whole truth about the assassination had yet to emerge. Seeing her father's clothing for the first time deepened her suspicions. Dalia learned about the holes from members of an Israeli documentary team who had come across the garments in the national archive in Jerusalem. After conducting their own probe (and producing an inconclusive film about it), one of them told Dalia cryptically that the mystery surrounding the clothing should keep her up at night.

In fact, it did. One scenario she kept replaying in her mind involved a bodyguard whirling around to shoot Amir but hitting her father instead. She wondered whether the security service that protected him would have covered up such a blunder to avoid yet more embarrassment—going so far as to have the pathologist leave the evidence out of his report. But Dalia also worried that raising any questions publicly or trying to have them investigated would give ammunition to the conspiracists. In a way, they had paralyzed her. Their accounts of the murder were so outlandish, she thought, and so clearly designed to exonerate Amir and the hardliners who had incited against her father that she vowed to avoid saying or doing anything that might give them momentum. In 2005, Dalia took possession of the clothes from the national archive and tucked them in a storage room at the memorial institute she ran in Tel Aviv, the Yitzhak Rabin Center, alongside her father's other belongings. They were still there when she mentioned them to me eight years later.

In early August 2013, a few weeks after those first meetings with Dalia, I sat down at the computer in my Tel Aviv rental to write her an email. I had met with Dalia several times in the preceding months while making progress on the research for this book. By then, my own view about the bits of odd evidence had been shaped in interviews with scores of people, including members of Rabin's security detail. "I want to be candid with you about this," I wrote. "With all the reporting I've done, I feel reasonably confident that the question marks surrounding the night of the murder . . . do not point to some cover-up.

"And yet, the hole in the shirt is a mystery. Having seen it with my own eyes, I find it hard to dismiss."

I asked in the email if I could take the clothes to the United States and have them inspected by an expert. I had spoken by then to several forensic examiners to find out whether it was possible nearly two decades after the event to determine what caused the holes in the garments, whether gunfire or something else. Crime-scene examiners who work privately often make their money by testifying on behalf of their clients. An investigative reporter I'd worked with and trusted in Washington, DC, had warned me to choose carefully—that the flaw in the profession is the vested interest examiners have in telling their clients what they want to hear.

Eventually, I got referred to Lucien Haag, a firearms specialist in Arizona whose credentials seemed unassailable. A former Phoenix police criminalist, he had been examining evidence from crime scenes for almost fifty years, including the Kennedy assassination and the FBI assault on Ruby Ridge. An article in the *Arizona Republic* described him as the Michael Jordan of his profession. On the phone, he sounded intrigued. If something other than a bullet caused the hole, it would be difficult so many years later to determine precisely what it was. But the important thing was to test the gunshot theory—to substantiate it or rule it out. That much, he was confident he could do.

Within a few days the cardboard box with the clothing sat in the foyer of my apartment. For Dalia, my proposition held appeal. She stood to get the answer to a question that had been gnawing at her for years—without having to initiate the procedure herself. Dalia seemed unsentimental about the garments. They were musty and soiled and held memories of a terrible ordeal. When I picked up the box from her office I had the feeling she was happy to be rid of it, even for just a few weeks.

My own calculations were mostly pragmatic. If Haag could exclude gunfire as the cause of the holes, it would help discharge the conspiracy theories altogether. If, on the other hand, a bullet had caused the defects in the front of the shirt and undershirt, the entire narrative of the Rabin assassination stood to be upended. That's the kind of information a writer wants to verify before embarking on a book—not after.

I opened the box and phoned Haag again. I wanted to know which garments he wished to inspect in addition to the shirt and undershirt and how best to pack them. The items had been strewn carelessly in the box for years, some in plastic bags, a messy heap of bloody remnants from one of the most significant events in Israel's history. I stretched out each piece on my dining-room table, which I had covered with long sheets of white paper. A washed out yellow tag attached to the suit jacket bore the Hebrew acronym for the police department's Criminal Identification Bureau, Mazap. The first thing Haag wanted to know was the composition of the dress shirt. A label on the inside seam listed it as 55 percent cotton, 45 percent polyester. Good news, he said. Burn traces were easier to detect on fabric that included man-made material. Then he instructed me to discard the plastic bags and wrap each garment in butcher paper. Mold tends to grow in plastic and can alter the chemistry of the evidence.

By now my flight was just two days away and I had visions of being arrested at either Ben-Gurion Airport or at John F. Kennedy in New York—or at least having to do some serious explaining. Haag said sniffer dogs in the baggage hall at Kennedy could potentially smell the blood in my carry-on, prompting a search. Customs agents might decide that the garments were a biohazard and seize them.

Working quickly, I drafted a letter for Dalia to sign, saying the Rabin Center had allowed me to take the clothing to the United States for a forensic exam. Then I called the Department of Homeland Security's customs bureau in New York. In an awkward exchange, I tried to explain why I needed to import the bloody clothes of a dead foreign leader. The spokesman on the other end of the line had not heard of Rabin and didn't seem particularly interested. I began thinking it was a mistake to raise the issue at all, that I should have just taken my chances. But by the next morning, I got an email from public affairs specialist Anthony Bucci: "Customs & Border Protection at JFK is aware of your arrival and you will be expedited. There will be no issues with the clothing."

The next day, I was on the plane with the clothes in the carry-on. The trace evidence from an Israeli tragedy would now make its way to a town in Arizona with a name that seemed to mock the entire endeavor: Carefree. Population 3,418.

———

ON THE NIGHT of the assassination, eighteen years earlier, I left my Tel Aviv apartment around seven p.m. and walked a few blocks to Kings of Israel Square. At the foot of the stage where Rabin and the other politicians and entertainers had started to gather, I showed my press badge, passed through a metal detector, and conducted a few interviews. Then I walked the length of the plaza, the size of several football fields, talking to people in the crowd.

By news standards, it was not a particularly significant event: a rally of Israeli peaceniks expressing support for their government's contentious agreements with the Palestinians. But the huge turnout—more than 100,000 people showed up—seemed to challenge the notion that Rabin's support was ebbing. In the arithmetic of the newswire—I was working for Reuters at the time—the event warranted a story of a few hundred words. At around nine thirty p.m., I phoned my editor to say I was leaving the area and would file from my apartment.

A few blocks away, the small black pager on my belt bleeped and vibrated with a message from the newsroom: Shots fired near Rabin, head back now. In the time it took me to race to the parking lot behind the square, I had just one thought: Did I leave the area prematurely, and would it cost me my first real job in journalism? At the scene of the shooting, several stunned witnesses told me they thought the prime minister had been hit. Using a bulky, work-issued Motorola cell phone we'd aptly named "the brick," I called the details into the newsroom. Then I sprinted to Ichilov Hospital, a half mile from the square, getting there in time for the announcement of Rabin's death.

For days after that, every interaction with Israelis, every outing, felt surreal. My newsroom rented a scooter from a local shop so that I could get through the traffic and cover the funeral and later the murder trial. Policemen had begun closing off main roads whenever Rabin's successor, Shimon Peres, moved around. They also put up roadblocks from the airport to Jerusalem to allow the stream of foreign leaders who arrived for the funeral to get around quickly and safely. The resulting gridlock added to the sense that all of Israel had been brought to a gloomy, eerie standstill, that nothing in the country was normal.

The murder had easily been the biggest story I'd covered. It was also the most depressing. Rabin's peace deals with the Palestinians had plenty of flaws and had triggered bursts of violence. Israeli fatalities from Palestinian attacks nearly doubled in the two years that followed the Oslo Accord compared to the two years that preceded it. But the agreements seemed to shift some big, important things to the inevitable column: a territorial bargain, a Palestinian homeland (even if Rabin never embraced it explicitly), and a veering away from the messianic drift that the 1967 war had set off in Israel. By deciding Israelis would no longer rule over Palestinians in the West Bank and Gaza, Rabin had struck a blow for the pragmatists over the ideologues. Through the barrel of Amir's Beretta, the ideologues had struck back.

And yet, the murder did not feel like the end. In the time that I had covered Israel and, later, followed events there from afar, I remained

244 ‹   KILLING A KING

convinced that Israelis and Palestinians would eventually reach a
workable agreement. No conflict could sustain itself forever, I told
myself with characteristic optimism (and how better to define an opti-
mist than someone who thinks the Israeli-Palestinian conflict can be
resolved?). Even in the bloodiest phase of the past two decades, during
the years of the second intifada, I believed that the broad trend lines
pointed toward conciliation.

In early 2010, after I'd been away from Israel for years, *Newsweek*
sent me back to the region to serve as the Jerusalem bureau chief. It
didn't take long for my assessment to shift. The country I returned to
was in many ways a more livable place. It felt safer, more prosperous,
and less troubled than it had in years. But the terrible violence and
hostility of the second intifada had left even the moderates among
Israelis and Palestinians feeling alienated from each other and simply
fed up. The fact that life in Israel was good despite the absence of
peace meant there was little incentive to revive the process.

In the first story I published during the new posting, I wrote that
the diplomatic arithmetic had changed. Many Israelis felt they had
nothing to gain from a resumption of negotiations. And since a peace
process would almost surely revive the suicide bombings and political
instability, they had plenty to lose. "A combination of factors in recent
years—an improved security situation, a feeling that acceptance by
Arabs no longer matters much, and a growing disaffection from politics generally—have for many Israelis called into question the basic
calculus that has driven the peace process. Instead of pining for peace,
they're now asking: who needs it?"

This analysis helped explain why Israelis had elected Netanyahu,
the hardliner, months earlier. There were other factors as well. The
Israeli settlement movement, which had viewed Rabin's Oslo Accord
as an act of treachery, had more than doubled in size since his assassination and greatly expanded its political power. Its representatives
in parliament would come to include Moshe Feiglin, who had been
convicted of sedition for organizing rowdy protests during the Rabin
era. The parliament I was now covering in Israel also included a
record number of Orthodox and ultra-Orthodox Jews—who form
the country's two fastest-growing communities and whose views on

the issues of war and peace are consistently hawkish. When Israelis reelected Netanyahu in 2013—for a third time in eighteen years—I wrote in *Newsweek* that the religious and right-wing parties opposed to ceding substantial portions of the West Bank might have something akin to a permanent majority. Even if they lost a vote, history seemed to be foreclosing on the possibility of a negotiated peace agreement between Israel and the Palestinians.

It was around this time that I made up my mind to write a book about the Rabin era. If the prospects of a peace agreement had shrunk to almost nothing in the intervening years, the assassination felt even more significant in retrospect. Had he lived, Rabin might plausibly have reshaped Israel broadly and permanently. In killing the Israeli leader, Amir had done better than the assassins of Lincoln, Kennedy, and King, whose policies had gained momentum as a result of their murders. During the years of his imprisonment, he had the satisfaction of watching Rabin's legacy steadily evaporate.

That was what I told Dalia Rabin at our first meeting. And how I'd come to possess her dead father's clothes.

———————

CAREFREE LIES ABOUT forty minutes north of the Phoenix airport, a desert town with adobe houses, huge boulder formations, and cactus plants almost everywhere you look. In the 1970s and '80s, it housed a film studio where some Hollywood hits were made, including one with Bob Hope. Now lined with golf courses and gated neighborhoods, the town has the feel of a Florida retirement community transplanted to the gold-tinted landscape of the Old West. Apparently it's marketed that way. A real-estate website I happened on listed Carefree's motto as "the Home of Cowboys and Caviar." On one of the nights I was there, I watched an hour of live bull riding at the Buffalo Chip Saloon, then dined at a fancy French restaurant.

In the desert heat people start their day early, so by six thirty I was already pulling into the Good Egg, a diner I spotted on the way to Haag's home. I had kept the carry-on close to me during two days of travel, imagining the awful prospect of having to tell Dalia I'd lost the clothes or let them get stolen. Now I wheeled it across the parking lot, lifted it into the booth, and ordered coffee and the morning special: peach cobbler pancakes. The dish seemed somehow in step with the broader juxtapositional weirdness. If Rabin's bloody clothes had any business in Carefree, the person who brought them there should obviously be eating peach cobbler pancakes. When they arrived, I tucked the suitcase under the table and out of sight.

Haag lives on the eastern ridge of Carefree, just in front of a huge nature reserve with high cliffs and dry riverbeds. When he's working on a case, he'll sometimes drive his SUV to a spot in the reserve and re-create the conditions of a certain shooting incident to deduce precisely what happened. He also has an indoor shooting range in his home with its own ventilation system. He moved to the area in 1965, after graduating from UC Berkeley, to take up a job at the crime lab of the Phoenix Police Department. Until his arrival, the lab had just one employee. Now it occupies a five-story building and employs 150 people, including one of Haag's two sons. Both young men followed their father into the profession.

We started the morning going over documents in Haag's backyard, where he warned me to watch for javalinas, a kind of wild pig that can show up unannounced. The folder I'd amassed included photos from just before and just after the shooting, police lab reports, and hospital documents detailing Rabin's wounds. After scrolling through several files, the sun was so bright that I could no longer see the screen of my laptop. We moved inside, reviewed the remaining documents, and then moved again, this time to his laboratory.

The room, sandwiched between the den and the living room, resembled a high school science class, with microscopes and beakers laid out on several large countertops and books stacked on shelves. It also contained objects not ordinarily found in a classroom—namely guns. Haag is a collector and he displays some of his firearms on a high shelf in the lab, including a Russian bolt-action rifle used in both world wars. He bought it in the Soviet Union during a visit in the '80s and has fired it about fifty times but says it bruises the shoulder in a way that, now in his early seventies, he no longer wishes to endure.

Two other rifles on the shelf looked like AK-47s but he corrected me and said they were AK clones—the kind that shoot only in semiautomatic mode, not in rapid fire.

Haag unzipped the suitcase, pulled out the box with the clothes, and placed it on one of the counters. He inspected the jacket first, noticed that the lower bullet hole had caused some tearing of the fabric, and said Amir was probably closer in when he fired that shot, almost at contact point. Then he unwrapped the shirt and, after inspecting the two punctures on the back, he turned it over and found the mystery hole. "Whoa, I'm really surprised," he let out, more expressively than anything else he'd said so far. But he quickly recovered his scientist timbre and issued a qualification. "Whoa doesn't mean 'Oh my God it's a bullet hole.' Whoa just means that's a very clean, sharply defined hole. . . . You certainly brought something different and very interesting."

Gunshot analysis involves mostly geometry and chemistry—figuring out pathways the bullets travel and testing for residue they leave behind. At one point during the morning Haag took a call from a lawyer and, when he returned, explained how geometry was going to sink his case. The lawyer represented a policeman who shot a young man dead and was being sued for damages. He hired Haag to help prove the policeman's version of events—that the man had been lunging at him when the officer discharged his gun. But the facts Haag gathered suggested the opposite: the man was actually backing away. Two findings led him to this conclusion. The bullet carved a straight tunnel through the midsection of the victim's body, a line that ran perpendicular to his spine. After exiting his back, it hit the wall behind him just a few inches up from the floor. "It's a straight path through the body and everyone agrees they were standing, facing each other," Haag explains. "So think about it. If a bullet goes through me as a standing victim and hits the wall low, I had to be leaning away to accommodate that."

With Rabin's shirt, determining whether a bullet had caused the hole was mainly a matter of chemistry. Most modern bullets have a lead core and a copper coating. They tend to leave traces of one or both elements on the clothes they penetrate, especially on man-made fibers. There's also lead in the propellant—the powder that sits in the case of the cartridge and ignites in the process of gunfire. When a bullet is discharged, lead vapors burst out of the barrel and can cling to fabric at close range, creating a ring of soot around the bullet hole. So Haag would be looking for three things—copper, lead, and soot. The traces of each tend to stick around for decades.

If any of the test results were positive, Haag said he would run other tests to determine the bullet type. Amir fired hollow points made by Winchester, bullets with rounded, carved-out tips instead of sharp, pointy ones. The Winchester hollow point—Silvertip is the brand name—has a nickel patina that makes it shiny and leaves a distinctive residue. But if a bullet had indeed hit Rabin from the front, it was unlikely to have come from Amir's gun. So the next step, should we get that far, would involve contemplating some unsettling scenarios—including the possibility that a second gunman may have shot the Israeli leader.

While Haag prepared the shirt for the first test, I described to him the conspiracy theories that had surrounded the murder and the way they had gained traction among significant numbers of Israelis, especially on the right side of the political map. One theory posited that rogue elements within the security establishment killed Rabin, using Amir as their patsy. Another laid the blame at the feet of Shimon Peres, Rabin's deputy and longtime rival within the Labor Party. The account that proved to be the most resilient put Rabin himself at the center of the plot, alleging that he helped stage his own shooting in order to raise his sagging approval rating—and died in some unintended twist.

Haag has honed a kind of doubt-but-verify approach to conspiracy theories, a paraphrase of Reagan's attitude toward the Soviet Union's disarmament in the 1980s. For an episode of the television series *NOVA*, Haag spent long hours reviewing the evidence of the Kennedy assassination and carrying out his own test fires. He said investigators tend to make more mistakes in high-profile cases than in just regular ones because "everyone is rushing around trying to do something." The Kennedy case was no exception. But none of the forensic or ballistic evidence he examined made him doubt the conventional narrative: that a lone gunman, not exceedingly smart, hatched a relatively crude plan to assassinate the most guarded man in the country and succeeded. "There's a natural inclination to want it to be more than that," he said. "It's got to take more than just one lone loser with a thirteen-dollar rifle to kill the president."

The Rabin assassination inspired similar incredulity. It had to take more than just one religious extremist, waiting in a parking lot for forty minutes with nothing but a handgun, to kill the prime minister. But the conspiracy theories that followed also served a political purpose. For members of the right wing, who took part in depicting Rabin as a traitor and a murderer for his peace deals with the Palestinians, the alternative narratives helped deflect a collective responsibility that many in the country felt they bore. If a right-wing zealot had indeed killed the Israeli leader, the right's incitement against Rabin might well have influenced him and contributed to the murder. But if a darker and more sinister plot lay behind the assassination—perhaps one orchestrated by Rabin himself or by the security agency sworn to protect him—their complicity would be washed away.

The conspiracy theories in the Rabin assassination have never stood up to any serious scrutiny. They endure in part thanks to those loose ends, including the testimony of witnesses at the murder scene who heard someone yell out, "It's not real" (or something similar) moments after the shooting. To the conspiracists, the odd detail suggested that the assassination was staged. But in one of the interviews I conducted, the former police officer who helped lead the murder investigation offered a somewhat more sober explanation—a complicated one, but the only one I've heard that actually tallies with the rest of the facts in the case. Dramatic events make people say or do odd things. Sometimes those things point to hidden information and help investigators uncover the real circumstances of a crime. But—and this is the part that's hard to accept in high-profile crimes—often they point nowhere, and mean nothing.

And still, there was the shirt. Haag folded it into the butcher paper, carried it across the house, and took it onto his back patio. He stretched it out on a table under the glaring midday sun and took pictures of the area of the hole using an infrared camera. With ultraviolet light streaming from the sun's rays, anything black would show up as white through the lens of the camera. If there were soot around the hole, embedded in the bloodstained fabric, he would see it in the viewfinder.

Haag stepped up onto a footstool and aimed the camera down at the shirt. "I don't think there's soot here," he said straightaway. He snapped several photos, scooped up the shirt, and walked back to his office adjoining the lab. Haag connected the camera to his computer and with a few mouse clicks brought up a close-up of the mystery hole. At maximum magnification, the shirt threads looked like coarse strands of rope woven together tightly. The hole itself appeared slightly oblong and the fibers around the margins looked almost perfectly clipped. "I can't remember the last time I saw something like this," Haag said. There was no sign of soot on the computer screen. His first test had come up negative.

Back in his lab, Haag sprayed a diluted ammonia solution around the hole in the shirt and then pressed a square of transfer paper onto the fabric. If there were copper particles around the hole, the solution would loosen them just enough for some to adhere to the paper. But the copper wouldn't be visible against the transfer paper. So Haag poured a few CCs of DTO—dithio-oxamine—into a pressurized bottle and sprayed the reagent onto the page. When DTO reacts with copper, the particles turn orange. Together we stared at the wet transfer paper for several moments, like a couple waiting on a home pregnancy test. Nothing happened. We were zero for two.

By now, Haag was speculating aloud what, other than a bullet, could have caused the defect. Insects can chew away bits of fabric in evidence storage rooms over time. But the hole was too clean and round to be the work of an insect, and how to explain the fact that the hole in the undershirt lined up? A cigarette could have burned a ring through both layers. Rabin was a heavy smoker. But under a microscope in polarized light, the threads along the margins lacked the clumped thermal effects associated with a burn (or a bullet hole, for that matter). Haag seemed to settle on the idea that the hole was caused on the operating table. In the emergency room, a doctor had thrust a tube into Rabin's chest cavity to drain the air and fluid that had accumulated. The procedure usually involves stripping the patient first. But in the chaos, in the rush to stabilize Rabin, maybe the instrument plunged through his shirt and undershirt. That would explain the clean shape and the lining up of the holes, he said.

When the third test—the one for lead—came up negative, Haag imagined himself on the witness stand, being cross-examined by an attorney. Could someone have lifted off all traces of copper and lead in a previous test or through some other procedure? Unlikely, he responded to his own question, but not impossible. To exclude even that remote possibility, he suggested a final test. He would cut out a small square of the fabric from somewhere else on the shirt and shoot a hole through it at close range. Then we could compare the hole he made with the mystery hole to see if they were similar.

By now, we were well into the afternoon in Arizona—nighttime in Israel. It was too late to call Dalia and ask for permission to cut out a section of the shirt. The question was left to me and it posed a dilemma. Dalia had entrusted me with her dead father's clothes and I was determined to bring them back safely. But she also badly wanted an answer to the question of the hole in the shirt. In that meeting at her office, it seemed more important to her than the garment itself, which had languished in a box for years. I told Haag to go ahead.

Working with a plain pair of scissors, Haag cut out a patch about five inches long and four inches wide. He used scotch tape to fix it to what looked like a block of yellowish gelatin. Haag described it as a tissue stimulant, a loaf of translucent silicone that behaves much the way the body's insides behave when struck with slicing metal. He suggested using the same gun and bullets Amir used, a 9mm Beretta with Winchester hollow points.

Together we walked over to his indoor range, a long, narrow room with thick walls and a soundproof door. He loaded a single hollow-point bullet into a magazine and clicked it into the Beretta. Then he handed me earmuffs and slipped a set on his own head. From six inches away, he pointed the gun at the gelatin block and pulled the trigger. Hollow points expand on impact, the metal in front peeling back and forming razor-sharp edges. They tend to cause more internal damage than regular rounds and stay lodged in the body—reducing the chance of a bullet passing through one person and injuring someone else. Most US police departments issue them to their officers.

Haag peeled off the fabric square and took it back to the lab. He placed it on the counter near the shirt so that we could examine both holes. They looked nothing alike. Haag's bullet had created an almost star-shaped perforation, with some vertical and horizontal tearing in the fabric. The threads along the margins of the hole were loose and uneven. After scrutinizing the panel and the shirt from different angles, Haag gestured that we were done. The chemistry alone had satisfied him that the mystery hole was not caused by the passing of a bullet. But the shooting test produced something more tangible—a physical piece of evidence that members of a jury could hold and pass around.

"I've been looking at bullet holes for forty-seven years or so. I shoot things for a living," he said, wrapping the shirt back in the butcher paper. "Everything I see says it's something other than a bullet."

———————

BY THE TIME I returned to Israel in September, the holiday season was under way—that three-week period between the Jewish New Year and Simcha Torah when children are out of school, government offices are closed, and any work at all feels strictly optional. I had sent Dalia a short email summarizing Haag's findings and we agreed to meet at her office so that I could give her a copy of his report. She walked from her desk to the door to greet me.

Dalia had worked as a lawyer in both the private and public sectors before her father was assassinated. She had no political ambitions and, except for her occasional involvement in high-profile legal cases, was not in the public eye. But the murder made her a national figure and the victory of Netanyahu over Peres in 1996 gave her a reason to enter politics—to help unseat him and get the country back on the peace track. She started campaigning for parliament in early 1999.

To the dismay of her mother and others, Dalia chose not to join the Labor Party. It was now led by Ehud Barak, a former army chief who had been Rabin's protégé but whose overture a few months before the election had put Dalia off. "He said, 'I need a Rabin on my list.' I didn't like his approach towards me." She aligned herself instead with the Center Party, won the sixth spot on the list, and just managed to enter parliament.

Her tenure lasted four years and included a stint as the deputy defense minister—a position that put Dalia in the core of her father's old milieu. But she never quite found her footing in politics. She left parliament in 2003 to establish an educational center in her father's name that includes a museum and an archive from his years in public life. The Cadillac in which Rabin was spirited to the hospital after the shooting is parked at the entrance to the center, on permanent display.

I gave Dalia a thumb drive with a copy of the report and the photos Haag had taken. She plugged it into her computer, brought up the first document, and scrolled to the key line: "The source of the sharply-defined hole in the front of the dress shirt and the likely associated hole in the front of the undershirt . . . were effectively *excluded* as being bullet-caused." Dalia said the conclusion came as a relief, though I had a sense that it wasn't exactly closure. She said she would go over the report slowly on her own.

Then we got to talking about the anniversary of the assassination, which was a few weeks off (Israel marks it officially according to the Hebrew calendar, which in 2013 put it around mid-October). Dalia said she dreaded the annual ritual. Her obligations start with the state ceremony in parliament attended by the Israeli prime minister—in this case, Benjamin Netanyahu, the man Dalia held responsible for much of the incitement against her father. Then she rushes from one public event to another in what feels like a failing endeavor to keep the memory of her father alive. She told me that the one engagement she looks forward to every year is the ceremony at the headquarters of the Mossad, Israel's intelligence agency. The employees gather along a spiral staircase and look down over the banister at a staging area on the ground floor, where a short observance is held. The security establishment's enduring solidarity with her father is palpable, she says.

Other events have left scars. For a while, Dalia would visit schools around the anniversary to talk about her father's legacy and about the Rabin Center's effort to promote democracy. At a religious girls' school in the settlement of Alon Shvut in the West Bank a few years earlier, she told the students about a program at the center that brings smart, underprivileged high school kids from outlying areas—including Arab-Israelis—to Tel Aviv and Haifa for a series of lectures on law and government. One girl raised her hand and asked why Arabs are included. Dalia explained that as citizens of Israel, they are equal members of society. "But they're not Jewish," the girl countered.

When she talked about her father's assassination and how it had highlighted the deep divisions in Israel, another girl raised her hand. She said it was actually Dalia's father who had created the divisions by agreeing to hand over parts of biblical Israel to the Palestinians.

The interactions, those and others, would not have been traumatic if Dalia thought the voices represented a small minority in Israel. But she has come to view the last twenty years as the story of a power shift from the likes of her father—secular, pragmatic, and moderate—to the advocates of Alon Shvut (and the settlement movement generally): ethnically chauvinist, uncompromising, often messianic. That the assassination would mark the birth of this new Israel is nothing short of horrifying to her. When a foreign correspondent asked Dalia at a small gathering of journalists a few years ago whether she and the Israeli mainstream had diverged at some point, she nodded without hesitation. "I don't feel I'm part of what most people in this country are willing to do."

And what of the Amirs? How have they fared since the assassination? Yigal Amir remains in prison, without the possibility of parole. He spent the first seventeen years of his sentence in total isolation. Since 2012, prison authorities have allowed him to study with other religious inmates for an hour a day, several days a week. Amir married while in prison and has a son he sees on visitation days two or three times a month. He can make at least one phone call each day but cannot talk to journalists.

His brother, Hagai, completed a sixteen-and-a-half-year sentence in 2012. He returned to his parents' home in Herzliya at age forty-four and found a job within weeks as a welder. The first time I met him, a year later, he was about to start a degree program in construction engineering. He showed me the second-floor bedroom he had shared with Amir growing up and the small shed behind the house where he tinkered with bullets to make them more effective at penetrating a car or an armored vest.

I wondered how people respond to seeing Hagai and the rest of the Amirs in public. Israelis recognize him and his parents from the media coverage over the years. His siblings are not familiar faces, but it's enough for them to mention the last name and the town Herzliya for some people to draw the connection. Yet the image I'd conjured of a family that remained stigmatized and isolated did not hold up. The brothers and sisters had all married. Four of them were university students at the time I conducted my interviews; one was doing a master's degree in psychology. The Amirs seemed to lead something close to normal lives. On one of the evenings I interviewed Hagai, he and the family had just returned from an outing with friends at the beach in Herzliya. On another night, they came from a wedding in Jerusalem. They were invited by the bride's father, a prominent right-wing activist. "We have a lot of support," Hagai told me. "People come up to us on the street and say it clearly."

If I had any reason to doubt it, Hagai's Facebook page seemed to bear it out. He created it soon after his release to post his own political observations and advocate on his brother's behalf. In a typical comment on his wall, one supporter wrote soon after Hagai came online: "We're all with you, Hagai Amir. We hope your brother will be freed soon." Another wrote: "The drinks will be on me." Within a few months, he had more than six hundred friends.

Hagai did not come to regret the murder during his years in prison. But his sharp hostility toward Arabs seemed to have softened and been redirected, chiefly toward the Israeli establishment—the government, the courts, the prison authority, the security agencies, and even the military. It made for some surprising conversations. In one of them, Hagai said Israel had a habit of launching unnecessary wars against the Arabs—a critique more commonly heard on the left than the right—and that generals and security officials needed them in order to justify their positions and budgets. He praised the work of civil-rights groups and said it was a mistake to give broad powers to the security agencies in order to suppress Palestinians because Israeli authorities would sooner or later use those powers against Jews as well. In the parlance of American politics, Hagai had become a libertarian.

In part, at least, the changes flowed from conversations he had in prison with Palestinians, including members of the Islamic Hamas group. That they found common ground should not be surprising. Outside prison, both Hamas and the Amirs played decisive roles in killing the Israeli-Palestinian peace agreements. Inside, Hagai came to view Palestinians as allies in the battle against the (mostly Jewish) guards, whom he regarded as dumb and vindictive. He told me that Arab inmates could not demand the rights they had coming to them in prison because their Hebrew wasn't good enough and they couldn't afford lawyers. And so, in what must have been a bizarre scene even by prison standards, Hagai sat in his cell and penned petitions to the High Court of Justice on behalf of Arabs, including a member of the Islamic Hezbollah group captured during fighting in southern Lebanon. Hagai showed me a handwritten note the Hezbollah man (he remembered him as Barzawi) slipped him requesting help in petitioning for a mirror, a bookshelf, and a hearing with the parole board.

Hagai told me his ambition now was to free his brother. In a diary he kept in prison that ran to five hundred pages, he hinted at ways he might try to spring Amir by force once he himself gets out of jail. But in my interviews with him, he said those ideas were unrealistic—that only political and legal pressure could force his brother's release.

Though the possibility seems unlikely, the fact that fully a quarter of Israelis now support a commuting of Yigal Amir's sentence makes it not quite unimaginable. Amir has already won several legal battles since his imprisonment, including the right to marry Larissa Trimbobler. An immigrant from the former Soviet Union, she began writing Amir in prison soon after the murder and later got permission to visit him. Larissa was married at the time, with four children. She divorced in 2003 and soon realized she was in love with Amir, she told me. When prison authorities rejected their request to marry, Larissa staged a wedding-by-proxy ceremony, with Amir's father standing in for the groom. After rabbis ruled that the procedure had the imprimatur of Jewish Law, the High Court of Justice ordered Israeli authorities to register the couple as married.

They also won a fight for conjugal visits, though not before Amir tried to pass semen in a bag to Larissa during one of her visitations. A son was born to them in the fall of 2007 and named Yinon, one of the biblical terms for the messiah. Larissa told me that Amir chose the name as a prayer for the coming of the messiah—not some megalomaniacal intimation that the boy was one. Still, it seemed to reflect the murderer's own sense of himself as a figure of historical and religious consequence. Jews circumcise their sons on the eighth day after the birth. In what Amir surely saw as yet another affirmation of God's support for the assassination, Yinon's circumcision ceremony fell on November 4—twelve years, to the day, after the murder.

Amir and Hagai have mostly rejected conspiracy theories about the murder over the years. In part, it was a matter of pride. The two men believe killing Rabin was a singular achievement, given all the obstacles, while the conspiracists pass the credit to others. But the family is divided on this issue. Geulah, the mother, told me she never believed her son fired the bullets that killed Rabin. And Larissa said Amir had come around to the idea that a retrial that focused on the loose ends in the murder investigation might somehow exonerate him.

If that's the case, the assassin now wants to have it both ways: to boast that he saved Israel from Rabin's betrayal—and hint that it might not have been him at all.

ACKNOWLEDGMENTS

I'm indebted to a good many people who agreed to share recollections, documents, and photographs for this book, including Dalia Rabin and her knowledgeable staff members at the Yitzhak Rabin Center, Naomi Rapoport, Dorit Ben Ami, and Braha Eshel. Of the scores of people I approached for interviews, very few turned me away. I would particularly like to thank Eitan Haber and Shimon Sheves for their help, and also Shlomo Harnoy, Nahum Barnea, Ofer Gamliel, Niva Lanir, Lucien Haag, and Israeli Channel 10 News.

When the book was just an idea, my wife, Nancy Updike, encouraged me gently but relentlessly until I ran out of excuses. Daniel Klaidman, a good friend and colleague, saw where I needed to go next and—as he has several times over the years—graciously helped get me there. My terrific agent, Gail Ross, educated me about book proposals and set the deadlines I needed.

Over a twelve-month period, I wrote the manuscript in libraries and hotel rooms, in the living room of a Tel Aviv rental and in a studio on the east side of Manhattan. When the New York City apartment felt too small, I worked on the roof of the building, overlooking the East River. With her usual generosity, Helen Rountree has made the apartment—and by extension the roof garden—available to us whenever we need it. She was also an early booster for the book. Charlie Updike and Beth Kaufman allowed me to stay in their house on Lake Champlain while I labored to complete the final chapters. Charlie also read the manuscript and offered valuable feedback, as did Howard Goller, Danny Kopp, and Stephen Kay, a loyal pal for as long as I can remember. Together, they saved me from embarrassing errors. Any remaining ones are my own. In Israel, Abby and the rest of the Pelegs provided delicious food and great company most Friday nights, along with their love and support. Nili Avidan took interest and offered insight, as did Dahlia Scheindlin, Bernard Avishai, and Sidra Dekoven Ezrahi. Tamar Vardi, a true friend over many years, helped with translations. David Blumenfeld and Bryan Meadan lent their artistic skills.

Being published by W. W. Norton is a privilege, made only better by the opportunity to work with John Glusman. His suggestions were always smart and his work on the manuscript sharp. I could not ask for a better editor. John's assistant, Alexa Pugh, made the production process a lot easier.

Finally, a huge helping of love and appreciation to my son and daughter, who have rich and absorbing lives of their own and yet still take interest in the things their parents do. And to Nancy. I'm lucky to be married to a gifted writer who helped me shape the narrative, who never lost interest, who read the manuscript and made invaluable suggestions. Thank you.

NOTES

Chapter 1

9 the most secular Israeli: Dennis Ross, *The Missing Peace: The Inside Story of the Fight for Middle East Peace* (New York: Farrar, Straus and Giroux, 2004), 91.

9 "Some Abu Ali": Aliza Wallach, interview with the author, June 17, 2013.

11 "We can blame Peres": Eitan Haber, interview with the author, August 5, 2013.

14 two old sumo wrestlers: Uri Dromi, interview with the author, May 1, 2013.

14 "That man ruined my life": Nahum Barnea, interview with author, December 3, 2013.

16 yellow stains on the insides: as described by Yehuda Hiss, Israel's chief pathologist, in Rabin's pathology report.

17 "He called me in the evening": *Rabin-Peres: Everything Is Personal*, directed by Arik Henig, Israel, 2007, Dragoman Films.

17 The "quintet," as Peres referred: David Landau, interview with the author, June 23, 2013.

18 "I told him, if you go": Shimon Peres, interview with the author, February 15, 2012.

21 On the day of the ceremony: Amos Eiran, interview with the author, July 2, 2013.

22 "We're only at the beginning": Dahlia Yairi, interview with the author, November 3, 2013.

23 "You don't invite the midwife": Ron Pundak, interview with the author, September 30, 2013.

25 "All right. All right": Bill Clinton, *My Life* (New York: Knopf Publishing Group, 2004), Kindle edition, chapter 35.

26 Rabin a regimented old soldier: Shimon Sheves, interview with the author, June 1, 2013.

26 "was sort of sizing me up": Bill Clinton, speech to the AIPAC Policy Conference, May 1995.

27 thwart the traditional Arab embrace: Clinton, *My Life*, chapter 35.

27 "Andrews, Bandar": Martin Indyk, *Innocent Abroad: An Intimate Account of American Peace Diplomacy in the Middle East* (New York: Simon & Schuster, 2009), 71.

30 "Your turn now": *A Prime Minister's Schedule,* directed by Shahar Segal, Israel, 1998.

31 become an apartheid regime: Clinton, *My Life*, chapter 35.

31 Israeli intelligence agencies had intercepted: Shimon Sheves, interview with the author, June 1, 2013.

31 "I can tell you that no doubt": Eitan Haber, interview with the author, February 18, 2013.

31 "If Golda was alive": Mahmoud Abbas, *Through Secret Channels* (London: Garnet Publishing, 1995), 214.

Chapter 2

35 he scored 144: According to a psychological assessment of Amir ordered by the court and conducted by Dr. Gabriel Weil in February 1996.

37 "He feels a sense of guilt": Ibid.

37 A student several grades ahead: Geulah Amir, interview with the author, August 8, 2013.

38 "Yigal was the enforcer": John Kifner, "The Making of Rabin's Killer," *New York Times*, November 18, 1995.

38 Most of the time, the Palestinians would pull: Nili Korman, witness statement, November 1995.

39 came to regard him as exceptionally smart: Avinoam Ezer, interview with the author, August 2013.

39 "must learn to fathom God's Will": Michael Karpin and Ina Friedman, *Murder in the Name of God: The Plot to Kill Yitzhak Rabin* (London: Granta Books, 1998), 23.

40 "Only through prayer and Torah study": Shlomo Amir, witness statement, November 1995.

40 He hadn't bothered cashing out: Hagai Amir, court records, 1995–1996.

40 who liked taking apart old radios: Geulah Amir, interview with the author, August 8, 2013.

43 After their service, he helped: Israel Shirion, witness statement, November 1995.

43 On recurring visits: Hagai Amir, court records, 1995–1996.

44 Amir outlined to Hagai: Hagai Amir, interview with the author, July 14, 2013.

45 a link in a chain of Jewish rebellion: Yigal Amir, court records, 1995–1996.

45 He and Hagai had both read *The Revolt*: Hagai Amir, interview with the author, July 14, 2013.

47 **"annihilation of Amalek":** Karen Armstrong, *The Battle for God* (New York: Ballantine Books, 2001), 346.

47 **"evil in the heart of Bar-Ilan":** "Murder Taints 'Tolerant' Campus," *Times Higher Education*, November 27, 1995, http://www.timeshighereducation.co.uk/99018.article.

48 **He agreed to let Amir pick up his notes:** Amit Hampel, interview with the author, August 4, 2013.

49 **Rabbis and students at the seminary:** Kifner, "The Making of Rabin's Killer."

51 **A photographer snapped pictures:** Yigal Amir, court records, 1995–1996.

51 **At home, he related the events:** Hagai Amir, interview with the author, July 14, 2013.

52 **Rabin liked to joke:** Niva Lanir, interview with the author, April 25, 2013.

53 **"Rabin is a traitor, Rabin is a traitor":** Noa Rothman, interview with the author, July 9, 2013.

54 **But he became skeptical:** Karpin and Friedman, *Murder in the Name of God,* 23.

54 **Amir divided Israelis into two camps:** Yigal Amir, court records, 1995–1996.

55 **blueprint for a "Jewish intifada":** Amir Gilat, "We'll Light a Fire," *Ma'ariv*, November 1, 1993.

56 **it wasn't just Israel fretting:** Nahum Barnea and Shimon Shiffer, "Taba First," *Yedioth Ahronoth*, October 15, 1993.

Chapter 3

60 **harbinger of bad news:** Noa Rothman, interview with the author, July 9, 2013.

62 **The bag Goldstein had carried:** The crime scene is described in Danny Yatom, *The Confidant* (Israel: Yedioth Ahronoth, Hebrew, 2009), chapter 9. See also, Jacob Perry, *Strike First* (Tel Aviv: Keshet, Hebrew, 1999), 271.

62 **"transferring these hostile Arabs":** Kiryat Arba election pamphlet, as cited in a memorial book for Goldstein titled *Baruch the Man* and edited by Michael Ben-Horin.

63 **"treasonous politicians":** Ibid.

63 **"He just threw his medical bag":** Eliezer Waldman, interview with the author, June 26, 2013.

64 **suspected that he received at least tacit approval:** Hezi Kalo, interview with the author, September 12, 2013.

66 **just as he expected Arafat to do with Hamas:** Perry, *Strike First*, 273.

67 **"ambivalence" of Israeli police officers:** Yehudit Karp, *Investigations of Suspicions Against Israelis in Judea and Samaria* (Israeli Government Press Office, 1982).

67 **Goldstein called his insurance agent:** Benny Barak and Avinoam Porat, "Two Days Before the Massacre, Goldstein Took Out a Quarter Million Shekel Life Insurance Policy," *Yedioth Ahronoth*, March 8, 1994.

67 "America's 'Gift' to Israel": Richard S. Gunther and Gary E. Rubin, "America's 'Gift' to Israel," *Newsday*, March 3, 1994.

67 He had been nursing a toothache: Nahum Barnea and Shimon Shiffer, "Rabin at 72. A Birthday Conversation," *Yedioth Ahronoth*, February 25, 1994.

68 "That's not how Zionism works": Eliezer Waldman, interview with the author, June 26, 2013.

68 "cancer in the body of Israeli democracy": Idit Zertal and Akiva Eldar, *Lords of the Land: The War over Israel's Settlements in the Occupied Territories* (New York: Nation Books, 2007), 47.

70 "In this whole process, the extremists are getting stronger": Yoel Bin-Nun, interview with author, May 2013. Bin Nun shared with the author some of the letters he exchanged with Rabin between 1992 and 1995.

71 "[The idea] was to break Rabin": Michael Karpin and Ina Friedman, *Murder in the Name of God: The Plot to Kill Yitzhak Rabin* (London: Granta Books, 1998), 69.

72 Rabin waited silently: Amos Eiran, who accompanied Rabin, interview with the author, July 2, 2013.

72 "He felt they were undermining everything": Uri Dromi, interview with the author, May 1, 2013.

73 "a saint, a great man": Patrick Anidjar, "Kach Extremists Who Backed Massacre Go Underground," Agence France-Presse, February 28, 1994.

74 "Hollow and superficial": Ed Blanche, "Israel Moves Against Jewish Extremists," Associated Press, February 27, 1994.

74 He also wanted an international force: Uri Savir, *The Process: 1,100 Days That Changed the Middle East* (New York: Vintage Books, 1998), Kindle edition, chapter 5.

76 "An IDF soldier, though Jewish": Elyakim Haetzni, "Civil Disobedience Now," *Nekuda*, January 1994.

76 "But if the government does": Zvi Zinger, "Settlers Calling on Soldiers to Refuse Evacuating Settlements," *Yedioth Ahronoth*, March 11, 1994.

77 "high likelihood of violent": Ehud Sprinzak, *Brother Against Brother: Violence and Extremism in Israeli Politics from Altalena to the Rabin Assassination* (New York: The Free Press, 1999), 251.

78 Ben-Yair, the attorney general, would come to regret: Michael Ben Yair, interview with the author, June 12, 2013.

80 an episode of *The Golden Girls*: Dennis Ross, *The Missing Peace: The Inside Story of the Fight for Middle East Peace* (New York: Farrar, Straus and Giroux, 2004), 131.

81 One of the bodies at the scene: Clyde Haberman, "Arab Car Bomber Kills 8 in Israel; 44 Are Wounded," *New York Times*, April 7, 1994.

82 "Keep Hope Alive": Said Ghazali, "Soldiers Shoot Stone-Throwers During Jackson Hebron Visit," Associated Press, April 8, 1994.

Chapter 4

85 Amir had been studying in the *kolel:* Michael Karpin and Ina Friedman, *Murder in the Name of God: The Plot to Kill Yitzhak Rabin* (London: Granta Books, 1998),16.

86 "You don't see a lot of people willing": Hagai Amir, interview with the author, July 2013.

86 he would have chosen a better target: Yigal Amir, court records, 1995–1996.

87 "deep emotional bond": Nava Holtzman, witness statement, November 1995.

87 She regarded her Gali as handsome: Geulah Amir, interview with the author, August 8, 2013.

88 a judicial commission to investigate: After deliberating for seven years, the Cohen Commission found no evidence that children were snatched from their parents. Most probably died of disease and malnutrition.

90 stop at Rachel's home: Rachel Adani, witness statement, November 1995.

92 "The objective he set for himself": Jacob Perry, *Strike First* (Tel Aviv: Keshet, Hebrew, 1999), 273.

94 "The Torah is the brain": Yigal Amir, court records, 1995–1996.

95 "There's no such thing as cognitive dissonance": Ibid.

96 "If he had a sense of humor": David Margolick, "Star of Zion," *Vanity Fair,* June 1996.

97 "The Likud has got to come to terms": "Senior Likud Figure Bucks His Party, Calls for Acceptance of Deal with the PLO," Jewish Telegraphic Agency, August 2, 1994.

97 and consorting with rabbis: Daniel Shilo, interview with the author, September 12, 2014. "There were many meetings in the home of Rabbi [Avraham] Shapira, many of them with the participation of Netanyahu. And from the home of Rabbi Shapira . . . there were repeated calls on soldiers not to evacuate settlements or military bases."

97 "We have an issue with political adversaries": Undated YouTube clip, https://www.youtube.com/watch?v=ms8si-ekSX4.

98 The three Israelis spent the week: Nava Holtzman, witness statement, November 1995.

99 When they got back to Bar-Ilan: Ibid.

99 To Hagai, Amir said he no longer wanted: Hagai Amir, interview with the author, July 1995.

99 the relationship might have distracted him: Karpin and Friedman, *Murder in the Name of God,* 168.

100 looking for a woman genuinely committed: Nili Kolman, witness statement, November 1995.

101 she would mimic his defense: Margalit Har-Shefi, witness statement, November 1995.

102 Adani, who had been pondering on his own: Yigal Amir, court records, 1995–1996.

102 They're paid by the state: Dror Adani, court records, 1995–1996.

103 he thought Amir intended the militia: Ohad Skornik, witness statement, November 1995.

103 But Amir felt certain: Yigal Amir, court records, 1995–1996.

104 he intended to shoot Rabin: Margalit Har-Shefi, witness statement, November 1995.

105 the rabbi advised against it: Ibid.

105 a holy martyr: Sefi Rachlevsky, "A Racist, Messianic Rabbi Is the Ruler of Israel," *Ha'aretz*, July 1, 2011.

106 "What is the rule about this bad government": Ehud Sprinzak, *Brother Against Brother: Violence and Extremism in Israeli Politics from Altalena to the Rabin Assassination* (New York: The Free Press, 1999), 254.

106 the rabbis were hoping with the letter: Daniel Shilo, interview with the author, September 12, 2014.

106 "If I did not get the backing": Yigal Amir, as quoted in the report of the Shamgar Commission, 89.

Chapter 5

110 "I will burn Gaza to the ground": Eitan Haber, interview with the author, February 18, 2013.

111 Arafat would be able to fight terrorism: Yitzhak Rabin, *Mabat*, Israel Television Channel 1, March 1, 1994.

111 settlers hired several hundred : Daniel Shilo, interview with the author, September 12, 2014.

112 The figure dropped by 79 percent: Israel's Central Bureau of Statistics.

113 "No doubt about it": Eitan Haber, interview with the author, February 18, 2013.

113 The first year of peacemaking: Roni Shaked, "Terror at an All Time High During Year of Peace," *Yedioth Ahronoth*, September 13, 1994.

115 "Don't worry. . . . We just want to trade": Jihad Yarmur, recounting the abduction for police investigators. Excerpts of his videotaped interrogation appeared in Levi Zini, dir., *Nachshon Wachsman: Countdown to Death*, Alma Films, 2010.

116 Soldiers were always heading off: Esther Wachsman, interview with the author, June 23, 2013.

116 first film screening in seven years: David Regev, "The First Screening of Movie in Gaza," *Yedioth Ahronoth*, September 18, 1994.

117 she felt immense relief at the evidence: Esther Wachsman, interview with the author, June 23, 2013.

117 A few loathsome kidnappers had reduced: Zini, *Nachshon Wachsman.*

119 "There's not a single Hamas person": Ibid.

121 **Esther asked Clinton:** Esther Wachsman, interview with the author, June 23, 2013.

122 **a government commission banned some interrogation:** The Landau Commission, 1987.

122 **Yes, she finally said:** Carmi Gillon, *Shin Beth Between the Schisms* (Tel Aviv: Yedioth Ahronoth, Hebrew, 2000), 220.

123 **"Not one person objected":** Zini, *Nachshon Wachsman.*

123 **they left the Defense Ministry separately:** Gillon, *Shin Beth Between the Schisms,* 221.

124 **Haber was mesmerized:** Zini, *Nachshon Wachsman.*

125 **"At this time, Israel Defense Forces soldier":** Israeli Ministry of Foreign Affairs, http://mfa.gov.il/MFA/ForeignPolicy/MFADocuments/Yearbook9/Pages/237%20Statement%20by%20Prime%20Minister%20Rabin%20upon%20notific.aspx.

126 **And Hamas had a track record:** Gillon, *Shin Beth Between the Schisms,* 221.

126 **"We have a rule":** Zini, *Nachshon Wachsman.*

126 **the operation was a go:** Gillon, *Shin Beth Between the Schisms,* 222.

127 **Lotan heard the man inside:** Zini, *Nachshon Wachsman.*

127 **"I understood from his expression":** Ibid.

127 **"They had a very traumatic visit":** Dalia Rabin, interview with the author, June 10, 2013.

128 **Esther noticed his eyes:** Esther Wachsman, interview with the author, June 23, 2013.

128 **"Yasser Arafat earned many points":** Gillon, *Shin Beth Between the Schisms,* 218.

128 **"He said, 'That's my red line'":** Eitan Haber, interview with the author, February 18, 2013.

129 **"Arafat is disappointed":** Nahum Barnea and Shimon Shiffer, "I Did Enough in the Negotiations with Assad." *Yedioth Ahronoth,* October 28, 1994.

130 **He informed neither Peres nor Rabin:** Yossi Beilin, interview with the author, July 7, 2013.

132 **"carrying the envelope":** Shimon Sheves, interview with the author, August 15, 2013.

132 **When Norwegian security men watched:** Nahum Barnea, "Peres Stumbled; The Norwegians Thought It Was an Assassination," *Yedioth Ahronoth,* December 11, 1994.

Chapter 6

134 **"May it be Your will that You heal me":** "The Viduy Confession Prayers," http://www.chabad.org/library/article_cdo/aid/364287/jewish/The-Viduy-Confession-Prayers.htm.

135 **But somehow, Shabak knew only about:** Hezi Kalo, interview with the author, September 12, 2013.

136 The last time a Jewish leader: The leader was Haim Arlosoroff. See Shabtai Teveth, *The Arlosoroff Murder* (Tel Aviv: Shoken, Hebrew, 1982).

136 "At the moment of crisis": Roni Shaked, "It's Difficult but the Extreme Right Can Be Infiltrated," *Yedioth Ahronoth* (Hebrew), October 29, 2004.

137 an emerging plot to murder Peres: Hezi Kalo, interview with the author, September 12, 2013.

138 he reminded himself that he had tried: Yigal Amir, court records, 1995–1996.

138 "If I'm going to act": Yigal Amir, court records, 1995–1996.

138 *din rodef* applied to Rabin: Margalit Har-Shefi, witness statement, November 1995.

138 Rosenbloom, who organized the protest: Shmuel Rosenbloom, witness statement, November 1995.

139 As a rule, the more radical the group: Carmi Gillon, *Shin Beth Between the Schisms* (Tel Aviv: Yedioth Ahronoth, Hebrew, 2000), 249.

139 Raviv seemed spellbound: Benzion Gopstein, interview with the author, February 3, 2014.

140 "We got very angry": Dani Dayan, interview with the author, July 30, 2013.

141 summoned him repeatedly for rebukes: Gillon, *Shin Beth Between the Schisms,* 247.

141 He bragged separately to Har-Shefi: Yigal Amir, court records, 1995–1996.

141 Geulah thought Amir was still brooding: Geulah Amir, witness statement, November 1995.

142 God would reward the person: Dror Adani, court records, 1995–1996.

143 "Rabin's character exemplifies": Uri Milstein, "Begin, Shamir, Sharon and Raful Are All Accomplices in the Big Lie Named Rabin," *Nukuda,* July 1995.

143 "There, they were forced to collaborate": Gillon, *Shin Beth Between the Schisms,* 239.

143 "They [Hamas] receive signals from both": Benjamin Netanyahu, *Mabat,* Israel Television Channel 1, March 30, 1995.

144 "pushes the extremists even further": Gillon, *Shin Beth Between the Schisms,* 237.

144 Instead, Shabak purchased an armored Cadillac: Ibid., 268.

145 "Are you out of your mind?": Ibid., 273.

146 So torn was Rabin that he offered: Ami Ayalon, interview with the author, July 29, 2013.

149 "He didn't think it was a real threat": Mordechai Alon, "I Could Have Saved Rabin," *Yedioth Ahronoth,* November 16, 1995.

151 "If you're wearing one": Dror Mor, interview with the author, June 10, 2013.

152 "We took it into consideration": Ibid.

152 "Dignitary Protection was a cocky unit": Shlomo Harnoy, interview with the author, July 3, 2013.

154 He also admitted to teaching two minors: The report of the Shamgar Commission.

155 He found Rabin alone in a back room: Carmi Gillon, interview with the author, June 6, 2013.

157 "He really wanted to kill Rabin": Dror Adani, court records, 1995–1996.

157 Occasionally, he raised the concern: Ibid.

Chapter 7

160 watched Arafat press his arm to Rabin's back: Martin Indyk, *Innocent Abroad: An Intimate Account of American Peace Diplomacy in the Middle East* (New York: Simon & Schuster, 2009), 1.

161 climbed the roof of a building: Yaron Kaner, "Eyal Seminar in Hebron, Organized by Yigal Amir," *Yedioth Ahronoth*, November 10, 1995.

162 At meals, Amir would stand up and announce: Ibid.

163 a sizeable gathering of extremists: Shai Fogelman, "Fifteen Years After Conducting the Pulsa Dinura Against Rabin, Avigdor Eskin Unites Right-Wing Extremists from Around the World," *Ha'aretz* (Hebrew), October 28, 2010.

163 "Angels of destruction": Ehud Sprinzak, *Brother Against Brother: Violence and Extremism in Israeli Politics from Altalena to the Rabin Assassination* (New York: The Free Press, 1999), 275.

164 "This is the ornament": "Itamar Ben-Gvir in His Youth," YouTube clip, uploaded November 15, 2010, https://www.youtube.com/watch?v=T7KkLWTc EYM.

164 "You better restrain your people": Michael Karpin and Ina Friedman, *Murder in the Name of God: The Plot to Kill Yitzhak Rabin* (London: Granta Books, 1998), 97.

165 When he spotted Har-Shefi on the street: Margalit Har-Shefi, witness statement, November 1995.

165 Ofir kicked and spat at policemen: Zvi Harel, "District Court Convicts Hebrew University Rabbi," *Haaretz*, February 14, 1997.

167 the Islamic Jihad leader who had boasted: Robert Fisk, "The Doctor Who Finds Death a Laughing Matter," *The Independent*, January 30, 1995.

167 Skornik would notice in a video: Ohad Skornik, witness statement, November 1995.

167 students talked about starting: Nili Kolman, witness statement, November 1995.

167 he suggested they drive to Shavei Shomron: Hagai Amir, interview with the author, July 2013.

168 discussed the counter-rally that rightists planned: Nili Kolman, witness statement, November 1995.

168 "We don't talk about things like that": Yuval Rabin, interview with the author, June 12, 2013.

168 Motti Naftali began directing: Motti Naftali, interview with the author, April 25, 2013.

169 It was a lesson they learned: Dror Mor, interview with the author, June 10, 2013.

170 "Rabin is going to be assassinated": Ibid.

170 defuse a crisis with Peres: Shimon Sheves, interview with the author, June 1, 2013.

170 "You bring Leah": Shahar Segal, dir., *A Prime Minister's Schedule,* Israel,1998.

171 a quick trip to the *mikva:* Hagai Amir, interview with the author, July 2013.

172 If Shabak had somehow been on to him: Ibid.

173 If a policeman approached: Yigal Amir, court records, 1995–1996.

173 "What a weirdo": Ibid.

173 if Rabin was wearing a bulletproof vest: Leah Rabin, *Rabin: Our Life, His Legacy* (New York: G. P. Putnam's Sons, 1997), 8.

175 the second bullet must come from: Dror Mor, interview with the author, June 10, 2013.

175 "It's not real, it's not real": Ofer Gamliel, interview with the author, July 23, 2013.

175 "Listen to me and no one else": Yoram Rubin, witness statement, November 1995.

176 did Cohen realize this elderly man: Naftali Glicksberg, dir., *An Unclosed Case,* Israel, Alma Films, 2005.

176 Gutman wanted Rabin in the surgery room: Gal Ochovski, "The Last Minutes of Rabin's Life," *Ma'ariv,* November 3, 2000.

177 "Don't worry, it's not real": Shai Glaser, *HaMakor,* Israeli Channel 10, November 10, 2009.

177 "Why aren't you at the hospital?": Rabin, *Rabin: Our Life, His Legacy,* 12.

179 At 11:02 p.m.: Ochovski, "The Last Minutes of Rabin's Life."

180 "From the look on his face": Bill Clinton, "Rabin Inspired Trust Even in Arafat," *Yedioth Ahronoth,* December 23, 2014.

180 "This idiot took my Yitzhak away": Shahar Segal, *A Prime Minister's Schedule.*

181 Amir delivered a full confession: Yuval Gershon, witness statements, November 1995.

182 "I did it": Motti Naftali, interview with the author, April 25, 2013.

183 How could you do this to me: Hagai Amir, interview with the author, July 1995.

184 The policemen and Shabak agents: Ibid.

Chapter 8

189 Gillon felt a constant anxiety: Carmi Gillon, *Shin Beth Between the Schisms* (Tel Aviv: Yedioth Ahronoth, Hebrew, 2000), 11.

190 "inconceivable reality": Leah Rabin, *Rabin: Our Life, His Legacy* (New York: G. P. Putnam's Sons, 1997), 20.

190 She roused her mother: Dalia Rabin, interview with the author, June 5, 2013.

191 House Speaker Newt Gingrich complained: Itamar Rabinovich, interview with the author, June 17, 2013.

191 Yuval mispronounced many of the words: Eitan Haber, interview with the author, August 5, 2013.

192 "In a democratic state, I'm allowed": Storer H. Rowley, "As Crackdown Looms, Settlers Tone Down," *Chicago Tribune*, November 10, 1995.

192 "You couldn't board a bus": Israel Harel, interview with the author, June 18, 2013.

193 "What did you people do to us?": Yedidia Stern, interview with the author, August 1, 2013.

194 She had agreed to host: Israel Harel, interview with the author, June 18, 2013.

199 "He's not mine anymore": Geulah Amir, *Mabat,* Israel Television Channel 1, November 9, 1995.

201 Frank had slipped into near catatonia: Mordechai Alon, "I Could Have Saved Rabin," *Yedioth Ahronoth*, November 16, 1995.

203 Shabak found itself on the defensive: Forty-six percent of Israelis said their faith in Shabak had been eroded, according to an opinion poll published in *Yedioth Ahronoth*, November 11, 1995.

204 a new survey showed him losing to Peres: *Yedioth Ahronoth*, November 10. The poll gave Peres 54 percent of the vote, Netanyahu 23, undecided 12.

205 Beilin had been planning: Yossi Beilin, interview with the author, July 27, 2013.

205 "Rabin became a saint that night": Nahum Barnea, interview with the author, December 3, 2013.

205 "I thought it was unfair": Shimon Peres, interview with the author, February 15, 2012.

206 Why didn't you urge Rabin to surrender: Uzi Baram, interview with the author, June 11, 2013.

206 "hypothetical, conditional willingness": Itamar Rabinovich, interview with the author, June 17, 2013.

208 "Based on everything we knew": Ron Pundak, interview with the author, September 30, 2013.

208 "Peres was very seasoned at timetables": Itamar Rabinovich, interview with the author, June 17, 2013.

209 fearing one of them might be tempted: Shlomo Harnoy, interview with the author, July 3, 2013.

Chapter 9

212 "There is simply no alternative": Amos Oz, "Israelis Will Not Stand for Fanaticism," *Newsweek*, November 20, 1995.

213 the woman married the mailman: Uri Savir, *The Process: 1,100 Days That*

Changed the Middle East (New York: Vintage Books, 1998), Kindle edition, chapter 9.

213 "The solution they were seeking was": Ibid.

214 If Palestinian terrorism picked up: Uzi Baram, interview with the author, June 11, 2013.

215 "If they would have attacked us": Hagai Amir, interview with the author, July 2013.

215 "The problem is these Torah authorities": Joel Greenberg, "Rabbis and Settlers Dispute Their Own Culpability in Rabin's Assassination," *New York Times*, November 9, 1995.

216 "I have no doubt in retrospect": Ofer Gamliel, interview with the author, July 23, 2013.

219 "The morale was low": Carmi Gillon, *Shin Beth Between the Schisms* (Tel Aviv: Yedioth Ahronoth, Hebrew, 2000), 359.

219 On the first Friday of the New Year: Dror Moreh, dir., *The Gatekeepers*, Israel, Cinephil, 2012.

220 Peres grew tired of Assad's dithering: Savir, *The Process*, chapter 9.

223 "I'm sorry to have to convey": Eitan Amit, "Nahum Barnea Came Back with an Empty Notebook This Time," *Yedioth Ahronoth*, February 26, 1996.

223 "You lost a vote": Yaron London, "History's Bloody Bargain," *Yedioth Ahronoth*, February 27, 1996.

224 Ayalon now faced a dilemma: Ami Ayalon, interview with the author, July 29, 2013.

224 "There were thousands of people around": Shimon Peres, interview with the author, February 15, 2012.

227 "He simply couldn't fathom": Douglas F. Schoen, *The Power of the Vote* (New York, William Morrow, 2007), 83.

227 The two men also had a history: David Landau, who co-wrote two books with Peres, interview with the author, June 23, 2013.

230 The fact that Gamliel had solved: Gamliel discussed the issue for the first time on the Israeli Channel 10 news show *HaMakor* on November 10, 2009, and later with the author. To this day, the Shabak man has never been identified.

231 The unit's company commander: Bennett would go on to become the leader of the right-wing Jewish Home Party. Whether he bore responsibility for the Qana mishap would be debated vigorously in the Israeli media many years after the incident. See Amos Harel, "Was Bennett Really to Blame for the Deaths of 102 Lebanese Civilians in 1996 Battle?" *Ha'aretz*, January 7, 2015.

231 "These were sleepless nights": Shimon Peres, interview with the author, February 15, 2012.

234 opinion poll conducted after the broadcast: Poll by Dahaf, published in *Yedioth Ahronoth*, May 28, 1996: Peres 51.5 percent, Netanyahu 48.5 percent.

235 the Israeli who voted twice: Thomas L. Friedman, "And One Man Voted Twice," *New York Times*, June 2, 1996.

235 Analysts would put the actual participation level: Daniel J. Elazar and Shmuel Sandler, *Israel at the Polls, 1996* (London: Frank Cass, 1998), 6.

236 Peres told her he would be home soon: Yossi Beilin, interview with the author, July 7, 2013.

Epilogue

240 the Michael Jordan of his profession: Jim Walsh, "Shooting Reconstructionist 'Michael Jordan of Profession,'" *Arizona Republic,* June 24, 2004.

257 Amir tried to pass semen: Eli Senyor, "Yigal Amir Attempts to Smuggle Semen," YNet, March 9, 2006.

INDEX